CONTENTS

PREFACE

The last three or four years has seen a remarkable explosion of interest in object-oriented programming languages and associated techniques for requirements specification, design, verification, and validation. We have seen industrial quality programming languages such as C^{++}, Objective C and Eiffel penetrate software developers, object-oriented software engineering has entered the curricula of colleges, and industrialists are starting to claim major productivity gains through using object-oriented programming languages.

This book is about this revolution. It describes how well-engineered software systems can be developed using object-oriented programming languages and, more importantly, software engineering techniques suited to such languages. A major theme of this book is that change is now a fact of life on every software project, apart from the most trivial, and that object-oriented techniques enable the software developer to cope with this change in such a way that it is no longer something to be feared.

It is worth stating at this juncture that my choice of programming language for this book was deliberate. I had a wide variety of languages to choose from, ranging from Ada to Small Talk, via Objective C and Loops. I decided to choose C^{++} for one major reason: that I think that it will be the major object-oriented programming language in the 1990s. Paradoxically, innovation in software development comes incrementally, and is often based on existing technology: programming languages, tools, operating systems and software development methodologies. My suspicion is that this will hold for object-oriented development in the future, and, indeed on limited evidence seems to be holding now; object-oriented programming languages that have a base in existing programming languages such as C seem to be experiencing the largest industrial take-up.

There are a number of more elegant object-oriented programming languages than C^{++}; however, they are still firmly based in an academic environment. C^{++} is a language that is now doing sterling service in the outside world, and I would have regarded it as a dereliction of duty to ignore it.

This book is intended for two mutually exclusive audiences. First, it is intended for those who wish to employ object-oriented techniques, and in particular C^{++} in their work-place. There are a large number of programmers out there who are C experts and are beginning to look to C^{++} as the next step in their work. This book is intended for them.

A second audience that I am aiming at is students studying software engineering—

either in a computer science course or an electronic engineering course. This book could act as a set text for software engineering courses, where the objective is to describe what the main activities of software engineering are, and how software developers set about producing software systems that are robust, correct, efficient, and easy to maintain. In order to help such students and readers who do not have any educational back-up I have provided a large number of worked examples or self-assessment questions (SAQs). Each of these is critically placed in the text, and I would advise you to complete each example before proceeding to the next part of the text.

A feature of this book—a feature that I would regard as a strength—is that for the most part I employ current software engineering techniques. This may come as a surprise to many readers; some may, in fact, see the book as a cynical attempt to climb aboard the object-oriented bandwagon by a software engineer associated with more conventional techniques. I would hope that this book would disavow the open-minded reader. The book emerged from a research project the aim of which was to answer the question: what new requirements specification, design, validation, and verification techniques are required for object-oriented development? The answer came as a surprise to me and to many of the industrialists and software engineers whom I have talked to; that existing techniques fit exceptionally well into the object-oriented paradigm and that the major difference is how they are used.

Finally, I would like to acknowledge some of the people to whom I am indebted. First, Professor Peter Henderson, now of Southampton University, then of Stirling University, who in a snow-bound restaurant in Stirling, convinced me that there was more to object-oriented programming than the hype that surrounded it. Second, to Professor Richard Housden of the Open University for his continual encouragement. Third, to my wife Stephanie who (to paraphrase P. G. Wodehouse) showed so much affection, concern, and attention during the writing of this book that she ensured that it was published three months later than it should have been.

Darrel Ince
Milton Keynes

INTRODUCTION

AIMS

- To describe current software development techniques.
- To provide a technical vocabulary that will be used in later parts of this book.
- To outline the major difficulties that software developers currently face.
- To describe briefly what is meant by the term *object-oriented programming language*.

1.1 INTRODUCTION

We have come a long way since those early days when we developed software using only primitive tools such as assemblers, and when everybody believed that the most important task that a software developer undertook was programming. The last thirty years has seen a revolution, both in terms of attitudes and, equally importantly, in terms of the technology that is available to even the most impoverished software developer. We now have good high-level languages such as Ada and Pascal, software tools that enable us to construct graphical specifications and designs, and sophisticated operating systems such as UNIX that, as well as controlling the resources in a computer system, provide a wealth of tools for program development.

In terms of changes in attitude we now no longer believe that programming is the be all and end all of the software development process. Indeed, many commentators now regard it as a relatively trivial task. We now organize a software project in ways similar to that of an industrial manufacturing project, with tasks such as system design and validation being regarded as vital—which if they were not performed correctly would lead to catastrophe.

Yet, even though our tools have improved and we organize our software projects better, there are still major problems with software development: many systems are still delivered late, are a nightmare to maintain, and only meet a subset of the requirements of the customer. This book describes a technology for improving the software process that relies on the notion of an object as the vital component in software development. However, before looking at this concept in detail in later chapters, and examining the reasons for the problems we encounter, it is worth looking in some detail at how a relatively organized company would set about developing a complex software system.

My aim in providing this description is twofold. First, to provide you with a vocabulary that will be used extensively in the remaining chapters of this book; and, second, to provide a context for the description of the problems that occur in software development which concludes this chapter.

1.2 CURRENT SOFTWARE DEVELOPMENT PRACTICES

Today's software project is partitioned into a number of phases—*requirements analysis, requirements specification, system design, detailed design,* and *programming.* Each of these phases corresponds to a distinct activity that gives rise to a document, or set of documents, which are then fed into the next phase. The starting point in any software project is a customer *statement of requirements.* This is a document, produced by the customer, that expresses their aspirations about a future computer system. The quality of the statement of requirements varies considerably: customers with little experience of software systems, specifications, and information technology will produce short, very abstract documents which, perhaps, only give broad hints about their requirements. The more sophisticated customer, e.g. a major computer manufacturer who is subcontracting a system, might develop a statement of requirements that is a multi-volume work containing descriptions of every facet of the system to be developed.

The statement of requirements is communicated to the software developer, who then carries out requirements analysis: the task of attempting to discover what the proposed system is to do. To carry out this task, analysts from the developer's staff study any existing systems— manual, automated, or semi-automated—that the proposed system is to replace, interview the customer's staff, and carry out some form of technical analysis of the statement of requirements.

When the process of requirements analysis is complete, the analysts write down a description of the properties of the system that is to be developed. This process is known as *requirements specification,* and gives rise to a document known as the *requirements specification,* often referred to as the system specification. This contains a detailed description of all the tasks that a system is to carry out, any constraints such as response time or memory utilization, and any design directives or implementation directives such as an insistence on a particular file organization for a database. The requirements specification also contains a number of appendices that address issues which, although important, are not directly relevant to the description of the system, e.g. appendices that detail the maintenance support for the system and the training of the customer's staff that will be carried out. The major feature of a requirements specification relevant to the subject matter of this book is that it contains a large amount of detail about what a system should do, i.e. its functions.

The requirements specification is a key document in the software project for a number of reasons. First, it is a major input into the next task in the project: system design. Second, it is used either in its final form or, more realistically, in outline form, by a project manager to estimate the resources that are required for a project. Third, it is used by quality assurance staff in order to develop the system tests and acceptance tests that will check the correctness of the system. Fourth, it is consulted by staff charged with the task of developing system documentation, when constructing the user manual.

Because the requirements specification is such an important document, the software developer will expend a large amount of resource on its construction, and will ensure that everything is defined in minute detail. Errors in the requirements specification that remain until

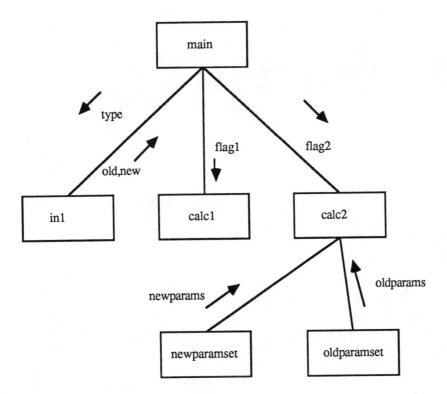

Figure 1.1 A system design notation.

late in a software project, say during system testing, have been a major cause of project overruns and have even lead to the cancellation of major projects.

The next stage in the development process is *system design*. This consists of processing the requirements specification and producing an architecture that implements the functions contained in the requirements specification, and also respects the constraints that are specified in that document. The architecture of the system is expressed in terms of self-contained chunks of program code which I shall call *modules*. If the programming language used was Pascal, modules would be procedures or functions; if the language was FORTRAN, then a module would correspond to a subroutine.

The system architecture can be specified using a number of notations—probably the most common class of notation uses graphics. An example is shown in Fig. 1.1. This shows the design of a system which contains six modules. The lines joining the modules are calls, and the items attached to lines represent the parameters that are passed between the modules. Thus, in Fig. 1.1, the module *main* calls the modules *in1*, *calc1*, and *calc2*, and the interface between *main* and *in1* is the collection of parameters *old*, *new*, and *type*. The arrows indicate the direction that data is passed between the modules. Thus, *type* is passed to *in1* and *in1* passes *old* and *new* to *main*.

The next stage in development is *detailed design*. During system design the staff allocated to this task will have specified what each module in the system should do. The task of the detailed designers is to take this description, and fill in the processing details inside the modules. These processing details are usually expressed in terms of some specialized detailed design notation, e.g. a flow chart or a program design language. An example of part of a module expressed in terms of a program design language is shown below. It counts up the number of items in the array *a* that are greater than the value *maxvalue*. The notation is very similar to that of a programming language, in that all the standard control constructs are used, the only difference being that it uses natural language for the specification of the detailed processing that occurs.

```
PROCEDURE Checkup(a, sum)
   BEGIN
   Set sum to zero
   FOR i FROM 1 TO n DO
      IF a[i] is greater than maxvalue THEN
      Add 1 to sum
      ENDIF
   ENDFOR
   END
```

The task of detailed design is an optional one. Many software developers prefer to miss it out, and program directly from the system design. Detailed designs tend to be used by software developers who are interested in portability—especially when they are implementing a number of versions of a system using a variety of programming languages. A detailed design represents a good, language-independent description of what a system does, and can be easily hand translated into any programming language—be it an assembler language or a very high-level language such as Ada.

After detailed design, *programming* starts. This involves the programmer taking a module specification, which is either extracted from a detailed design—when such a document is constructed—or from a system design when it is not. If a developer constructs a detailed design, the process of programming is easy: all it involves is a hand translation of the detailed design into the program code of the chosen implementation language. However, if the developer has not constructed a detailed design, then programming is a more intellectual task, which involves selecting an algorithm that carries out the processing required by the system design.

This marks the end of the development activities in the software project. Fortunately, this is not the whole story. Overlaid with all the developmental activities that have been previously described, there is the continual application of a series of activities which check that the developer is carrying out software tasks correctly, and that the system that is being specified and programmed meets user requirements. These tasks are collectively known as *verification* and *validation*.

1.3 VERIFICATION AND VALIDATION

Verification is concerned with checking that a particular task has been carried out correctly, e.g. checking that a programmer has correctly implemented a detailed design is an example of verification; validation is concerned with checking that a system meets customer requirements, e.g. system testing: executing a system in order to check that it meets customer requirements is an example of validation.

There are many verification and validation activities that occur during a software project. Because many of them occur during object-oriented development it is worth introducing them at this stage of the book. In this section they will be described in the order in which they occur in the conventional software project.

During requirements analysis and requirements specification two validation activities are carried out and one validation activity is started. The first two activities are the software requirements review and prototyping; the third activity is preparing for the system testing and acceptance testing phases.

A *review* is a meeting of a number of staff who spend some time—no more than two hours—reading a document or a segment of program code, and checking it for correctness. Reviews are highly effective: staff who attend such reviews tend to bring a fresh mind to a problem, and are able to check a document or program code more thoroughly. Many programmers, analysts, and designers find it very difficult to detach themselves from what they produce, and hence find it very difficult to detect errors. The technical review overcomes this problem in that staff who are completely detached from a document, or software product, do not have any misconceptions about that product.

Normally a review involves between three and five members of staff. In a requirements review, which is attended by five staff, these would normally be the analyst who produces the requirements specification—or more realistically the part of a requirements specification—that is being reviewed, a member of the developer's quality assurance department, a member of staff from another project, another analyst, and a customer representative.

The requirements specification is examined in detail, together with the statement of requirements. The participants main concern is that the requirements specification actually represents an adequate description of the system that the customer wants. The meeting also concerns itself with problems such as ambiguities and contradictions in the requirements specification. A review is an error detection process, and not an error rectification process, and hence there is little discussion about what needs to be done in order to improve the specification—all that is produced is an action list of errors that have been discovered, and need subsequent attention.

A second validation activity that can occur during requirements analysis is *prototyping*. This involves the early production of a version of a system that can be used as a learning medium by both the developer and the customer. There are a number of ways of developing such a prototype. If the application is for a commercial data processing system, then a fourth-generation programming language would, almost invariably, be used. Such languages enable large amounts of functionality to be expressed in a small amount of programming code. Other techniques for prototyping involve the use of very high-level languages such as LISP and PROLOG, the UNIX operating system, relaxing the quality assurance standards on a project, or only implementing part of a system.

Prototyping is a highly effective process for carrying out requirements analysis. Requirements specifications are becoming so complex and large that both the customer and the developer have major difficulties understanding them. A prototype represents the most concrete manifestation of a software system that is possible, and is able to give the customer an exact and complete idea of what will be delivered.

Another validation process that occurs towards the end of the requirements specification is the process of deriving the system tests and acceptance tests. These tests are the final checks on a system which confirm that it meets user requirements. The system tests and acceptance tests are carried out at the end of the development of a system—after all the correctly programmed modules of the system have been brought together. The acceptance tests are carried out in the environment in which the system is to be installed—each test being witnessed by the customer or a representative. These tests are crucial since, if the system fails an acceptance test, the customer has every right to refuse to take delivery of a system and hence pay for it. Also, the failure of an acceptance test often involves the developer in a large amount of respecification and redesign.

Because the acceptance tests are so critical, the developers carry out a series of preliminary tests in their work-place. These so-called system tests have, as a subset, the acceptance tests, but also contain a large number of other tests which give the developers a large amount of confidence that there will be no embarrassment during the acceptance test phase. The major difference between the system tests and the acceptance tests is that items of equipment, such as a nuclear reactor or an aeroplane, will not be available in the developers' work-place and, hence, will need to be simulated—either by software or by special-purpose hardware.

During the latter stages of requirements specification the developers will start to develop the system and acceptance test suite. By the end of the system design phase they will have a description of the tests expressed in outline form. An example of such an outline is shown below. It represents some of the tests for a stock control application.

TEST 1.4 — This test checks that when an order is processed by the system and the order is for an item that is out of stock then a suitable message is displayed at the originating VDU.

TEST 1.5 — This test checks that when the query command is processed by the system that the correct price of the item that is queried is displayed on the originating VDU.

TEST 1.6 — This test checks that when the back orders command is processed by the system that the list of orders which cannot be currently satisfied is displayed.

There are a number of reasons why the system test process is started so early. First, it helps the developers' analysts in carrying out requirements analysis. One of the toughest questions to ask of a statement in a requirements specification is how do I test that? Many analysts have reported to me that they carry out their job better if there is a member of the quality assurance department continually looking over their shoulder at the requirements specification, asking hard questions about how functions and constraints are to be checked during system testing. It is an excellent way of detecting functions and constraints that are expressed ambiguously, together with platitudes.

A second reason for starting the development of the system tests and acceptance tests early is in order to predict the resources required for these activities. The high-level management of a software company would look askance at a project manager who asks for staff for acceptance testing and system testing a few days before those activities started. They require as much notice as possible. A set of outline system tests provide the basis for at least a rough estimate of project resources early in a project.

The final reason for preparing the system tests and acceptance tests early is that many software projects either require special-purpose testing tools, or the development of large test data suites. Only by deriving the system tests and acceptance tests early, will the developers be able to anticipate these needs well in advance of requiring them.

After requirements analysis and requirements specification is complete, system design starts. The main validation and verification activity associated with this activity is the design review. The conduct of such a review is similar to that of the requirements review. The major differences are that the customer is usually not invited to such reviews, and the nature of the questions asked will be different.

A design review concentrates on two types of issues. First, it addresses issues concerning the degree to which the system design meets the description of the system contained in the requirements specification. Second, it concentrates on structural issues: is the specification of a module's function expressed clearly and correctly, are there any features of the design that will give rise to problems during software maintenance and will the design produce a system that will satisfy memory constraints?

An important activity started during system design is *integration testing*. During the later stages of the design process the developers decide on an integration testing strategy. Integration testing occurs during the integration process. The developers build up a system a few modules at a time; after each addition of modules, a series of tests are carried out in order to check that the interfaces between the integrated modules and the system that is being built up are correctly implemented.

There are a number of decisions that software developers have to make about integration and integration testing. First, they have to decide on an overall strategy. There are essentially three options for integration: top-down integration, bottom-up integration, and inside-out integration. Each has its advantages and disadvantages. For example, top-down integration enables an early, albeit partial, version of a system to be available, but is not very good at detecting errors in modules that lie at the bottom of a system. Another decision that has to be made is the granularity of integration: the number of modules that are to be added at a time. The developers may decide on an overall figure, for example, that three modules are to be integrated at a time, or may decide on integrating a variable number of modules at a time, for example, they may integrate one module when that module is very complex and integrate twenty when the modules are relatively simple.

Another decision that the developers have to make is whether to execute any early system tests during integration. The developer may find that after carrying out a number of integrations, enough of the system has been constructed for some system tests to be executed. It is often a good idea to carry out these tests: a maxim for all software developers is that if it is possible to check something early in the software project, then check it, and save yourself the large redesign and respecification costs that would arise if the checking was carried out later.

By the end of the system design phase the developers will have constructed an *integration and test plan*. This plan will specify the order of integration, what modules are to be integrated, the degree of testing that is to be carried out, and a list of any system tests that are to be exercised.

As early as the latter stages of the system design process, coded and tested modules will start emerging from the project—usually from subsystems that have been designed early. The testing that these modules undergo is known as *unit testing*. This involves the programmers who programmed a module developing test data which checks out the function of the module. For example, if the module sorted an arbitrary collection of integers, the programmers would check the module with one integer, fifty integers and a large number of integers; they would also select a sequence of integers that was already sorted, a sequence that was already sorted except for one integer and a sequence of integers that was sorted in reverse order. After this functional testing is complete, the programmers check that their test data has achieved a high coverage of some structural element of their module—typically they might check that their test data has exercised all the statements in a module and a very high proportion of branches.

The tested modules are then placed in a project library and withdrawn from this library during integration testing, as and when they are needed. Eventually, after all the integrations have taken place, and all the integration tests are complete, the final system will emerge from development. The only validation and verification activities that remain will be system testing and acceptance testing. By this stage of the software project the outline system tests, which, you will remember, were generated during the late stages of requirements specification and the early stages of system design, will have been expanded out until they have become step-by-step descriptions of the tests to be carried out. In this state they are known as *test procedures*. An example of a test procedure is shown below. Ideally, such procedures can be given to staff who have little knowledge of the system that they are to test.

TEST-PROC 3.4 Attach test file ATEST14.TST to the system stored in file SYSV3.OBJ. Execute the system and type in a variety of product numbers between 1 and 1000 when prompted by the character =. If the product number is not found in the product database then a message: error - unknown product, will be displayed. A list of the product numbers that are in the test database can be found in the file PRODT.TXT, use this to check on the correctness of the response.

The test procedures for the system tests are then executed against the final system. If there any errors the system is debugged, the error rectified, and the test repeated, together with any tests that exercise the program code that was modified when the error was rectified. Eventually, the system will have passed its system tests, and all that remains is the execution of the acceptance tests. By the beginning of the system test phase the customer, in conjunction with the developers, will have selected the subset of the system tests that will be the acceptance tests. These tests will be applied to the software in its operational environment. If the developers have done their job correctly, then the execution of the acceptance tests will be a formality!

1.4 THE PROBLEMS OF SOFTWARE DEVELOPMENT

The previous section has described what a well-organized software developer would do in order to produce a software system. It is a large improvement over how we did things two decades ago. However, major problems still occur. The aim of this section is to describe these problems.

1.4.1 Software maintenance

Software maintenance was not described in the previous section, although it includes many of the activities which form part of conventional software development. Software maintenance is the process of modifying a system when it is in operation. There are two mistaken views about software maintenance. The first is that it solely consists of rectifying errors committed during development, and the second is that it is not an important activity. Maintenance activities can contribute as much as 75 per cent to the software spending of a developer and consist of three distinct processes: *corrective maintenance*, *perfective maintenance*, and *adaptive maintenance*.

Corrective maintenance corresponds to the popular view of the maintenance process: the detection and rectification of errors committed during development. Perfective maintenance is the process of improving a system in some way, e.g. replacing an inefficient algorithm by a more efficient one, or changing a system so that it can be executed on a more powerful computer.

Adaptive maintenance is the process of modifying a system in response to changes in customer requirements. These requirements could change for a number of reasons. A list of reasons is given below:

- The air defence system that has to be changed in order to cope with advances in air technology of a potential aggressor. Often this means modifying such a system in order to achieve a faster response time.
- The accounting system that has to be changed in order to comply with changes in financial laws and new financial instruments introduced by a government.
- The management information system that was working well for its current users. However, it has to be changed because newly hired senior staff have different ideas about management and require different information.
- The purchasing system that has to be changed because the company that uses it has merged with another company who have a different system.

Rather than respond to such changes by building a new system, a developer will modify an existing system. Because a software system is a reflection of the real world, and because the world is dynamic, this form of maintenance becomes a major cost item for software developers.

Although I have discussed change in terms of maintenance, the situation is even more serious, because many of the changes can occur *during* a software project—especially medium and large projects which can last a number of years. Consequently, if you cut a time-slice through a project, you will find that a number of activities are being carried out: if the time-slice was extracted during detailed design you will find staff carrying out detailed design, together with staff carrying out redesign and respecification, either due to changes in requirements, or because errors have been detected. You might even find some staff carrying out the programming of modules that form part of a subsystem whose design is complete.

The more I see of industrial software projects, the more I tend to the point of view that there is no such thing as development: the only activity that the software developer actually carries out is something akin to software maintenance—where functionality is gradually added to a system in a highly dynamic way, and where the concept of a phase has to be replaced by the concept of a task that will, invariably, be carried out in parallel with other tasks.

Developers who use current software development techniques find major difficulties in coping with change—whether the change occurs during development or during software maintenance. Typically, what happens is that systems are designed in such a way that modifications degrade their structure, with a consequent effect on the subsequent development processes. Many project managers have reported to me that very early into the maintenance process, a change that might have taken a day to implement at the beginning of maintenance, now takes a week to implement.

Now, not all the blame for this can be put at the door of current approaches to software development. Often poor management practices are to blame for some of the problem. For example, it is fairly typical for a software developer not to insist that the same quality assurance standards that are used during development are employed during software maintenance. Nevertheless, even the best organized software developer still finds major problems with change.

1.4.2 The requirements specification

The requirements specification has traditionally been the most troublesome document on the software project and, unfortunately, as has been said earlier, it is also the key document. The requirements specification suffers from many problems. In order to highlight these problems I shall consider a requirements specification written in natural language. In many ways this is the worst case. However, it is worth examining documentation in this form because it graphically demonstrates the problems that the software developer faces.

There are now a large number of specification notations that rely heavily on graphical notations where some of the problems that I will discuss are lessened. However, they are not lessened to the extent that the requirements specification has a sufficient quality that it enables us to feel that major improvements are not possible. For example, graphical specifications still lean fairly heavily on natural language text.

A requirements specification exhibits a number of problems. There will be ambiguities in the text with statements such as

> The system will receive a message. If it receives an error message the system should signal an alarm. After receiving the message the system will be revert to its previous state.

Now there is an inherent ambiguity in this: does the word *message* in the last sentence refer to the error message or any message? Such a sentence can be interpreted in two ways, and a misinterpretation that is not detected early in the project could lead to a large amount of re-design and respecification if a designer interprets the sentence in the wrong way.

There is also the problem of contradictions occurring in the requirements specification. Functional descriptions, which may be separated by many pages of text, could be at variance with each other. A statement that all the commands in a chemical plant monitoring system will be logged to a file for archival reasons, may be followed by a statement, many pages later, that a particular command will not be logged, perhaps for efficiency reasons. Such contradictions lead, at best, to the embarrassment on the developers' behalf when they ask the customer later in the project which functional requirement is to be deleted; at worst, the developers may have to carry out a large amount of redesign and respecification because they followed one of the statements that occurred in the contradiction.

Requirements specifications also suffer from omissions. For example, a system operates under a number of conditions and, as the number of conditions increases, there is an exponential increase in the number of combinations of conditions. As a microcosm of this problem, consider the implementation of a command that is part of a chemical plant monitoring system.

This command has three parameters: the first parameter is a chemical reactor name, the second and third parameters are times. The function of the command is to display the average temperature between the two times. There are a number of conditions that may occur when this command is typed in: a reactor could be under maintenance or functioning, the first time could be typed in incorrectly, the second time could be typed in incorrectly, the chemical reactor name could be typed in incorrectly, the second parameter could be chronologically later than the first time, and so on, you can probably think of at least another ten conditions. Even with such a simple command, there are many combinations of conditions which must be considered by the analyst when writing a requirements specification.

When it comes to higher-level functions in the requirements specification this number of combinations can be massive. It is no surprise, therefore, that omissions occur in a requirements specification—omissions that, if not detected early in the software project, could lead to serious redesign and respecification.

Another problems with a requirements specification is that the functions of the system tend to be intermingled randomly at a different level of abstraction. For example, in a purchase order system there will be statements at a high level of abstraction such as

> The purpose of the system is to maintain stock holding information and purchasing information for a large multi-national company who manufacture electronic components used in the oil industry.

together with statements such as

> When the back order command is typed with a valid product number the system will respond with a list of the back orders for a particular product. Each line of the display will show the quantity ordered, the date the order was placed and the customer who made the order. This list will be ordered according to the customer priority.

which are at a low level of abstraction and, hence, contain rather a lot of detail. More often than not, this lack of organization in the requirements specification is compounded by the presence of platitudes, descriptions of stored data, non-functional requirements such as response times, design directives, and implementation directives.

This gives the analyst major problems when interviewing staff at different levels of a company. For example, a major activity for an analyst is to check over parts of the requirements specification with members of staff from the customer's company who are expert in the business area that the part of the requirements specification describes. Such staff do not want the document that they are presented with cluttered with extraneous detail; e.g. the chief accountant of a company that is having a purchase order system developed wants to know about high-level financial reporting, not the detailed format of the commands typed in by enquiry clerks. It also gives major problems during change—either during software maintenance or during the project—when a large amount of effort is spent in interpreting the jumble of information that is presented to the staff who are charged with implementing a change.

Another serious problem with the requirements specification—one that afflicts all requirements specifications irrespective of what notation is used to express functionality—is size. All but the smallest systems have requirements specifications which comprise hundreds of pages, with expressions of functionality making up the majority of the pages. This means that it is very difficult for both the customer and the developer to gain an idea of the nature of the system that is being developed.

1.4.3 Functionality problems

The previous section contained a description of software development which was essentially function driven: the developer established what a system is to do early in a project, and produced

(a)

(b)

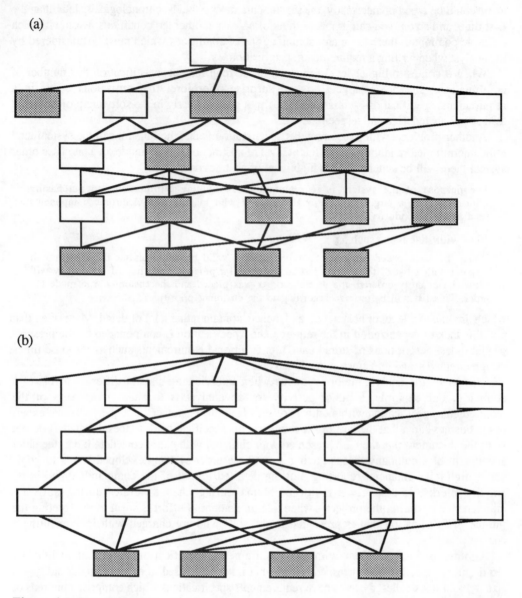

Figure 1.2 Two different types of architecture.

the documentation and the code of the system using the functional part of the requirements specification as a major input. Unfortunately, it is the functional part of the requirements specification that is most volatile. Consequently, when modifications occur, the functional part of the requirements specification will change quite radically, and thus all those documents that depend on this key document and the program code will change to the same degree. In this book I shall outline a development technique that is not so heavily rooted in functionality, where considerations of functionality are delayed until quite late in the software project, so that changes only affect system documentation at a late stage and for a short period.

1.4.4 Architecture problems

System architectures—particularly those of systems that have undergone even a small amount of software maintenance—exhibit a number of problems. One example of a problem is shown in the design depicted in Fig. 1.2(a).

This shows a system architecture where a number of modules refer to some stored data, e.g. a linked list. The modules that directly refer to the stored data are shown shaded. If a maintenance change necessitated a change to this data, e.g. to increase response time, then the staff who carry out this change will need to examine every module that references this data, and carry out a large number of modifications—for what often is a relatively small reason. This book will describe a technique whereby references to stored data can be minimized and localized, where an architecture similar to Fig. 1.2(b) can be achieved. This system architecture has the property that references to the stored data are localized to a small number of modules.

Another problem with system architectures is that modules often carry out a large number of functions, e.g. a module might input some data, check it for validity, process the data in some way, and then output the data. When a module is overloaded with functions, major maintenance problems occur. What happens is that all the functions become so coupled together, e.g. by the fact that they use the same variables, that a change to one of the functions invariably means that changes have to be carried out to the other functions. Usually a good indication that this problem is afflicting a system is that many of the modules have large parameter lists, or the specification of the modules are long and consist of sentences joined together by a number of occurrences of the word *and*.

A further problem with system architectures is that modules may become closely coupled together by virtue of the fact that they use the same global data—where a change to one module necessitates a change to all the modules that are connected to it. The concrete manifestation of architecture problems is a phenomenon known as *system ripple*. System ripple occurs when a change is made to a system with a poor architecture. A change to one module necessitates changes to other modules connected to it, these modules give rise to changes in the modules that are connected to them, these further changes then give rise to a higher number of changes in other modules, and so on. This ripple effect means that even small changes can consume large amounts of resource.

1.4.5 Reusability

Even though developers may have constructed a large number of systems before, they will, almost invariably, start anew when developing a system—even though they may have developed modules similar to the ones developed in the past, the first inclination is to program such modules afresh. There are good reasons for this lack of planning. First, the software development methods of the past have encouraged the development of modules that are overloaded with functionality, and highly connected to other modules in a system. Such modules cannot be reused directly and need modification. Such modification can use as much resource as programming from scratch. Another problem is that modules in one system are never quite the same as the modules required for another system; some small modification is necessary. In poorly designed systems this modification can use up a large amount of resource.

There have been a number of success stories in terms of reusability. However, these have normally involved libraries of modules which manipulate simple data types and which have a single well-defined function, e.g. subroutine libraries for numerical analysis, where the most complex object that is manipulated is a two dimensional array of real numbers. This book introduces a technique that is capable of generating structures that can be reused time and time again—even when these structures are complex. It demonstrates that using object-oriented development techniques, and an object-oriented language, results in a library of reusable components that require very little work to incorporate them into a new system.

1.5 WHAT IS AN OBJECT-ORIENTED PROGRAMMING LANGUAGE?

Object-oriented programming languages are languages in which objects can be implemented, together with facilities for ensuring that the implementation of objects can be hidden from the programmer, and facilities that enable a high degree of reusability to take place. This statement is rather platitudinous, and it is the aim of this section to explore this statement in a little more detail. Later in this book you will see many of the ideas worked out in practice in a language called C++, a superset of the C programming language that we all have come to love and hate.

Objects are found in all applications—a plane in an air-traffic control system is an object, an invoice in a purchasing order system is an object, and a student in an educational enrolment system is another example of an object. Object-oriented programming languages implement objects as data structures and modules which access the data structures. They enable a programmer to produce an entity known as a *class* which describes the data structures and the modules.

Figure 1.3 shows the structure of a typical class, in this instance a class that describes a queue. Associated with this class would be a description of the stored data that makes up the object, together with a description of the operations that allows access to the data—the operations being implemented as modules—and some mechanism for specifying what facilities of the class can be accessed by the programmer who employs the objects described by the class in an application.

This, then, is the base idea on which object-oriented programming languages are based. The various facilities that are associated with objects in a language, the number of these facilities, and the quality of their implementation, are a good guide to the object-orientedness of a programming language. The remainder of this section describes these facilities.

The first facility that an object-oriented programming language possesses is that of providing a means whereby access to a data structure is restricted. For example, the designer of the queue object described in this section would, almost invariably, want to prevent a programmer from manipulating the base data structure that implements the queue. If such manipulation was allowed it would lead to the development of a system rather like that shown in Fig. 1.2(a), where references to the underlying data structures are found scattered throughout the system.

Such a system is a software maintenance headache since a change to the underlying data requires, as a minimum, that the programmer implementing the change examines every module

CLASS

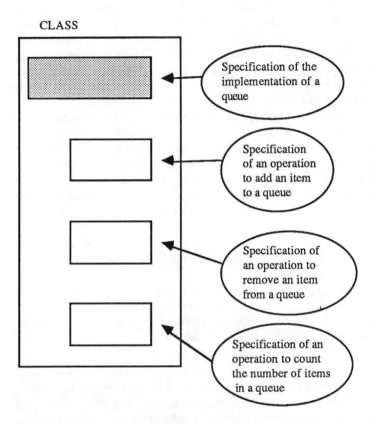

Figure 1.3 A class that specifies a queue.

that references the data structure. In practice, it also leads to a vast amount of change necessitated by modifying each module that refers to the internal details of the data structure. The facility that allows access to a system to be severely restricted is known as *information hiding*: the information about a data structure is hidden beneath a series of operations that only allow access to the data structure via parameters. So, for example, the operation of adding an item to a queue would be implemented as a module that had two parameters: the first would be the item to be added, and the second would be the queue which would be added to.

Another feature of an object-oriented programming language is *polymorphism* or, as it is sometimes called, *genericity*. This allows the software developer to define the data and operations that implement an object via the class mechanism, and instantiate the class for a variety of components in the data part of the class. For example, an object-oriented programming language would enable a developer to implement a queue class for, say, integers, and then use that class for a queue of messages in a communications system, a queue of spool files in an operating system, or a queue of back orders in a purchasing system. Moreover, this instantiation of a new instance of a class is usually a matter of writing a few extra lines of program code. Polymorphism allows a developer to build up a library of reusable objects, and contributes greatly towards the ability to develop reusable software.

A further feature of an object-oriented programming language is *inheritance*. What this term describes is the ability of the developer to define a new class that inherits many of the feature of an existing class. For example, a commercial data processing system developer may have already defined a class for purchase order objects which would describe an implementation in terms of a data structure that would hold information about the name of a customer making an order, the customer's address, the products being ordered, etc., and a list of operations which communicate with data described by that class.

If another application came along, say for a slightly different system which handles orders for dangerous chemicals, where the purchase order contains information about handling instructions for the items to be delivered, then the developer is able, using an object-oriented programming language, to define a new class which mainly consists of items from the old purchase order class, together with new extensions and operations which handle the new special case. In general, a good object-oriented programming language should allow a class to inherit properties from more than one class, and inherit properties more than once from the same class.

A final facility that should be provided by a class is dynamic memory management where the underlying compiler software allows an object to be created when it is required, and deallocated when it is no longer needed.

The degree to which a programming language can be called object-oriented is dependent on how many of the above facilities have been implemented, and the degree of simplicity with which they have been implemented. There is a broad spectrum of languages which could be described as having object-oriented properties, ranging from languages such as Ada with a small number of facilities, up to the programming language SmallTalk which has, as its base facility, the object, and where every other facility of the language is integrated with this idea of an object. The language C++ described in this book lies in the top quarter of the object-oriented language spectrum: it is certainly nowhere as sophisticated as SmallTalk, but still contains a considerable amount of object-oriented facilities, albeit that some of the facilities have been implemented in what might seem a slightly eccentric manner.

My suspicion is that of all the programming languages that have object-oriented facilities, it is C++ that will be the most popular and long-lived. This is not because it is an elegant language, but because it is built upon an existing, popular programming language—C. The history of software engineering still only occupies three and a half decades. However, it has lasted long enough to show us that radical change does not occur in software development, but that change, dampened by the fact that we have a massive software maintenance mountain, is an evolutionary process that takes place in increments—increments that, more often than not, are based on an existing technology, programming language, or development method.

1.6 FURTHER READING

An excellent textbook that describes the type of conventional software engineering which has been the subject of this chapter is Pressman (1987), it also contains a good discussion of object-oriented techniques. A splendid book which describes software engineering techniques that can cope with change is Lamb (1988). If you have had your appetite whetted for prototyping, the first three sections of Hekmatpour and Ince (1988) contain a good review of the techniques that can be used to deliver an early version of a software system. Lientz and

Swanson (1980) was the first treatment of software maintenance that indicated that there were major problems with this part of software development. Yau *et al.* (1978) was the first paper to point out the ripple effect that occurs in systems when one change gives rise to a series of changes. Lehman has been at the forefront of research into the dynamics of systems that change during development and maintenance. The most approachable account of his work can be found in Lehman (1985). The best introduction to object-oriented techniques is Meyer (1988). This not only contains an excellent description of the problems with conventional development, but also describes the advanced object-oriented programming language Eiffel.

BIBLIOGRAPHY

Hekmatpour, S. H. and Ince, D. C. (1988) *Software Prototyping, Formal Methods and VDM*, Addison-Wesley, Reading, Mass.

Lamb, D. A. (1988) *Software Engineering, Planning for Change*, Prentice-Hall, Englewood Cliffs, NJ.

Lehman, M. M. (1985) Programs, cities, students—limits to growth, in *Program Evolution*, Ed. Belady, L. L. and Lehman, M. M., Academic Press, New York.

Lientz, B. P. and Swanson, E. B. (1980) *Software Maintenance Management*, Addison-Wesley, Reading, Mass.

Meyer, B. (1988) *Object-oriented Software Construction*, Prentice-Hall, Englewood Cliffs, NJ.

Pressman, R. S. (1987) *Software Engineering—A Practitioner's Approach*, McGraw-Hill, New York.

Yau, S. S., Collofello, J. S. and MacGregor, T. (1978) Ripple effect analysis of software maintenance, *Proceedings COMPSAC 78*, pp. 60–65.

2

OBJECT-ORIENTED PROGRAMMING

AIMS

- To describe in some detail the main concepts of object-oriented programming.
- To outline the main advantages of object-oriented programming.

2.1 INTRODUCTION

The path to object-oriented software development has been a long and interesting one. It started with one of the earliest high-level programming languages, Simula 67, progressed via modern ideas on data abstraction, and is currently exemplified by modern object-oriented programming languages such as Eiffel, Loops, and SmallTalk. It is associated with modern software development methods which place data at the heart of development, rather than the functions of a system. The main ideas behind object-orientation are: data abstraction, inheritance, polymorphism, and dynamic binding. The aim of this short chapter is to describe these ideas in outline, later chapters will discuss them in much more detail, including their implementation in the programming language C++.

2.2 ABSTRACT DATA TYPES

The critical idea behind object-oriented programming is the *abstract date type*. An abstract data type is a collection of data and the operations on that data. A specification of an abstract data type concentrates on describing data, not by its structure, but by the collection of operations that operate on it. Software engineers who design in terms of an abstract data type, say a stack, are less concerned with the structure of the stack—whether it is implemented by an array or a linked list—but rather the effect of the operations on the stack. They are concerned, for example, that when an item is pushed onto the stack, and then popped off, the stack remains unaltered.

A direct result of this concentration on properties is that the user of an abstract data type should not be worried about the way that a data type is represented in the computer. As an example of an abstract data type, consider the queue. This is an abstract data type used in many applications: queues are found in operating systems, commercial data processing systems, and communications systems—to name a few. An object-oriented programming language enables a system designer to define the form of queues that are available— e.g. whether they are linked lists, arrays, or some other implementation—and specify the operations that are available to the programmer who uses the abstract data type. The mechanism that achieves this is known as the *class*. A class is a template for describing data, and the operations on that data. An example of a class is shown below. Each instantiation of a class in a program is known as an *object*. The actual structure of a class will vary, depending on the object-oriented programming language used. The description below is not taken from any particular language, but just illustrates the general principles. Later in the book you will see how classes can be implemented in the language C++.

```
class queue
private:
   queuearr: array[1..20] of messages;
   queuepointer :=1;
public:
   additemq (m:messages);
   integer countq();
   remitemq (var m:messages);
end class
```

The first line defines what follows to be a template for the abstract data type `queue`. There are two parts to the class: a private part headed by the keyword `private`, and a public part headed by the keyword `public`. The private part describes any parts of an object that cannot be used by a programmer. The two private parts in the class above are `queuearr`, which holds up to 20 message items, and a pointer `queuepointer`, which points at the next location in a queue at which an item can be added. The specification of `queuepointer` states that when an object of type `queue` is declared its `queuepointer` part will be initialized to 1.

The public part of the queue declares that a number of parts of a queue object are going to be available to any programmer who uses queues. First, the subroutine or procedure `additemq`, which adds a message m to the queue will be available, followed by `countq`, which returns with the number of messages in a queue, and, finally, `remitemq` which removes a message from a queue and sets m equal to the message.

The class above does not show the procedures associated with the class; in an object-oriented programming language they are written as they would be in conventional languages such as Pascal or C. Some languages insist that they are included in the class, others, such as C++, insist that their code is written outside the class. However, this is just a small syntactic detail which can be glossed over. I will not show the code of these procedures, as it will be the same as code in any other high-level procedural language.

Objects of type `queue` can now be declared in a program. For example, the queues in and out can be declared as

```
queue in, out;
```

If a programmer wants to find out the number of items in the queue in and set the variable `nitems` equal to this total, all that he or she would write is

```
nitems := in.countq();
```

If the programmer wishes to add a message m1 to the queue out then all that would need to be written would be:

```
out.additemq(m1);
```

Those of you familiar with languages such as Pascal will notice that what the class mechanism does is to promote the idea of a procedure as having the same status as data types such as integer and character. This is an idea that, at first, seems, quite strange, but which most programmers feel very happy with after a short time.

The components of the class that are declared private cannot be accessed by any programmer, apart from the programmer who develops the public facilities of the class, when these facilities are implemented. This means that statements such as

```
in.queuarr[i]:=m1;
```

are illegal. This way of declaring objects has a major advantage: the code that uses the objects defined by classes will not contain references to the internal data structures of the classes. This means that when a system that uses classes needs changing, e.g. during maintenance, all the changes tend to be localized to classes. For example, a change to the internal structure of a queue will only require changes to the procedures that form part of the queue class. Since the main processing code of a system that uses the queues will not have any reference to the internals of a queue, there will be little change needed.

This idea, known as *information hiding*, is crucial to producing systems that are easy to maintain. Although it was developed independently of object-oriented programming languages it has, quite rightly, been embraced by the designers of such languages.

Abstract data types are now regarded as such a fundamental part of object-oriented programming languages that many commentators regard the development of software systems using such languages as purely the manipulation of abstract data types, with the facilities described in the remainder of this chapter supporting this process.

2.3 POLYMORPHISM

When you have developed a number of computer systems—even systems for widely different application areas—you will notice that a high degree of commonality between the abstract data types that are used. For example, virtually every computer system that I have programmed has required a table. The items in the table may be different: in commercial data processing systems they might be entities such as employees, while in an operating systems they tend to be entities such as processes and files. Nevertheless, much of the software that we develop is often replicated in structure from one application to another. Object-oriented programming languages allow classes to describe general objects which can be oriented towards a particular application. This feature is known as *polymorphism* or *genericity*.

An example of polymorphism is that of the queue. Queue objects are used in a large number of diverse applications. A class declaration which reflects this is shown below

```
class queue [t]
private:
    queuearr: array[1..20] of t;
    queuepointer :=1;
public:
```

```
    additemq (m:t);
    integer countq();
    remitemq (var m:t);
end class
```

This declaration is very similar to the previous one, except for the introduction of the text `[t]` in the first line. This states that the class `queue` will be parameterized over a type `t`, which can be replaced by any type when the queue is used in an application. For example, if the queue was to be used in a message transmission system, then an example declaration might be

```
queue [messages] in, out;
```

This would declare two queues `in` and `out` which contain messages. However, if the queue was to be used in a commercial data processing application, where purchase orders were to be stored, then the program code declaring the objects `back_orders` and `current_orders` would be

```
queue[purchase_orders] back_orders, current_orders;
```

Thus, via polymorphism, object-oriented programming languages enable a library of basic abstract data types to be written, which can then be reused from application to application.

2.4 INHERITANCE

A major property of an object-oriented programming language is *inheritance*. To describe this concept in detail, consider the example of an employee record in a personnel system. In such a system there will be a number of categories of employee, but, basically, they will share the vast amount of data that describes them. For example, each employee will have a works number, a tax code, an address, a salary, etc. This means that a class can be defined which describes an employee. Its private part will contain the data on each employee, while the public part would normally contain procedures that enable objects of the class to be manipulated, e.g. procedures to change a tax code, to modify a salary, and to indicate a change of address.

Unfortunately, some employees will differ from others. For example, there may be a set of employees called managers who own company cars, and it is felt that the personnel records of these employees should contain details of the car they currently drive, in case, for example, an accident is notified to the company. Also, there may be employees whose salary is made up of a basic salary together with performance-related bonuses calculated using factors such as their sales performance.

An object-oriented programming language allows a programmer to define a base class *employee* which contains common data and operations and also allows the programmer to develop new classes that reflect different categories of employee, by inheriting many of the properties of an employee together with some new ones for the category of employee being considered. For example, the class below defines objects called senior managers who have a car:

```
class senior_manager inherit employee
private:
    current_car: cars;
public:
    integer calculate_car_tax();
end class
```

This states that a new class `senior_manager` will contain all the private and public parts of `employee`, together with a private item of data `current_car` which holds some identification of the current car being owned, and a procedure `calculate_car_tax` which calculates the tax allowance that the company car attracts.

Objects described by the class `senior_manager` can be declared, and use all the facilities of the class `employee`, together with the procedure `calculate_car_tax`. The process of a class being given the facilities provided by another class is known as *inheritance*; where a class inherits the properties of two or more classes, it is known as *multiple inheritance*.

Another facility connected to inheritance is the ability to redefine a facility provided by a class. For example, if we assume that the class `employee` contains a public procedure `calc_pay` which calculates an employee's pay, then a number of classes derived from this class may require a new version of `calc_pay` to take account of particular features of that type of employee. For example, there may be a class `salesman` whose pay is partly calculated from an annual salary, but is supplemented by a bonus formed by adding some proportion of monthly sales. An object-oriented programming language allows a class for this employee to be defined which redefines the procedure. For example, the header

```
class salesman inherit employee;
redefines calc_pay;
```

notifies the compiler for the programming language that the version of `calc_pay`, provided as part of the class `employee`, will be replaced by another procedure with the same name. This code would be written by the programmer who develops the new class and, somehow, differentiated from the original `calc_pay` procedure—usually by prefixing the name of the procedure by the class name.

2.5 DYNAMIC BINDING

The final facility provided by an object-oriented programming language is *dynamic binding*. This describes the ability of a programming language to determine the dynamic form of an object during execution. For example, assume that in the personnel system described in the previous section, there are two classes: `employee`, which describes the vast bulk of employees in a company; and `manager`, which describes employees who manage the company. Suppose these two classes each had a separate public procedure `print_details`, which prints the details of objects described by each class. Dynamic binding is exhibited in the following fragment of code

```
employee e;
manager m;
.
.
.
e:= m;
e.print_details();
```

Which version of `print_details` would be used? An object-oriented programming language would be able to see that instead of holding an employee object, e is currently holding a manager object and would apply the print procedure associated with that object.

This ability to sense the type of the object is crucial, and enables object-oriented programming languages to reduce the amount of programming necessary in large software applications. The example used in this section is a good one to illustrate this point. If an object-oriented programming language was not used, then the code of the system would require some sort of flag embedded in the data for each employee, to indicate what sort of employee he or she was. In order to carry out the printing process a case statement would be required to sense which sort of flag was contained in the employee, and then call the procedure associated with this employee.

2.6 THE ADVANTAGES OF USING OBJECT-ORIENTED LANGUAGES

There are a two advantages in using an object-oriented language. First, the facilities for data abstraction encourage the development of systems that, when modified, only require changes to relatively small parts of the system. Second, the facilities for polymorphism, dynamic binding, and inheritance enable a software developer to build up a basic library of classes that can be reused with little extra effort for new applications.

For example, a commercial data processing software company would soon build up classes for invoices, delivery notes, reminder letters, purchase orders, and queues, which can be used in a variety of retailing applications. In this way a high degree of reusability can be achieved and novel techniques such as prototyping—described later in this book—can be applied during the requirements analysis stage of the software project.

One of the most important points that should be made about object-oriented programming, object-oriented programming languages, and object-oriented software engineering is that it radically changes the attitude the software developer takes towards development. Instead of concentrating on functionality—what a system should do—the developer has to concentrate on the underlying data. This is a major theme of the remainder of this book, which attempts to show that although the culture change for object-oriented methods is great, much of conventional software engineering can be used in developing systems using the object-oriented paradigm.

2.7 SUMMARY

Object-oriented programming languages are languages that enable a software developer to define objects via a mechanism known as the class. By doing this, such languages provide the means to produce easily maintained systems and also give the developer who has built up a library of abstract data types the ability to produce a system with very little effort indeed.

3

AN OBJECT-ORIENTED APPROACH TO SOFTWARE DEVELOPMENT

AIMS

- To describe, in outline, the software development method used in this book.
- To describe, in outline, the validation and verification techniques that support the software development method described in this book.

3.1 INTRODUCTION

The remaining chapters of this book will describe a software development method that is based mainly on considerations of the data inherent in an application. The whole development process that will be described is driven by the idea of an object—not just during programming, but during all the other activities in the software project. Since this chapter is expository in nature it will contain no self-assessment questions. Each section of the chapter represents a particular grouped set of tasks in the development method.

3.2 THE IDENTIFICATION OF ENTITIES, ACTIONS, AND ATTRIBUTES

The first stage in the development method is the identification of entities. An *entity* is an object in an application which has associated with it a set of data and a series of actions. An action is an event that operates on an entity during a moment in time which cannot be decomposed into any further actions. For example, the placing of an order by a customer in a purchase order system is an example of an action. In the case of this action it affects the purchase order entity.

Two other concepts are also important, that of an *entity attribute* and an *action attribute*. The latter is the data associated with an action. For example, the action of placing an order for a number of commodities would be associated with a series of data: the name of the customer who placed the order, the address of the customer, the purchase order number, a collection of commodities to be ordered, and so on. An *entity attribute* is the subsidiary data which is associated with an entity. For example, in a system for a hire car operation an obvious entity is the car; associated with each car would be the registration number, the type of car, its current mileage, data describing its service history, and so on.

Requirements analysis in our development method consists of processing a statement of requirements, removing all the problems such as inconsistencies, ambiguities, and platitudes, and then carrying out the following five-stage process:

- Discover the entities in a system by looking at the base objects that the system manipulates.
- For each identified object list the items of data associated with these objects, these will be the entity attributes.
- Look at the external events that occur in the application and discover how these are communicated to the system.
- Define the actions that need to respond to the events.
- Identify the action attributes for each action.

As an example of this, consider a system for booking theatre seats. The first step involves identifying the entities in such a system. Typical entities for the theatre booking system would be a customer and a seat. The second step would identify the entity attributes. For a customer these would be the name, the address, and a telephone number by which the customer could be contacted if a performance that has been booked is cancelled. The next stage is to look at the external events in the system. There would be a number of these. For example, a customer could telephone and book a seat or a series of seats, or a customer might telephone and cancel a seat booking.

Other external events might be associated with the system manager, e.g. the system manager may set up a new configuration of seats in the theatre's auditorium—the theatre may have quite a large repertory of productions, some of which require space normally taken up by seats. Also, the system manager may want to change the charging policy for seats, depending on the production time: a matinee, for example, would normally involve cheaper seats than an evening performance.

The next stage is to look at how these events are communicated to the application as data. For example, the process of a customer cancelling a seat booking would involve the customer communicating over the telephone or turning up in person and providing the booking staff with details such as the seats cancelled and the performance data.

Finally, the actions that are required by the system to respond to external events are listed and the data associated with each action described. For example, the action of booking a seat would be a typical action identified in a theatre booking system. The data associated with this action would be the name of the customer, the customer's address, the seats required, the performance details and whether it was for a matinee or an evening performance.

Once this part of the analysis has been completed the analyst should have produced a list of actions, action attributes, entities, and entity attributes. The remaining part of the analysis process is to order the actions in time.

3.3 ORDERING ACTIONS IN TIME

Actions occur in a distinct order in time: certain actions preclude other actions following them in time or preceding them in time, other actions insist that a particular action has to precede it or another action has to follow it. An important part of the requirements analysis process is to document the temporal relationship between actions. Examples of such temporal relationships are the following:

- The action of creating a purchase order has to precede any other actions on that purchase order.
- The action of cancelling a seat has to follow the booking of a seat.
- The action of returning a car to a car hire company has to follow the hiring of the car.

In this text a graphical diagram known as an *entity life history* will be used to describe this time relationship. An example of this form of notation is shown in Fig. 3.1. This shows the ordering of actions on the entity *car*, which is an entity in a system for a car hire company. The top level of the diagram gives the name of the entity. The next level states that a car will first be obtained, it will then undergo hirings and finally will be disposed off. The box marked *hire body* describes what the hiring part of the system involves: it first involves customer hirings, followed by maintenance on a car. The box marked *customer hire* describes the fact that a repeated number of hirings is to take place, the asterisk in the box *hirings* indicates that all the boxes underneath it are to be repeated a number of times. Finally, the boxes underneath the box marked *hirings* show that a customer hire is always followed by a return. This diagram, therefore, describes a situation whereby a car is obtained, and then a series of actions consisting of a series of hires and returns followed by a maintenance action is executed, the whole process being terminated by the action of disposing of a car.

Such diagrams are a good aid to validation and verification: they enable the analyst to discover whether any events in the system have been missed. Indeed, in Fig. 3.1, an event has been missed: that of a customer crashing a car, and the car being written off. However, we will leave the discussion of how this is specified until the next chapter.

The final process that affects the entity life history diagram is that of annotating it with basic operations. A basic operation corresponds to some operation on an entity—e.g. updating the maintenance record of a car—or some top-level processing code, e.g. program code which prompts the clerk who uses the car hire system for car details. An example of an entity life history annotated with basic operations is shown in Fig. 3.2.

Each basic operation is represented as a square box with a number in it. A description of each of these boxes is shown below:

1. A hire car is created.
2. The clerk at the hire company gives details of the car, e.g. its registration number and its make.
3. The car is updated with its make.
4. The car is updated with its registration number.
5. The clerk at the hire company gives the details of the customer, e.g. name, address, telephone number, and so on.
6. The clerk at the hire company gives the hire period of the car.
7. The customer details are added to the car.
8. The hire period of the current hire is added to the car.
9. The car is marked as being hired.

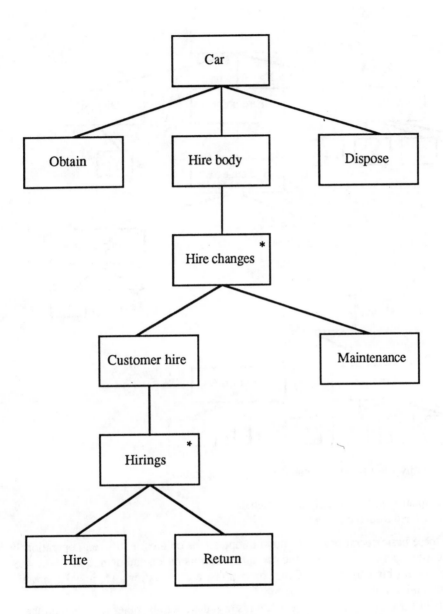

Figure 3.1 An example of an entity life history.

10. The car is marked as having been returned.
11. An invoice is prepared by the system.
12. The clerk at the hire company gives the details of the maintenance that is to take place.

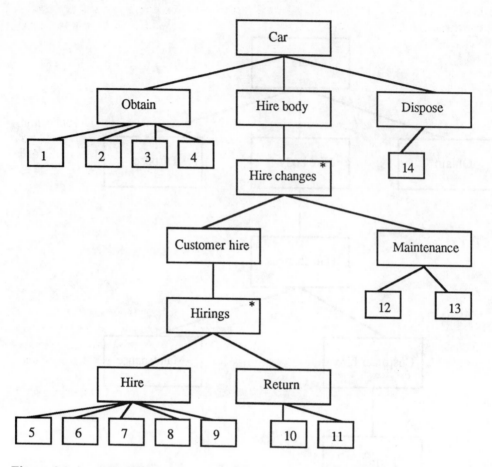

Figure 3.2 An entity life-history annotated with basic operations.

13. The car is updated with details of the maintenance.
14. The car is deleted from the system.

A number of these basic operations correspond to operations on a car entity, e.g. operation 1 creates a car entity, operation 3 updates the car entity with its make, and operation 7 adds the details of the current hirer to the car. Other operations, e.g. operations 11, and 12, are all concerned with top-level processing.

Now this is just one example of an entity life history, there will be other entities with their life histories which will have operations associated with it. For example, when a car is disposed of, it is normal for the details of the car to be written to an archive; thus, if anybody wants to know who bought the car from the hire company that information can be found easily—perhaps in response to a request from the police. This means that another entity in the system might be an archive record, such a record will have its own entity life history and will be associated with operations such as creating an archive record and updating an archive record with the name of the purchaser of a car.

It is worth pointing out that addition of the basic operations can be carried out during requirements analysis or during design; however, it is important that it is finished by the time that the design is complete.

3.4 DEVELOPING THE DATA DESIGN

The next stage in the development process is to design the data associated with an application. The processes that were described in the last two sections will have given rise to a number of entities and basic operations. The next stage is to develop some description of the stored data that will support these entities, and a description of the basic operations that will be required. The concept that we shall introduce in Chapter 6 is the *abstract data type*. This is a data type which lies at a high level of abstraction, and has associated with it a series of operations. A number of abstract data types will be presented in Chapter 6. In this section we will briefly outline one: the sequence.

A sequence is a collection of data items that are stored in some predefined order. For example, a set of personnel records stored in order of an employee's tax number is an example of a sequence, as is a queue of spool files in an operating system. In the former, the sequence order is determined by information in each element of the sequence; in the latter, the order is usually determined by the order in which items join the queue.

The entities identified in the analysis part of the development process will give rise to abstract data types, and it is the purpose of the data design task to specify those abstract data types in terms of the stored data and the operations on the data. The operations will correspond to basic operations which annotate the entity life history. ,

The specification of abstract data types, as described in this book, is simple; an example of the specification of a queue data type is shown below:

queue = SEQ OF spool_files

INVARIANT a queue is in ascending order of *spool_ file* priority

OPERATION add(item:spool_files)

WR q: queue

For this operation to be defined *item* must not already be in *q*. After the operation has completed *item* will be added to *q* in a position determined by its priority.

OPERATION remove(item:spool_files)

WR q: queue

For this operation to be defined *q* must contain at least one item. After the operation has been completed the head of *q* will have been removed and placed in *item*

OPERATION count(number: Integer)

RD q: queue

When this operation has been completed *number* will contain the number of items in the queue *q*.

The first line states that the abstract data type queue will be a sequence of spool files, the assumption being that spool files have been defined elsewhere. The keywords SEQ OF signify that a sequence of spool files that has some implicit ordering is declared. The next line defines a data invariant: this is a condition that must be true for queues *throughout* the execution of the system that uses queues, namely that after each operation has been applied to a queue it will remain ordered on some priority criterion.

Following the data invariant is the specification of three operations. The first defines the operation of adding an item to a queue, the item to be added is *item*, the queue to which it is added is *q* (which acts very much like a global variable). The keyword WR indicates that *q* will be written to, i.e. updated. The text following the definition of *q* defines the processing associated with the operation. The text for the *add* operation describes a condition that must be true *before* the operation is successfully executed and what is true after the operation is executed. The specification of the operation *remove* follows the same pattern: header, parameter, global variable, text that states what must be true before execution and text that describes what happens after execution.

The final operation is *count*, which counts the number of items in a queue *q*. This operation differs slightly from the others. First, the keyword RD is used, this signifies that *q* will only be read and not updated. The second difference is that there is no text that states what must be true before the operation is executed. The reason for this is that the operation will always be able to be executed, irrespective of the number of items in *q*.

This, then, is a sample specification of an abstract data type. Notice that it does not specify any implementation: the sequence could be implemented using either an array or some form of linked list; this decision is made a little later.

At this time in the project, when the data design has been expressed in terms of abstract data types the developer will start developing outline descriptions of the tests that will be applied to the abstract data types in order to check that the operations work well together. This is a form of integration testing. For example, one test of the implementation of the queue abstract data type that a developer will note down at this stage is a test in which an item is added to a queue, the number of items in the queue checked, an item removed and the number of items in the queue checked again.

3.5 IMPLEMENTING ABSTRACT DATA TYPES

The next stage in the process of object-oriented development is that of implementing the abstract data types. Here a decision is made about the implementation of the abstract data type—one that has been delayed until now. In this book the programming language C++—a language based on C but with a number of facilities for the definition and manipulation of objects—is used for implementation. The facility in C++ that allows us to implement abstract data types is the class. An example of a class is shown opposite.

This defines a stack of integers implemented by means of an array of integers `stckarr` and an integer which points to the top of the stack `topelement`. Three operations, implemented by means of C functions, are provided. The first initializes a stack by setting the stack pointer to zero. The code for this is shown in curly brackets. The other two operations are `push`, which places an integer on the stack, and `pop`, which returns the top element of the stack. The code for the last two procedures are defined separately, elsewhere in the program code which contains the stack class.

```
class stack {
   int topelement,
   stckarr[20];
public:
   void initstack(){topelement = 0;}
   void push (int);
   int pop();
}
```

The class definition is split into two parts separated by the keyword `public`. All the information before the keyword `public` cannot be used by a programmer who uses objects described by stack. So, for example, it would be illegal for a programmer to use the variable `stckarr` anywhere in a program. However, everything after the keyword `public` can be used by a programmer. This means that the three functions can be used, but nowhere will the programmer be allowed to manipulate actual data structures; this is an example of the implementation of information hiding discussed in the previous chapters.

Once a class has been defined, the public elements are then implemented; in the case of the stack class this means that the two C functions `push` and `pop` provided for stack manipulation would be developed. Each function would be programmed, its functionality would be checked by means of a unit test, and the programmer would ensure that a large proportion of some structural test metric such as 100 per cent statement coverage or 85 per cent branch coverage has been achieved

The next stage is to carry out the integration tests identified in the previous stage. Here the programmer would test object operations in combination with each other, not only operations on the same type of object, but also on other objects.

3.6 SPECIFYING FUNCTIONALITY

At this stage of the software project all the objects required will be programmed and certified correct. The next stage in the process is to write down what the system is to do, and this involves the development of the requirements specification. In this book a graphical notation known as a data flow diagram will be used for the expression of functionality; an example of a small data flow diagram is shown in Fig. 3.3. This shows the flow of data through a system, and how the data in a system is transformed to other data. Figure 3.3 shows the specification of part of an airline booking system. Users interact with the system by means of a command and a series of parameters. Square boxes represent either sources of data or consumers of data. Bubbles represent processes that transform data into other data.

First, bubble 7.1 splits a command typed in by a reservation clerk into its components: a command name and a number of parameters. The command name is then checked for correctness: if it is incorrect then an error message is produced; however, if it is correct then it is passed on to the part of the system that executes the command.

The parameters are checked by bubble 7.2: if they are correct they, like the command, are passed on for processing. However, if they are incorrect an error is produced that is displayed on

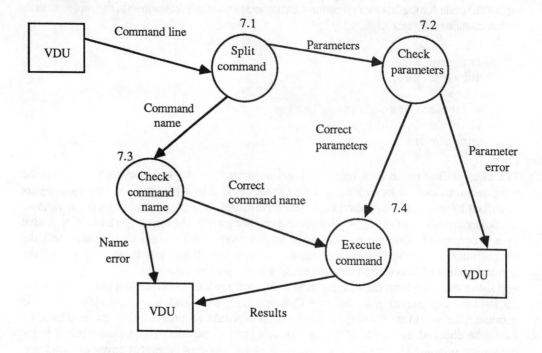

Figure 3.3 An example of a data flow diagram.

a VDU. At this stage do not worry about the numbering in the diagram, all that you should feel confident about is that a data flow diagram is capable of describing what a system should do.

One activity that has to be carried out towards the end of requirements specification is the process of generating the system tests. These tests, which will act as a final check of the system, can only be generated after the requirements specification is complete and have to be left to this late juncture.

3.7 FINAL CONSTRUCTION OF THE SYSTEM

At this stage in the project the system consists of a series of objects and operations, and the requirements specification. The final part of the development process is to develop some top-level program code which calls the functions specified in the classes associated with the system.

The code is developed by first producing a detailed design of the top-level code using a program design language. The program design language used in this book looks, in many ways, like a programming language, apart from the fact that it contains natural language descriptions where detailed processing would occur, e.g. when carrying out a numerical calculation. An example of a fragment of program design language is shown opposite.

It shows the top-level design of a system for administering a library, and describes the repetitive process of a library transaction being read and execution taking place; the transaction representing either the borrowing of a book, the return of a book, or the close down (termination) of the system. Two program-like constructs are shown: a while statement and a case statement.

1   Read in library files
2   While the closedown command has not been initiated
3.1   Read the transaction type
3.2   Decode the transaction
3.3   Case transaction type of
3.4   Borrow: process borrow transaction
3.5   Return: process return transaction
3.6   Terminate: process system termination transaction
4   Close down library files

The process of developing the design of the system consists of a refinement process, whereby the functions of a system are written down at a high level and are then gradually refined until the design can be directly translated into program code. Much of the design will not require too much translation, as it will consist of calls on operations that affect objects which have been already been implemented using the class facility.

    Once the design has been completed and hand translated, the system is then system tested, and then acceptance tested by a subset of the system tests chosen by the customer.

3.8 SUMMARY

This chapter has shown, albeit briefly, how object-oriented development, as described in this book, is carried out. The main difference between this form of development and that outlined in the first chapter is that the data plays a more important part and is considered well in advance of the functionality of the system.

    It is worth pointing out that what has been described in this chapter is an ideal model: where functionality only pops up towards the end of the development process. In practice, functionality will intrude into the early parts of the object-oriented software project, in that the developer will have to ask the customer about what a proposed system is to do in order to derive entities and abstract data types, and will always keep some notes on functionality for reference during the project. Nevertheless, the feature of object-oriented projects that distinguishes them from more conventional software projects is that the data plays a much more important part in the process of development.

4

MODELLING DATA

AIMS

- To describe how the data items in a statement of requirements can be captured and modelled.
- To outline the major deficiencies in a statement of requirements.
- To describe the major features of a statement of requirements.
- To outline a procedure whereby entities in a statement of requirements can be discovered and their life histories specified.

4.1 INTRODUCTION

This section starts the detailed description of the development method which will be further described over the next seven chapters. The stress in this chapter is on examining and specifying the data that forms the kernel of an application. An important point, which cannot be stressed too many times, is that at this stage in a software project employing object-oriented techniques, we are not too concerned with what a system does; this aspect of development is left until quite late in a project and, consequently, is dealt with at a later stage in this book.

4.2 THE STATEMENT OF REQUIREMENTS

The customer statement of requirements is the first document to be processed by a software developer. The size and quality of the statement of requirements will really depend on the sophistication of the customer who produced it: a small hardware company with little experience of information technology will produce a statement of requirements which may take up a few paragraphs of poorly written text, while a sophisticated customer, say a computer manufacturer subcontracting some software, might write a detailed multi-volume statement of requirements which is almost a requirements specification.

No matter who produces the statement of requirements it will, almost certainly, contain problems—the number of problems varying with the sophistication of the customer. This chapter examines these problems in depth. It is important to point out that although this chapter deals with the statement of requirements, many of the problems discussed here surface in the requirements specification. First, it will be useful to examine the categories of statements that are made in the statement of requirements. It is worth stressing here that examples from each category will be found liberally sprinkled throughout a statement of requirements, almost at random.

4.2.1 Constraints

The first category is *constraints*. These will either be *product constraints* or *process constraints*. Product constraints are constraints that limit some feature of the software system that is being developed. For example, a common constraint for real-time software is that certain actions should be completed within a specified time period—usually a stringent period. Process constraints are constraints that limit the process of producing a system. For example, a statement of requirements might insist that the software developer use a particular programming language for development.

SAQ Examine the sentences written below and categorize them as product or process constraints. The statements are as follows:

- The system should occupy no more than 34k of memory.
- The developer should ensure that the system communicates with our existing software systems using the communications protocol described in Appendix C.
- The system should make all calls to the file system in the UNIX operating system via the standard file utilities.
- The developer should ensure that the quality assurance standards used are roughly equivalent to those specified in British Standard 5750.
- The system should respond to the reactor closedown command within 500 milliseconds.

SOLUTION The first statement is a product constraint. The second statement is again a product constraint: it tells the software that the system must have a particular feature. You might have been tempted to think of it as a process constraint, as it instructs the developer to ensure that something is done to ensure that something happens. The third statement is a product constraint; however, it contains some elements of a process constraint as, indirectly, it instructs the developer to employ a particular operating system. The fourth statement is a process constraint as it instructs the developer to carry out the development in a particular way. Incidentally, even though this statement is very laudatory, it stinks: the phrase *roughly equivalent* can be interpreted in so many ways. Detecting such loose phraseology will be dealt with in a later part of this chapter. The fifth statement is a product constraint. ❑

All constraints are important: as their name suggests, they constrain the developer in a particular way, and hence cut down the possible system solutions that can be produced. Consequently, the developer's analysts should spend a considerable amount of time investigating constraints. They should attempt to ask hard questions about whether a particular constraint is necessary, or could be relaxed. For example a developer who is constrained to develop a system with an average response time of 500 milliseconds could, almost certainly, deliver the equivalent system with a response time of 1500 milliseconds more cheaply, and with a greater chance of delivering the system on time and within budget.

4.2.2 Platitudes

You will find platitudes in a statement of requirements. These are statements that everybody—customer and developer alike—can agree on. They state universal truths. For example, the standard platitude I see in many statements of requirements is that the system to be delivered should be user friendly; it's almost as if the phrase was hard-wired into the word-processor that was used to construct that document. Everybody agrees that systems should be user friendly, but there are considerable disagreements about how it can be achieved.

Platitudes are usually easy to detect. The temptation, however, is to ignore them. This is often a mistake: almost invariably, there is something serious and exact behind a platitude. For example, a statement about user friendliness in a system for monitoring and controlling a nuclear reactor usually means that the customer is saying that the interface to the system must be developed in such a way that the operator of the nuclear plant should not make a mistake when communicating with the system—even during periods of maximum stress.

> SAQ Write down some other possible meanings for the platitude *the system should be user friendly*.
>
> SOLUTION Some interpretations are shown below:
>
> - The system should use an advanced window interface with a hardware mouse attachment.
> - Short commands should be provided as well as long commands.
> - That if an operator made a mistake in a command or a parameter, the system should attempt to guess what the operator intended and present the guess to the operator for confirmation.
> - The system should provide help facilities.
> - The system should provide full error checking and feedback to the user as soon as an error has been discovered.
>
> You can see that even the most harmless platitude is capable of multiple interpretations. ❑

Because platitudes often hide important facets of a system it is wise for the analyst to explore platitudes very thoroughly. Some platitudes can be deleted—for example, I saw such a platitude some months ago which stated that the system to be developed should be capable of being executed on the computer for which it was intended—but many can be expanded into functions and constraints.

4.2.3 Design and implementation directives

A design and implementation directive is a statement that directs the developer to develop a system in a particular way. A design directive is concerned with the design part of the development process, while an implementation directive is concerned with directing how the developer should carry out the programming process.

Design and implementation directives are rather similar to process constraints. This book takes the view that a process constraint is a reasonable constraint on the developer, while an implementation directive or design directive is an unreasonable constraint, which takes away much of the responsibility from the developer. This is a slightly fuzzy division which depends on local circumstances. For example, a directive to use a particular programming language for implementation might be very reasonable if the customer is maintaining the system, and the language is the one with which the staff are most familiar. However, if the customer has no intention of maintaining the system, then insisting on a particular programming language can be regarded as an implementation directive: it could be that the developer is able to find a programming language that will deliver a well-structured system with a lower response time.

SAQ Categorize the following as either design directives or implementation directives:
- The system should be programmed in Pascal.
- The system should be split up into three subsystems: one for monitoring, one for control, and one for management information.
- The system should use an indexed sequential file which has the employee name as a key.
- The passwords for staff should be stored in a table.

Assume that they are all unreasonable.

SOLUTION The first statement is an implementation directive. The second statement is a design directive. The third statement is an implementation directive. The final statement is a design directive. ❑

4.2.4 Functions

A function is some expression of what a particular system is to do. Functions will be scattered throughout a statement of requirements almost at random. They will also exist at different levels of abstraction. For example, a system that administers a warehouse may contain a high-level functional description of the system in terms of the movement of items into and out of warehouses. At the same time, it might contain detailed instructions about the commands that should be used by the warehouse staff, and staff who interact with the system from outside the warehouse.

As will be seen later in this chapter, functions are important because an analyst will extract the properties of the data that a system uses from functional descriptions. However, at this stage in the software project all that the analyst needs do is to identify all the functions, and partition them out into a separate section of the requirements specification.

SAQ Which of the following statements are functions?
- The system should detect any warning message issued by a remote radar.
- The system should respond to warning messages within 2 seconds of them being received.
- The system should keep track of stock in the three warehouses that the company owns.
- When the OUT OF STOCK command is typed the system will respond with a list of products that are currently out of stock at all three warehouses.
- The developer should implement the NEW ITEM command in a way that all possible errors in the command will be detected.
- The developer should use the COBOL programming language.

SOLUTION The first statement is a function, expressed at a high level of abstraction. The second statement is a constraint—a product constraint. The third statement is a function, expressed at quite a high level of abstraction. The fourth statement is again a function, this time expressed in some detail. The fifth statement is also a function, although it can be criticized on the basis that it is rather vague. The final statement is a process constraint, it could be an implementation directive if it was not a reasonable request. ❑

4.2.5 Trade-offs

The final category of statement found in the statement of requirements is the trade-off. A trade-off is a statement that gives the developer guidance on which particular factor to optimize if there is a possible design choice between two factors. For example, a common trade-off is that between response time and memory utilization: the more memory an algorithm uses the slower it becomes, and vice versa. Wise customers will list any trade-offs that they want considered, and provide direction about which factor to maximise; in the case above they may instruct the developer to maximize the response time at the expense of memory — this is a very common trade-off.

SAQ Categorize the following as constraints, functions, trade-offs, platitudes, design directives, or implementation directives:

- The system should respond to a valve closing by issuing the close message on the main console and all subsidiary consoles.
- We regard both portability and response time as important. However, we regard the latter as of paramount importance.
- The system should monitor the state of all communication lines attached to the satellite computer.
- The system should be developed using a few well-understood principles.
- The developer should structure the system as a series of five subsystems.
- All error messages should be logged.
- The system should employ VSAM type files for all the system files.

SOLUTION The first statement is a function. The second statement is a trade-off in which the customer tells the developer to aim for response time in preference to portability. The third statement is a function. The fourth statement is a platitude. The fifth statement is a design directive. The sixth statement is a function. Finally, the seventh statement is an implementation directive. Of the two directives, the fifth statement is a true directive. The seventh directive may be a product constraint if the reason for having VSAM files is a valid one; for example, the system from whose statement of requirements the directive has been extracted may need to interface with another system which has this type of file organization. ❑

4.3 PROBLEMS WITH THE STATEMENT OF REQUIREMENTS

Statements of requirements contain many errors, and it is the aim of this section to describe the nature of these errors.

4.3.1 Omissions

A major error that is encountered in a statement of requirements is omission. This usually occurs because the customer has expressed functions and constraints in too high-level a manner, or has just forgotten about some facet of a system. Consider the functional statement below. It is taken from a statement of requirements for a system to process results from a wind tunnel experiment. Such an experiment consists of placing a model in a wind tunnel, attaching pressure sensors to the model, and measuring the stress on the model at discrete times during the experiment.

The statement below describes one command that is used by engineers who interrogate the database of readings produced after an experiment.

The AVPRESSURE command takes three parameters: the name of a pressure monitoring point, a time and another time chronologically later than the first time. The function of the command is to display on the originating VDU the average pressure for the monitoring point over the time period delimited by the times.

There are a number of omissions in this statement.

SAQ Can you think of any omissions that this statement suffers from? Assume that this is the only reference to the command in the whole of the statement of requirements in which it is contained. It might be worth thinking of the type of question the analyst might ask in investigating this function.

SOLUTION The omissions are discussed in the text that follows this question. ❏

The first omission is that there is no description of the error processing that should occur. There is no description of what should happen if the engineer mistypes a monitoring point name, or if the times that are typed in are invalid, e.g. 26:88. There is also no discussion of what should happen if the second time is chronologically earlier than the first time. Should the system ask the user whether the second time is the start of the period, or treat it as an error?

These omissions are rather easy to detect. Unfortunately, there are more subtle omissions. Monitoring instruments sometimes malfunction: they give erroneous readings—usually zero values. What should happen if, for the specified time period, the file contains malfunction readings? One solution is to specify this as an error. However, this is rather drastic. What if the file contained thousands of readings and only a few were in error. The average produced will still be pretty accurate. In this case the average should be displayed, together with the total of malfunction readings in the data. If the number of malfunctions was very high then, almost certainly, an error message should be displayed.

There is another omission—again a subtle one. What if the engineer had asked for a time period for which data was not available, or only partially available? For example, data taken between 11:53 and 12:06 may have been requested—even though the wind tunnel experiment was only started at 12:35. In this case an error message will be displayed. However, what should the system do if the user had asked for data for a period where only a small time space in that period did not have any data associated with it? For example, the average between 12:33 and 14:44 may have been requested and the experiment started at 12:35 and finished at 14:50. There are two possible responses: the harsh one of displaying an error message, or the more realistic one of displaying the average but, at the same time, informing the user that the data was incomplete.

Omissions affect the whole of a statement of requirements and not just the functional descriptions. For example, a statement of requirements which describes the communications equipment that is to be used by a software system may omit important features of that equipment such as the transmission rate, the accuracy of the data that is provided by the equipment, the format of the data, how long the data is available for reading, and the error characteristics of the equipment.

4.3.2 Ambiguities

Natural language encourages ambiguities. I find it very difficult to write more than a page of text without including statements that are capable of a number of meanings. A typical ambiguity in a statement of requirements is contained in the following extract:

> When the OPERATING command is typed the system will be placed in operating mode, and all messages to the subsidiary VDUs connected to the system should be displayed in bold. The messages to main VDUs should be displayed as normal. The messages should be queued using a first-in, first-out priority mechanism.

This rather innocuous statement can be interpreted in a number of ways. The problem arises with the third sentence. Does it mean that all the messages that are processed are to be queued using the specified queueing discipline, or is it a reference to messages that are sent to main VDUs?

4.3.3 Contradictions

A statement of requirements also contains contradictions; these are often easy to detect if they are close to each other in the text. However, such contradictions are often separated by pages of text. By the time a contradiction is read and processed by the analyst the original statement that was contradicted may have been forgotten. A typical contradiction might involve the statement that all commands are to respond within a few milliseconds of being invoked, with the details of one command implying that response time is irrelevant for this particular command.

4.4 PROCESSING THE STATEMENT OF REQUIREMENTS

The aim of this section is to describe how a statement of requirements is processed, the actions that the analyst has to carry out before the objects inherent in that statement of requirements are identified, and how the operations associated with them are described.

Figure 4.1 shows the process. The first stage is for the analyst to discover the obvious problems in the statement of requirements. These will normally be platitudes. On discovering a platitude the analyst should check with the customer whether there is anything behind the platitude: the previous chapter showed that many platitudes have some functionality hidden behind them, and are often inserted into a statement of requirements because of problems that customers have in expressing themselves. If the platitudes hide some functionality, then the analyst should insert the description of the functionality into the statement of requirements.

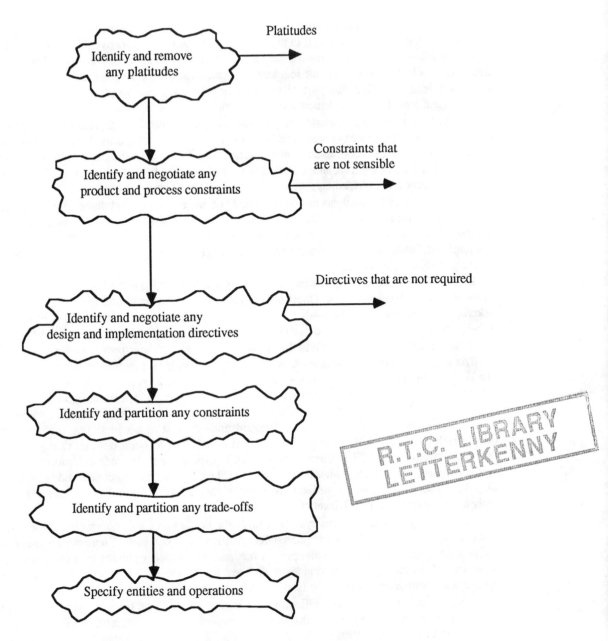

Figure 4.1 The requirements specification process.

The next step is to identify any product constraints, process constraints, implementation directives, and design directives. Remember that the difference between a constraint and a directive is sometimes a hazy one. The major questions that should be asked by the analysts are: is this statement necessary, and are there any circumstances which I do not know about that make this statement a sensible one and, hence, categorize it as a constraint? If there is nothing that can be found that makes the analyst consider the statement as a constraint, then the customer should be encouraged to drop what is, in essence, a directive. If this is agreed, then the developer's job will be much easier; however, if no such agreement is reached then the directives should be inserted into the requirements specification in a separate section—it would be a good idea to divide this part of the specification into two sections: one for design directives and the other for implementation directives.

The constraints should be treated in a similar way, i.e. identified and partitioned into two subsections: one for process constraints and one for product constraints. It is important to point out that although this description of partitioning might give the impression of being relatively straightforward, it is an intellectually very difficult task, as the analyst will be on the look out for contradictions, ambiguities, and omissions while carrying it out.

Once this part of the analysis has been carried out, the analyst should detect any trade-offs and then place them in an appendix. Until now the actions of the analyst will be the same, irrespective of the type of software development carried out—whether it is object-oriented or conventional, function-driven software development. The next stage is where the two styles of software development diverge.

In conventional software development the analyst will investigate thoroughly the functions of the system to be constructed. Questions concerned with the actions of the system will be asked. An attempt will then be made to build up a hierarchy of functions, sub-functions, sub-sub-functions, and so on, which describe the processing that occurs in the system, and relate these various categories of function to the product constraints that have been discovered.

The approach adopted in this book is to delay this process of function identification until the last possible moment in the software project, but concentrate on the objects or entities in a system and specify both the operations and the time sequencing of operations associated with these entities. This has the advantage that functionality, which is the component of a software system that is most prone to change, is delayed until the last moment, so that the duration over which changes might occur is minimized. It is only fair to point out that this approach has some disadvantages. First, customers are used to expressing their needs in terms of what a system should do for them, rather than in terms of the data and the effect operations have on that data. There will, almost invariably, be some adverse reaction from the customer who has only experienced function-led development before.

The second problem concerns system testing. It is normal on a software project to develop the system tests as soon after the requirements specification is complete. There are a number of reasons for this. First, it enables the project manager to predict resources for system testing and, second, by asking the question 'how do I test this?', the analyst is able to detect many poor features of a requirements specification such as ambiguity and platitudes.

Delaying the requirements specification process until later in the software project will give the project manager problems with resource estimation. Unfortunately, there is no easy solution to this problem. What can be said is that this disadvantage is small compared with the immense flexibility object-oriented development gives the developer. Also, since the requirements specification will be delayed, the hard questions about its contents could be delayed until very late in a project—almost to a position where if any errors are discovered, they could lead to severe and serious redesign and respecification. However, Chapter 4 will describe a technique that enables the object part of a requirements specification to be validated with a high degree of confidence, and eliminates many of the errors that would be detected by asking hard questions about the testing of a system just after requirements specification is complete.

So, at this stage in the requirements specification process, the analyst will reserve a section in the requirements which will be called *system functions* and fill this in later. The major work that is carried out at this stage is to identify the entities in the system and the operations that they are associated with. This would be placed in a section of the requirements specification which will be called *system entities*. The process whereby this is carried out, and the notations used, will be described in the next section of this chapter. However, before progressing to this part of the chapter it is worth describing some of the peripheral parts of the requirements specification that will need to be constructed in this part of the project.

First, a hardware requirements specification must be written. This will describe the hardware base on which the system is to be implemented and, eventually, run. If there are any differences between the hardware environment used for development and the eventual target environment, then these should also be specified. As well as computing equipment, any other hardware used, such as communications equipment, should be fully specified. So, for example, if a communications link is used, then this section should detail properties such as the format of the data provided by the link, its transmission rate, how erroneous signals are manifested, etc.

The requirements specification should also include a section that describes how maintenance of the system is to be carried out. For example, how errors reported by the customer are to be communicated to the developer, how quickly errors will be dealt with, and how any requirements changes will be processed by the developer.

Another section will include details of training: when training sessions are scheduled, what training materials are to be provided, and what level of staff are expected at which training sessions. A wise developer will schedule some preliminary training, as much in advance of delivery as possible. A major problem with developing a software system is that the analysts often do not meet the real users of a system, and have to base their analysis on conversations with customer staff who might be very removed from the application area. By scheduling training sessions as early as possible, the developer ensures that errors, committed by analysts through defects in the information flow between them and the customer, are picked up earlier than acceptance testing.

A further section to be included in the requirements specification is a description of any support software that is required for the development process. This will detail what software tools are needed. For example, the developer may require a software tool that produces large files of data which are used in system testing and acceptance testing. It is important that if these tools are to be developed in-company, then they are specified in the same way as the software that is to be constructed. For example, an error in a software tool that produces test files with a certain data distribution could mean that an erroneous response time of the system might be demonstrated during system testing, and that the real data would slow the system up during acceptance testing, and lead to considerable redesign and reimplementation.

It is important that such software tools are specified as accurately as the software under development, and also that the same quality assurance techniques are used to validate and verify them. Once the requirements specification process is complete, the requirements specification, apart from function details, is carried forward into the next stage of the project: design. It is important to point out that the requirements specification is not the only document that will have been developed by the end of requirements specification. The developer will also have produced a quality plan, which details how it will be ensured that the final product meets user requirements, and an outline project plan, which details all the tasks that are to be carried out, together with the resources required for each task.

> SAQ Read the statement of requirements that follows this question. Point out the deficiencies in it. If you can detect six deficiencies then you are doing well. Cover up the text following the statement as it contains the answers.
>
> SOLUTION The answer to this question is reproduced in the text, and follows the statement of requirements. ❑

The following is the statement of requirements mentioned in the previous question.

> The system is aimed at giving sales clerks information about orders that are currently placed by a large number of customers—over a thousand. Normally, on average, 50 orders will be stored for each customer. A number of commands should be provided for the sales clerks. These commands should be easy to use.
>
> The computer on which the system is to be implemented will be a PC clone with 1 Mb of main memory.
>
> The DISPLAY command will display the orders currently stored for a particular customer.
>
> The OUT OF STOCK command will print all the orders from customers which refer to items which are currently out of stock.
>
> The REMOVE ORDER command will remove an order from those stored.

There are a number of things wrong with this statement of requirements. First, the description of the computer to be used is inadequate, e.g. there is no mention of any file storage device, something that the system will almost certainly need. The implication in the text is that the orders have already been entered into a file, and only a small subsystem is to be developed. However, it is worth checking on this—the customer may have assumed that the orders will appear magically inside the computer.

There is also the platitude about the system being easy to use. It will be necessary for the analyst to discover the technical capabilities of the staff who are to use the system, before implementing any facility that might help them when using the system.

There is no discussion of how customers and orders are to be represented; should they, for example, be identified uniquely using integers or their names? Also, there is no specification of the error processing that should occur when a command is typed in. For example, what if an invalid customer identifier was typed in when the DISPLAY command was initiated?

There is also a subtle design directive: throughout the statement of requirements there is a reference to *commands*. This seems to imply that the interface to the system is in terms of commands, expressed as a combination of characters, rather than something like a WIMP interface.

There is also a problem with the words *display* and *print*. Do they mean the same thing? Commands that use the word *display* could be asking for data to be displayed on a VDU screen or a similar device, while commands that use the word *print* could be implying that a hard-copy device is used. This would need to be clarified.

4.5 ENTITY ANALYSIS

Entity analysis is the process of identifying the underlying data features of a system. This section describes how entity analysis is carried out, and how entities are documented, together with the actions that are associated with them.

In order to examine some of the concepts that will be discussed in this section, consider the expression of functionality taken from a statement of requirements

> When the order command is executed the purchase order clerk will provide the identity of the customer, and a list of items ordered. The order will be stored until it is processed by the supply subsystem.

This is the type of specification of functionality that can be found in a wide variety of statements of requirements and requirements specifications. Sutcliffe (1988) has characterized this as something akin to the ripple on the surface of a pond when a fish comes near to the surface. That is, it is an external manifestation of something important that is hidden below the surface: in the case of the fish pond the important entity is the fish, while in the case of the purchase order system it is the purchase order.

The analysis that will be described in this section will ignore the external manifestations—the functions—and concentrate on the important entities that lie below the surface. The technique and notation that will be used is borrowed from the front end of a development method known as Jackson Structured Design (JSD), a method developed by the British industrialist Michael Jackson. JSD has, as its main aim, the development of systems that can be easily modified—both during development and during maintenance. One of its main features is that it considers the functionality of a system at a late stage during development.

The important concept in the early stages of JSD is the *entity*. The view taken in this book is that an entity is an object of interest in the application that is being computerized, together with a set of data descriptions about the entity and the actions associated with the entity.

For example, in the example given above, the entity that is being described is the purchase order. The actions that a purchase order suffers are: creation, when a purchase is notified by a customer; amendment, when an order is changed during the period before it is satisfied, e.g. the supplier of an item on the purchase order may discover that the item is out of stock and the customer, on being told this, orders another item; and, finally, purchase order deletion or archival, when the purchase order has been satisfied. The data associated with a purchase order entity would be various. For example, it would contain the name and address of the customer, the settlement terms, the items to be ordered together with the order quantities, and the delivery address.

It is important to point out that the actions that occur on an entity are time ordered, and this time ordering can be specified accurately. Also, some actions, when they have been carried out, can never be repeated for a particular instance of an entity. For example, the purchase order entity first suffers an action which creates it. It may then be affected by a series of amendments ranging from zero up to a high number. Finally, when the purchase order entity has been dealt with, and the customer is happy, the entity is deleted or archived. At no stage after a purchase order has been created can it be created again. It is important to point out that entities can be people such as purchase order clerks, documents such as invoices, or inanimate objects such as transducers.

Before looking at the process of entity analysis in a little more detail, it is worth writing down some definitions.

- *Entity* An entity is an object of interest in an application which has associated with it a series of actions. Typical entities include purchase order, library book, switching message, invoice, clerk, and library borrower.
- *Action* An action is an atomic event associated with a particular entity. By atomic I mean that it is an event which cannot be split up into its components. Examples of events include a clerk inputting a purchase order, an invoice being amended, or a thermocouple being read.
- *Action attribute* An action attribute is some data associated with an action. For example, when a purchase order is communicated to a purchasing system, the attributes associated with this action are the purchase order number, the address of the customer, the items ordered, and so on.
- *Entity attribute* An entity attribute is an item of data associated with an entity that is read, or updated by an action associated with the entity. For example, in a conference booking system the entity *room* will have an attribute that represents the number of people the room can hold.

Before proceeding further it might be worth gaining some practice in identifying actions and attributes.

SAQ In a computerized library system a major entity that the system manipulates is the book. What actions would you associate with the book entity in such a system, and what entity attributes would you expect a book to have?

SOLUTION The actions would be create a book, borrow a book, return a book, and delete a book. The first action would occur when a book was bought for the library, or when a book previously thought to be lost, turned up again. The second action occurs when a borrower removes a book legally. The third action occurs when a borrower returns a previously borrowed book. The final action occurs when a book is removed from the library stock, perhaps because it is in a very poor condition, or because it has been removed without the library staff having been notified. The entity attributes would be: the name of the book, its serial number (a unique number which identifies the book), its ISBN number, the author(s), the publisher, a flag which indicates whether the book is borrowed or on the library shelves, and some identification of the person who has currently borrowed the book. ❑

4.5.1 Identifying entities

Sutcliffe (1988) contains good advice about identifying entities; although the advice is not exact, I have found that it identifies the major entities in a system quite easily. Briefly, the advice is to ask three questions: what application problem is the system that is to be built solving, what are the goals of the system, and what are the objects that the system responds to or manipulates?

Applying this advice to a library system gives us the fact that the problem that is being solved is the one of keeping track of the borrowings and lendings in a library. There may be a number of goals, e.g. to provide accurate information on current book borrowings, to keep track of popular books that are being borrowed, to keep track of books that should be in the library stock but have disappeared, and to provide information on the frequency of loans by users. The objects that the system responds to, or manipulates, are borrowers and books.

It is clear after answering the questions that the two main entities that are important to the library system are books and borrowers. *Book* is the entity that it manipulates and *borrower* is the entity that the system responds to. The borrower carries out a series of actions that are associated with action attributes, and these actions either read or update the attributes of the book entity. For example, a borrower who returns a book provides the system with the action attribute of the book's serial number. This action results in two entity attributes being modified. First, the attribute that describes the book's status—whether it is borrowed or on the shelves—is updated to show that the book is on the shelves; second, the attribute that identifies the current borrower is modified to show that there is no current borrower.

SAQ Have I missed out any entities in the previous discussion of the library system?

SOLUTION Yes, there is one entity that is not major, but is quite important: library staff. Library staff will create the initial details for a book when it is purchased, or is found after being regarded as lost. Consequently, this entity will be associated with the action of creating a book which would have action attributes such as the title of the book and the serial number of the book associated with it. Library staff will also be associated with the action of modifying book details, e.g. they may modify an attribute that had been typed incorrectly when a book was created. ❏

In the library system example I might have been tempted to specify that there were only two entities: library staff and books. After all, library staff are really the people who would input a book's details when it was returned. However, this would be wrong.

SAQ Why would ignoring borrowers as entities be a wrong step in the analysis of the library system?

SOLUTION Because they provide data that is important to the functioning of the library system, e.g. the name of the borrower, which needs to be stored along with book details. ❏

4.5.2 Identifying actions

Again Sutcliffe (1988) gives good advice on the identification of actions. He states that in order to identify the actions in a system, a four-step process should be adopted. First, identify all the external events that happen in the application. Second, find out how these events are communicated to the system that is to be developed. Third, from the previous step, identify the system inputs, these will be action attributes. Fourth, identify the actions associated with the attributes discovered in the third step.

As an example of this consider the external event in the library system of a book being received by the library from a borrower. The event will be communicated to the system by means of the book's serial number being typed in by a library assistant. This means that the book serial number will be an attribute and the action that is associated with it is that of returning a book to stock.

In order to describe this four-step process in more detail, consider a simple room booking system for a hotel. The external events that could occur in such a system are as follows: a room is booked, a room is vacated by a customer, a room booking is modified by a customer, and a room booking is cancelled by a customer. We shall also consider actions carried out by booking staff at the hotel: a room may be removed from availability, e.g. when it is being redecorated, and a room category may be changed, e.g. the addition of a minibar, better bed, and coffee-making facilities would upgrade the room to a higher class.

The first event—that of a room being booked—will be communicated to the system by the customer phoning the time period of the booking, the type of room required, and the name of the customer, together with subsidiary items such as the address and telephone number of the customer.

The external event of a room booking being modified by the customer will involve the customer providing his or her name and the booking period, together with information about the amendment. There may be two types of amendment: the first is to amend the time period, the second is to amend the type of room required. Therefore, there will be two actions associated with this event: that associated with modifying the period of a booking and that associated with modifying the type of room required.

When a room is vacated, this event is communicated to the system by the customer turning up at the reservations desk and giving his or her room number; the system will look up the current day and will then effect the process of notifying the system that the customer has left.

When a booking is cancelled, the customer will provide his or her name and the period of the booking. The system will then expunge the details of the booking. It is important to state that this is a very simple hotel booking system. For example, the fact that a customer, such as a company, is capable of booking blocks of rooms, say for a conference, is not considered.

When a room is taken out of service, this is communicated to the system by a member of the booking staff providing the room number and the period over which it is non-available. When a room category is changed, a member of the booking staff provides the number of the room, the date on which the new category takes force and the new category.

Given that we have now identified the system inputs, the actions can be extracted. Some of the actions are shown below, together with their attributes:

- *Booking* Attributes are customer name, time period of booking, and type of room.
- *Type modification* Attributes are the name of the customer, the time period, and the new type of room required.
- *Period modification* Attributes are the name of the customer, the time period and the new time period.
- *Vacation* Attributes are the name of the customer and the current day.
- *Cancellation* Attributes are the customer name and the time period.
- *Removal* Attributes are the room number and a time period.
- *Category change* Attributes are the room number, start date and the new category.

It is important to point out that the actions that have been defined above are atomic: they cannot be decomposed into further actions. Also, I have ignored a number of other actions that could also occur in a realistic hotel reservation system. For example, a customer could book a period, stay in the hotel and decide to change room in the middle of his or her stay, or decide to leave early. These are all actions and would have to be identified.

At this stage it is important to point out that actions can be associated with a number of entities. For example, in the hotel system there are a four entities: *customer*, *room*, *booking*, and *booking staff*.

The booking of a room is an action associated with a customer, a booking, and a room. These common actions are important for two reasons. First, they establish a link between entities—a link that will, eventually, be reflected in the implementation of the system. For example, in the room booking system this will almost invariably mean that there will be some physical way of connecting together room data, booking data, and customer data by means of a data structure. Second, it provides a time ordering constraint on the system. For example, a room cannot be marked as being booked until a customer has actually phoned in a booking.

4.5.3 Tying actions and entities together

Once actions and entities have been identified, together with their attributes, it will be necessary to document this relationship. In this book the form that this documentation will take is as follows:

- A list of all the actions that the system processes.
- A list of all the entities together with their attributes.
- A list of all the actions grouped together under the entities that they are associated with, and listed with their attributes.

An example of this documentation is shown below for some of the hotel booking system.

System actions

- A customer phones in a booking for a room.
- A customer phones in a cancellation of a room.
- A customer phones in, changing the type of room required.
- A customer phones in, modifying the booking period for a room.
- A customer arrives at the hotel to take up his or her booking.
- A customer leaves the hotel at the end of the period that was booked.
- A member of the booking staff places a room out of action.
- A member of the booking staff changes the category of a particular room.

Entities

- *Room* Attributes: room number, category of room, date of start of service, date of finish of service.
- *Customer* Attributes: customer name, address, billing address, telephone number.

- *Booking staff* Attributes: staff name.
- *Booking* Attributes: booking period, customer name, room number.

Actions

Customer

- *Book* Customer books a room. Attributes: customer name, address, billing address, category of room time period, telephone number.
- *Cancel* Customer cancels a booking for a room. Attributes: customer name, time period.
- *Room change* Customer changes a category of room already booked. Attributes: customer name, time period, updated category.
- *Period change* Customer changes the period of a booking. Attributes: customer name, old period, period change.
- *Arrives* Customer arrives at hotel to take up his or her booking. Attributes: customer name, arrival date.
- *Leaves* Customer leaves the hotel. Attributes: customer name, leaving day.

Booking staff

- *Change category* A member of the booking staff changes the category of a room. Attributes: room number, staff name, new category, start date.
- *Remove room* A member of the booking staff removes a room from service. Attributes: room number, staff name, time period.

Room

- *Create* A room is created with the start day on which bookings can be made. Attributes: room number, category, start date.
- *Delete* A room is removed by specifying the last day on which that room is to be used in its current state. Attributes: room number, final date.
- *Removed* A room is removed from use for a particular period. Attributes: room number, time period.
- *Category change.* A room category is changed. Attributes: room number, staff name, new category, start date.

Booking

- *Booked* A booking is registered for a particular period. Attributes: customer number, customer name, address, billing address, telephone number, time period.
- *Cancelled* A booking for a particular period is cancelled. Attributes: room number, time period.
- *Modified* A booking for a particular period is modified. Attributes: customer name, old time period, new time period.
- *Deleted* A booking is deleted when a customer books out. Attributes: customer name, current date.

- *Makecurrent* A booking is made current when a customer arrives and is allocated a room. Attributes: room number, current date.

Some explanation of the specification would be useful at this stage. The system actions are those corresponding to the main events that happen to the system. The attributes of the entities are straightforward enough and correspond to stored data that will be needed for the system to operate. The entities and actions are, for the most part, straightforward. However, it is worth concentrating on the room entity and the three actions that it suffers.

The first action is that of creation. This corresponds to an operation that is executed when the system is first started up. However, it is also invoked when a room category is changed. The changing of a category of a room from a particular date can be seen as the creation of a different room from that date. This is taken care of by the creation action. This action affects the entity attribute of room which gives the starting day of use of that particular room. The second action that a room suffers is that of deletion, when its last day of use in that particular category has occurred the room will be deleted. Finally, the last action associated with a room is removal: it will be removed for a specified period, e.g. for redecoration.

This, then, is the list of overall system actions, the entities and their attributes, and the actions that each entity is associated with. There are a number of points that should be made about the process that I have described. First a didactic one: the hotel system above bears little reality to a practical one. This was done in order to keep the detail to a minimum for teaching the concepts of entity analysis. For example, when a member of the hotel booking staff changes a category of a room, they have to interrogate the system in order to see whether there is anyone staying in the room past the date on which the room was upgraded. If there was, then either that guest would be moved to another room of the category booked, or the start date of category modification would have to be moved further into the future. This means that booking staff will need some form of enquiry mechanism, a mechanism that has been ignored in the previous discussion.

The next point to be made about the hotel system that has been described is the amount of duplication that occurs. For example, the actions associated with the customer are also associated with rooms; this is as it should be, as there is an intimate connection between them. However, this duplication is not strictly necessary. Customers and booking staff are, in a very real sense, outside the system and are providers of input data. The main entities manipulated by the system are rooms and bookings. Therefore it is only necessary for the designer to concentrate on this part of the specification. However, it is worth listing out *all* the entities in a system as above: in the next chapter, which deals with validation, you will see that descriptions of entities outside the system boundaries provide a good cross-reference check on the correctness of a system. However, it is worth stressing that only those entities inside the system boundary will be passed to the designer of the system. In the case of the booking system above this would mean that only the details about the room and booking entities and their associated actions would be used by the designer.

4.5.4 Ordering actions in time

Actions associated with entities occur in a particular order. For example, the action of cancelling a particular booking in the hotel booking system has to happen after the booking has been created. Another example is that a modification of a booking phoned in by a customer has to occur after the action of creating a booking has occurred. The final stage of the entity analysis is the specification this ordering of actions.

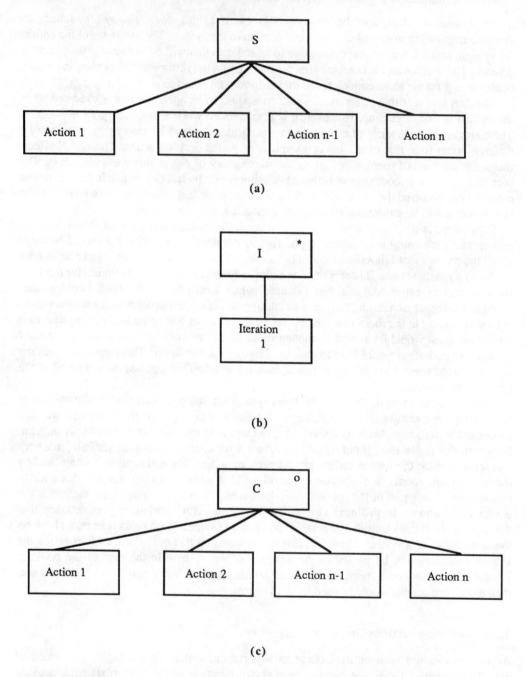

Figure 4.2 Diagrammatic conventions for describing the lives of entities.

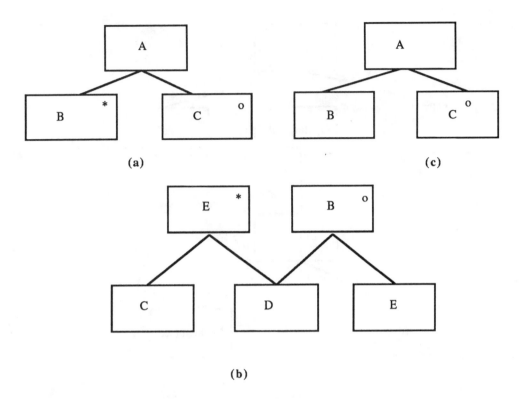

Figure 4.3 Illegal entity diagrams.

In order to do this a graphical notation is used. The elements of this graphical notation are shown in Fig. 4.2. A number of temporal relationships are shown in this diagram. Figure 4.2(a) shows that a sequence S will consist of action 1 followed by action 2, and another $n - 2$ actions; (b) shows that a certain iteration 1 will be executed a number of times, and that the iteration will be contained in box I, the convention used in this book in the diagrams is that for iteration only one box will be iterated; and, finally, (c) shows that a number of actions from action 1 to action n will be conditionally carried out depending on the processing in C. Figure 4.2(a) acts very much like a sequence of programming statements; (b) is equivalent to looping; while (c) is equivalent to a case statement. Each category is identified by a symbol, or lack of symbol, in a box.

A series of actions that are carried out one after another, in sequence, are shown with no symbols, iteration is indicated by asterisks, while condition is denoted by circles. It is important to point out that iteration can occur zero times, i.e. the actions that are iterated may not occur at all.

Another convention that must be observed is that boxes at one horizontal level, which emanate from a parent box, must contain the same symbol. Also there must be no cross-linking of boxes. Figure 4.3 contains a number of illegal combinations of boxes. Figure 4.3(a) shows two different symbols at the same level; (b) shows cross-linking; and (c) shows a box with no symbol used in a sequence followed by a box containing a circle.

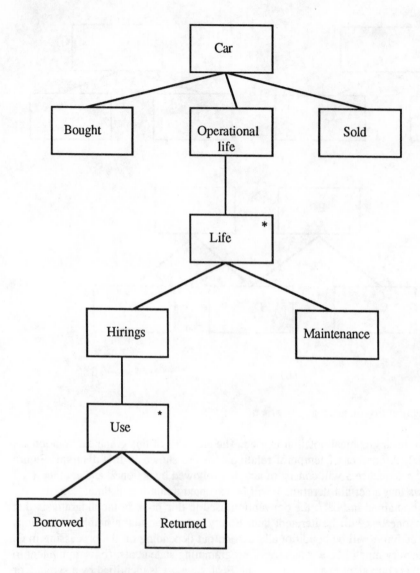

Figure 4.4 The life history of a hire car.

The processes of sequence, iteration, and condition can be combined together to form a diagram which describes the life history of an entity. This diagram is known as a process structure diagram or an entity life history. An example is shown in Fig. 4.4. This describes the life history of a car in a car hire system. It shows that the car is bought by the hire company, and then has a history of being borrowed and then returned, interspersed with periods of maintenance. The car is finally being sold off when its mileage reaches a particular figure. The first level of the diagram shows that the car is first purchased and then undergoes an operational life and is then sold, the operational life consists of an iteration which consists of an iteration of customer hirings followed by maintenance activity.

SAQ Write down a diagram that describes the life of a book entity in a library system. Assume that the book can be notified as being lost and can also be found after being lost.

SOLUTION The diagram is shown as Fig. 4.5. A library book is first purchased, it then undergoes an operational life, and is sold when it becomes unusable. Its operational life consists of a iteration of borrowings, being lost, being found and returned. Notice that a book can only be notified as being missing after it has been borrowed. In a more realistic system it could be notified as being missing before a borrowing, say, during a stock taking. This is a good example of one of the issues that an entity life history can highlight. ❑

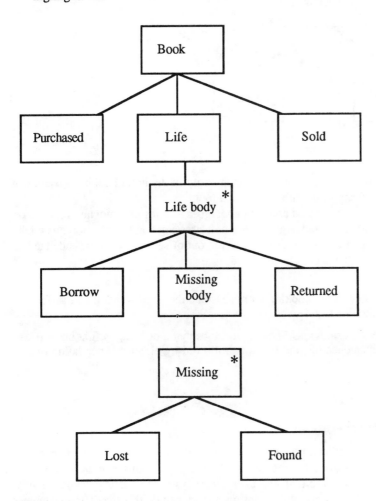

Figure 4.5 Solution to assessment question.

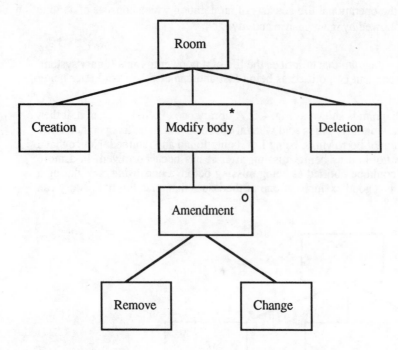

Figure 4.6 The life history of a room.

The timing of the actions that were identified for each entity in the hotel booking system can now be described. Figure 4.6 shows the life history of a room.

As you can see, a room is first created and then undergoes a series of removals from use or category changes and, finally, is deleted. Again it is worth stressing that the iteration box could stand for a zero iteration, i.e. a room will never be taken out of service before it is deleted, a highly unlikely event but one that should be specified.

SAQ Draw the life history of the booking entity, assume the actions that it can suffer are: booked, cancelled, modified, and archived.

SOLUTION The diagram is shown as Fig. 4.7. It shows that a booking is first booked and then undergoes a sequence of modifications followed by either a cancellation or archival. ❑

4.5.5 Specifying basic operations

The previous subsections have shown how entities are identified, how actions associated with entities are discovered, and how the time ordering of these actions can be represented diagrammatically. The final and important step in entity analysis is to create a bridge between the entity analysis task and the process of data design. In order to do this the diagrams created during entity analysis are decorated with smaller, numbered boxes representing basic operations.

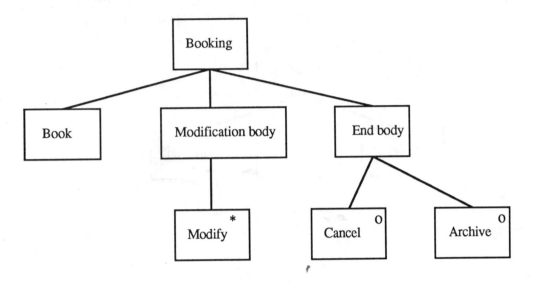

Figure 4.7 The life history of a booking.

A box representing an action will be annotated with smaller boxes which represent the low-level operations that are executed when that basic operation is carried out. Some of these basic operations will eventually be implemented as subroutine calls on stored objects, and provide an input into the design stage of the development method described by this book. In some cases these operations will be in one-to-one correspondence to the actions with which they are associated; however, you will find that often a number of primitive operations are executed when an action is carried out.

An example of the use of primitive operations is shown in Fig. 4.8, which specifies the entity life history of a hire car to which primitive operations have been added. The life history of this entity consists of the car first being bought, then undergoing an iteration of actions which first consist of an iteration of hirings and returns, followed by maintenance.

Figure 4.8 contains a number of numbered boxes corresponding to primitive operations, and will eventually be implemented either by operations on objects or by top-level program code in the system. The action of buying a car is associated with the primitive operation 1 which registers the car with the system. The action of hiring a car is associated with primitive operations 2 and 3. Operation 2 involves the car hire company obtaining details about the hirer, and operation 3 is the process of booking a particular car out to the hirer. The action of returning a car is associated with primitive operation 4, which involves a bill being calculated, and with operation 5, which marks a car as being returned.

Maintenance is associated with operations 6 and 7, which involve the car being marked as being maintained and then being returned to use. I am assuming here that in the car booking system there is an entity called *maintenance history* that will be adjusted with details of the maintenance such as the mileage of the car and the mechanic's name; however, this processing should not be specified here but should be specified as a primitive operation for the entity *maintenance history*. Finally, operations 8 and 9 are associated with the retiring of the car.

Operation 9 removes a car from the booking system and operation 8 archives details of the car to a removable long-term storage medium, say a floppy disk or magnetic tape.

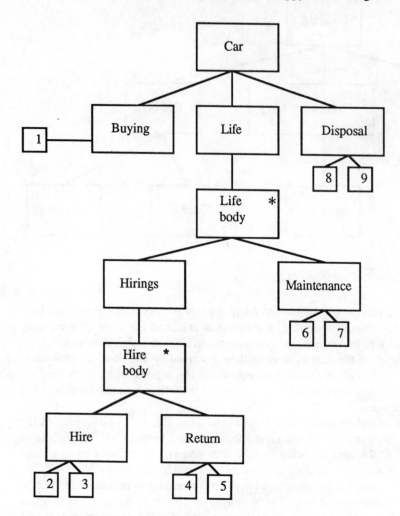

Figure 4.8 The life history of a car and its low-level operations.

Some of these operations affect objects directly, e.g. operation 9, which removes a car from the system. Other operations are concerned with calculations or producing reports. For example, operation 8 is an example of this type of operation. Normally the basic operations are added during the later stages of entity analysis: once the details of each entity and the time ordering of the entity actions has been decided upon. It is also worth stressing that, at this stage, the actual physical details of the implementation should be ignored, details such as whether the archiving medium is magnetic tape or floppy disk, the detailed format of reports, and the range of values of variables should not intrude upon the analysis. They only get in the way of the analysis.

One final step is required which concerns the basic operations: that of detailing what each operation does. At this stage I would recommend that only the details for basic operations that affect the entity under consideration are specified. Details of other processing, such as the production of reports, or the calculation of values such as an account balance or a customer bill, can be dealt with when entities such as account and bill are being considered. Since the following stage in the development cycle, described in the Chapter 6, is the design of the data that is to manipulated, it is important that primitive operations that affect entities are specified before this phase commences.

As an example of this process consider the car hire example. There are four operations which deal with the car entity. Operation 1 registers a car with the system, operation 3 involves a car being associated with a hirer, operations 6 and 7 involve the car being marked as being maintained and then being returned to service, and operation 9 involves a car being disposed of. In this book these operations will be specified in natural language. Each operation is specified by its number on the entity life history diagram, the name of the operation, any parameters and a natural language narrative that describes the effect of the operation. These operations will be processed during data design and refined so that they can be eventually implemented.

1. createcar(carnumber, type)—The effect of this operation is to inform the system that a new car of a particular model *type* described by *carnumber* is to be registered.
3. hireout(carnumber,hirer)—The effect of this operation is to associate the car whose registration number is *carnumber* with the customer *hirer*.
6. maintain(carnumber)—The effect of this operation is to mark the car whose registration number is *carnumber* as being maintained.
7. hirable(carnumber)—The effect of this operation is to mark the car whose registration number is *carnumber* as being able to be hired.
9. remove(carnumber)—The effect of this operation is to remove the car whose registration number is *carnumber* from the system.

A number of points should be made about these basic operations. First, that each operation is associated with the number of a basic operation in the entity life history. Second, that the operation of registering a car uses both the car number and its model, both of these will be action attributes and attributes of the entity *car*. Other operations solely require the use of the registration number, which will be unique for each car.

The final point, which has already been dealt with previously, but bears repetition, is that some primitive operations, which might be assumed to be associated with cars, will be associated with other entities in the system. For example, in a car booking system there will be an entity *booking*, which will deal with the reservation and booking of a car and will include details such as the period of booking. A basic operation that will occur in the hire system is for a customer to place a booking for a car. This will form part of the entity life history for bookings.

Another example of this will be the process of maintenance where the primitive operations for maintenance associated with the car entity are only really concerned with marking a car as being maintained, and not with updating the car's maintenance history. There will be another entity in the system that models the maintenance history, and operations that maintain this entity will be specified in its entity life history.

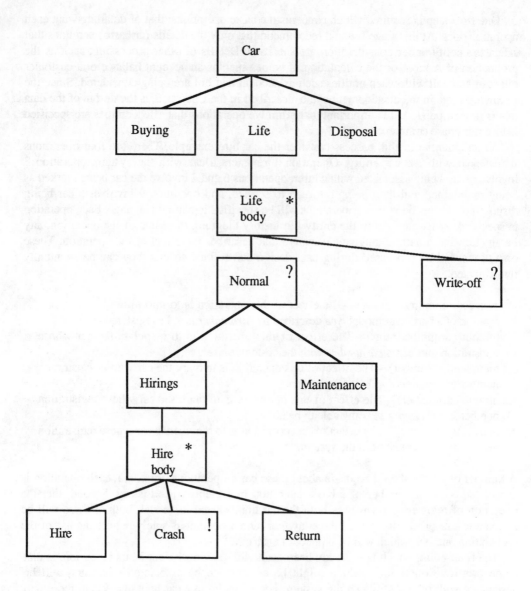

Figure 4.9 An example of abnormal termination.

4.5.6 Coping with disaster

One major omission in this chapter has been a description of what should be done when an abnormal or error event occurs. For example, in the car booking system a customer may try to book a car for a period during which maintenance has been planned. This subsection describes some notational devices that allow for this in the specification of the entity life history. A box marked with a question mark is either a posit box or an admit box, the former shows that normal processing is occurring and marks a point to where backtracking occurs, the latter indicates a point in the processing where actions associated with the backtracking to a posit box are processed. A box marked with an exclamation mark is known as a quit box and represents an action that will give rise to backtracking. An example of this is shown in Fig. 4.9

Here, a crash has occurred between the hiring and returning of the car, causing the vehicle to be written off. In this case the system backtracks to the boxes marked with question marks and takes the branch labelled 'write-off'. Remember that this action only occurs if the car is written off, our diagram indicates that if a smaller crash that does not involve a write off occurs, then the car is returned, and then has the possibility of being maintained, where the meaning of maintenance is that work is carried out on the car to improve it in some way.

4.6 SUMMARY

This chapter has described how entity analysis is carried out. First, the system inputs are identified, and these are then listed as system actions. The entities in a system are then identified and the actions that are associated with them are listed, these actions being extracted from the list of system actions. The attributes of each entity action are listed and the stored attributes of each entity are identified. Once this process of identifying actions, entities, and attributes is complete, the entity life histories are specified in terms of the temporal ordering of actions they suffer. The last step in the process is to identify basic operations that are used in each entity life history. These primitive operations will either involve subsidiary processing, such as producing a report or making a calculation, or will be actions that affect entities. It is important that the latter type of primitive operation is specified in some detail so that it can be input into the next stage of the development process: data design. The detailed descriptions of the other types of primitive operations can be left for later in the software project.

4.7 FURTHER READING

There are few tutorial accounts of JSD in existence. One of the best is Sutcliffe (1988) which, as well as describing the main components of the method, contains two good case studies. Cameron (1983) contains a selection of papers on JSD and another Jackson-inspired technique JSP. Although JSD has moved on a little since this collection was published it still describes the essence of the method.

BIBLIOGRAPHY

Cameron, J. R. (1983) *JSP and JSD: the Jackson Approach to Software Development*, IEEE Computer Press, New York.

Sutcliffe, A. (1988) *Jackson System Development*, Prentice-Hall, Englewood Cliffs, NJ.

5

VALIDATING THE DATA MODEL

AIMS

- To describe the various techniques that can be used to validate a data model.
- To describe how data model reviews are organized.
- To introduce briefly the use of prototyping as a validation technique.
- To describe how a preliminary test plan can be constructed from the data model.

5.1 INTRODUCTION

Chapter 1 briefly discussed the fact that there is a need for validation and verification activities on the software project. In the past, these terms have normally been associated with testing. However, testing suffers from a major problem: it is carried out too late in the software project; at a time when, if an error committed early on in a project was discovered, extensive reworking would be necessary.

Testing is a vital activity, even in object-oriented software development; nevertheless, a number of techniques can be used in the early stages to reduce the amount of resource required for respecification and redesign when a test highlights an error late in the software project. It is worth stressing at this point that these techniques do not affect the amount of resource required for activities such as system testing and acceptance testing, it is just the resources consumed by reworking that will be affected—but affected drastically. There is an industry rule of thumb which states that the cost of rectifying an error will add an order of magnitude to the cost of reworking each time a phase is completed in which the error was not detected. This chapter discusses three topics: technical reviews, prototyping, and the generation of scenarios.

5.2 REVIEWS

One of the common experiences that programmers have is that of staring at a program listing for a number of hours in order to detect an error, only for a colleague to walk into their room, look at their listing, and discover the error in seconds. This has certainly happened to me and, early in my career, I found it a very depressing experience: that another member of staff, whom I regarded myself as being equal to, seemed to have superior debugging skills. In a moment of depression I confided to a senior programmer why I was so depressed. He came up with the reason for the seemingly better debugging skills of my colleagues.

What seems to happen in programming—and in other software tasks as well—is that we have a major attachment to our work. Producing a program or design is very much like giving birth and, metaphorically, our programs and designs become the software equivalents of our children; as with our children, it is very difficult to look dispassionately at them and find many faults. Certainly when I started looking at my colleagues' programs I discovered that my debugging skills had increased tenfold!

One of the major problems is that we often have an erroneous view of what a program does: we may assume that a particular subroutine is executed when a certain combination of data values are encountered, or that a particular path is taken through a subroutine when a particular item of data is read.

In order to overcome this problem of staff having a technical blindness when it comes to their own products, a number of developers have initiated a series of technical reviews. A review is just a meeting of a number of people who read and comment on errors in a particular project document. This document can be a project plan, a requirements specification, a data model, a system design, program code, or a test plan.

Reviews have been found exceptionally useful for two reasons: first, they are a collective process where a number of staff take a dispassionate look at some software document, and second, they can be held early on in the software projects, in order to detect errors that, if they slip through, are capable of causing catastrophe. Pressman (1987) has described a number of principles and guidelines for the organization and conduct of technical reviews.

First, ideally, three to five staff should be involved in a technical review. In the review of the data model, which might involve five members of staff, this would typically be a chairperson, usually a senior member of staff from the project; the analyst who prepared the part of the data model being reviewed; a member of the quality assurance department; a customer representative; and a member of staff from another project who has no interest in the project being reviewed.

The member of the quality assurance department is an important representative on the review. Usually in large companies such staff are charged with the responsibility for developing system tests and acceptance tests, and are able to probe any weaknesses in the data model by asking hard questions about how particular combinations of operations would be tested. It is also important for a customer representative to attend. After all, they are experts in the application area, and are best able to detect errors in interpretation made by analysts. In later reviews, which tend to be more technical, customer representatives can be omitted.

A point which should be made about the chairperson—or as he or she is sometimes called the *moderator*—is that the project manager should not chair such reviews. There are two reasons for this. First, project managers have other pressures on them that they often see as being much more important than software quality. These will be the number of days to the date of release of the software and the amount of budget remaining for their projects. Consequently, there will be a subconscious tendency for managers to skimp the task of chairing the reviews in order to sweep problems under the carpet. The second reason is that a review is a bruising experience for the member of staff whose work is being reviewed. Often such work is torn to pieces. If the manager is in attendance there will be a tendency for staff who have their work being examined to regard the presence as some sort of personnel evaluation exercise, and become exceptionally defensive, rather than have the very open attitude to errors that is a prerequisite for the successful review.

The second guideline is that review meetings should not last more than two hours. Reviews, when run properly, are intensive and exhausting. Most people's span of attention is no more than two hours; after this time they tend to lose interest in the topic of a review— very quickly.

It is also important to point out that time should be devoted to preparing for a review. What the participants who attend a review are doing is debugging, this is not something that can be done in a few seconds, but requires time for reflective thought. Pressman advises that advance preparation should take no more than two hours per person.

An important point to be made is that it is the document that is the subject of a review, not the person who developed the document. This is an important point, because a review can be quite a harrowing experience for the staff whose documents or program code is being reviewed. Nobody likes criticism, and at a review the staff involved have to take two hours of implied criticism. The role of the moderator is key in a review: he or she has to organize and run the meeting in such a way that the product is decoupled from the person that produced it.

There are a number of strategies aimed at depersonalizing a review. A simple one is never to refer to errors as errors, but as problems. One particularly good moderator that I know of announces, at the beginning of the review that, from the start of the review, the document or program code being reviewed is the collective responsibility of the attendees in the review. The blame for any errors that remain after the review has been completed is divided equally among the participants. Another moderator that I know of always tries to encourage positive remarks about a program, e.g. that it is well-structured or easy to read, as well as encouraging the error-detection process.

Another guideline is to set an agenda and stick to it. Reviews can meander quite a bit with a solution to a problem being aired, followed by a discussion of similar problems encountered on other projects, followed by a discussion of an old project that some of the participants worked on; eventually, ending up with a general free for all about office politics, sexual politics, and the quality of the eating houses in the area.

An important point related to keeping to an agenda is that the moderator should not allow the review to be taken up with discussions about how an error should be rectified. A review is an extremely useful validation and verification technique for detecting errors. It is less good at remedying errors. The only person who is really capable of removing an error is the person who produced the document under review. It is, of course, impractical to ban all discussion about how an error can be eradicated. However, this should be brief and along the lines of 'we had that problem with one of our programs, ring Geoff up and he'll tell you how he coped with it'.

The agenda for a review should be quite simple. Normally, the first item that should be dealt with is any general points about the item for review. Next, the participants should work through a check-list of overall points about the product. This should be followed by a detailed reading of the item. The amount of time that is devoted to each of these activities will depend on the item that is being reviewed. However, the final activity—i.e. of reading the item, line by line—will take up the majority of the time of a review.

It is important that the moderator or a secretary take written notes during a review. In particular a list of errors—or rather problems—is produced. There are two reasons for this. First, attendees will forget about what went on in a review. It may be days before the member of staff who produced the item that was reviewed gets around to changing it. The second reason for taking written notes is that quality assurance staff will be required to ensure that reviews are being carried out correctly, and any actions outstanding have been dealt with. They usually do this via formal audits and spot-checks. A set of minutes, together with a list of outstanding problems, is necessary for them to do their jobs.

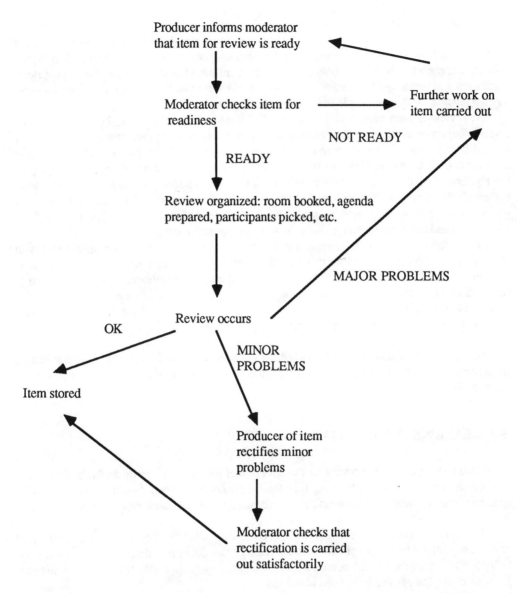

Figure 5.1 The review process.

A final point to be made about reviews is that each type of product that is being reviewed should have a check-list associated with it. For example, programs or subroutines would have a check-list that contains instructions about detecting unsafe programming constructs, non-initialized variables, non-conformance to coding standards, overcomplex interfaces, and convoluted program code.

The review process is shown in Fig. 5.1. First, the item to be reviewed is produced and the staff who produced it consider that it is near to being correct. This is often an iterative process, whereby whoever produced the item checks specifics with colleagues. The member of staff who produced the item then informs whoever is to chair the review that the item being reviewed is ready. It is sent to the moderator who then evaluates whether it is, in fact, ready. If it is, the review is organized: the room booked, participants informed, and copies of the review item, together with current guidelines for the item type, are circulated. Finally, near to the meeting day the agenda for the meeting is sent to all participants.

The review is then held, and a problems list produced together with the minutes of the review. Copies of these are sent to each of the participants of the review and at least one copy is filed in the project library. There are a number of outcomes of a review. First, the review may have been totally successful. In this case the item is passed and stored in the project library. Eventually, it will be frozen, along with all the other similar items that have been reviewed. For example, the requirements specification will be reviewed a chunk at a time, and when the whole of the requirements specification is deemed to have been satisfactorily reviewed it is frozen, and any further changes are monitored and controlled rigorously.

The second outcome of the review is that there may be some small errors associated with the item that is being reviewed. In this case the item is regarded as having passed the review. The member of staff who produced the item then makes any amendments, and shows them to the moderator of the review who signs the item off as fully passing the review. The third outcome is that there are major problems with the item. In this case the item is then modified and has to be re-reviewed, preferably with the same members of the original review being present.

This, then, is how reviews are organized. How can they be employed on a project that uses object-oriented techniques and, in particular, the form of entity analysis that is described in Chapter 3?

5.3 REVIEWS AND ENTITY ANALYSIS

There are two aspects to the review of the data model produced by entity analysis. First, there will be the almost routine checking that the notations have been employed correctly. For example, that a condition box in an entity life history has the same type of box at the same level of the diagram.

The second aspect is concerned with determining whether the model has an internal consistency, and whether it actually reflects reality. The document that should be considered will be made up of the textual descriptions of the entities together with the entity life histories for each of the entities that have been identified.

A list of questions that should be considered by the staff in a review are shown in the following paragraphs..

- *Is there an operation associated with an entity that is mirrored in an operation associated with another entity?*

This question is really only relevant when a full entity analysis is carried out which involves objects out of the scope of the system. For example, in the hotel booking system we considered objects such as customers and booking staff. One typical operation that was identified and associated with booking staff was the booking of a room. This operation was mirrored in an operation which created a booking entity.

• *Are all the system actions associated with an application specified?*

This would involve the review team stepping through the operation of a system and looking at all the actions that would affect the system. In order to achieve this it is a good idea to have a detailed description, or narrative of the detailed processing over a typical period of the system's lifetime. For example, with the hotel booking system it would be a good idea for the analyst concerned with specifying the system to have written such a narrative and provided it for the review team. A typical extract from such a document is shown below. It describes what happens in the hotel booking system:

> A customer rings in to book a room. The reservation staff ask the customer the name, the address, telephone number, and any billing address. They then ask the customer for the period of the booking and the room category. The customer may ask for confirmation of the booking, in which case a confirmation letter is sent out. Also, the reservation staff ask the customer to send in written confirmation of the booking.

> A customer telephones in a cancellation. The reservation staff ask for the name and also for the period of the booking. The booking is cancelled. If the booking is cancelled on the same day as the booking starts, a cancellation fee is charged and the customer is billed. The cancellation fee depends on the category of room cancelled. If the booking was not cancelled on the same day, then no billing takes place.

From this description of the system the review team might check that the system actions that are listed are reflected in the description. For example, that there is a system action corresponding to the cancellation of a room.

• *Have all the entities been identified and are the attributes correct?*

Again, a useful document that helps in this is the narrative which describes what happens to a system over a time period. From this, the team can decide whether the correct number of entities have been identified, and whether there are any omissions. Each attribute should also be examined in detail, and the question asked: why is this attribute needed? Usually an attribute is needed in order to support some internal processing. For example, in the hotel booking system, a billing address is required for some customers whose company are paying for their stay in the hotel. The members of the review team should be satisfied that each attribute is associated with a particular piece of processing that occurs in the system narrative. Also they should be sure that each item of processing in the system narrative corresponds to some entity attribute.

• *Is the list of entity actions consistent with the system actions?*

The system actions give a high-level view of the processing components that make up a system. Each system action corresponds to one or more entity actions. For example, in the hotel booking system the system action of taking a room out of service corresponds to the removed action associated with the room entity.

• *Are the entity life histories a correct reflection of the states that an entity goes through?*

Entity life histories are very useful diagrams which allow the review team to check that the analyst has understood conceptually what each entity action does. The review team should be asking questions about the ordering of the actions. For example, would the system cater for a number of consecutive operations whereby a whole series of category changes occur to a room. They should also be asking questions about whether some action can occur only in certain circumstances. For example, in the hotel booking system, has the entity life history shown that a booking can only be cancelled after it has been booked?

- *Do the entity life histories show actions that are in a sense extraordinary and occur infrequently?*

For example, does the system cater for a customer leaving the hotel without formally booking out. This could happen if the customer did not wish to pay the bill. It could also happen when a customer is taken ill and is rushed into hospital.

- *Is the description of the entity actions adequate?*

The review team should satisfy themselves that there is no ambiguity in the description of the operations. As has already been stated in this book, natural language is a difficult medium in which to construct exact documents; so particular attention should be paid to this aspect of the data model. However, since the description of the entity actions for each action will be short, there is less chance that there will be problems with this part of the document, as compared with the problems that occur with functional specifications in conventional software development.

These, then, are a selection of the questions that should be asked in the review of the data model. At the same time that the data model is being validated, quality assurance staff should be constructing some tests that will be carried out at an early stage of the project in order to ensure that the entity actions work correctly in conjunction with each other, and in order to carry out a preliminary check that the detailed functioning of the system is correct.

5.4 SCENARIO GENERATION

Scenario generation is the process whereby the entity life history diagrams are examined and the actions combined into a sequence of actions that would naturally occur in the application. The staff charged with quality assurance would examine the entity life history of a booking and might generate the following sequence of actions for the hotel booking example:

Sequence 1:   A booking is created and is then cancelled.

Sequence 2:   A booking is created, suffers a number of modifications of the period, the booking is deleted.

Sequence 3:   A booking is modified.

Sequence 4:   A booking is deleted.

Sequence 5:   A booking is created, made current, and then deleted.

The first sequence describes the common occurrence of a customer making a booking and then cancelling. The second sequence describes the less common occurrences of a customer who cannot decide about a booking. The third sequence describes what happens when a booking, which has not been created, is modified. The fourth sequence describes what happens when a booking that has not been created is deleted. The fifth sequence—a common one—describes what happens when a booking is made, the customer arrives, and then leaves the hotel.

These sequences are known as *scenarios* and represent both typical and atypical combinations of actions that occur during the lifetime of a system. In general those sequences that represent extraordinary events will be the ones that test out a system thoroughly. For example, the scenario of a non-existent booking being cancelled is a much harsher test than the scenario of a customer making a booking, arriving at the hotel, and then departing normally.

The scenarios are normally written in outline after entity analysis has been completed, and after all the reviews of the data model have occurred. There are a number of reasons for generating these scenarios. First, they will be used in the first test of the implementation: at a later stage in the project staff will implement the primitive operations that annotate the entity life histories and combine them together into tests. These primitive operations will, of course, be tested in isolation, but there is also a need to test them in combination. By setting up tests corresponding to these scenarios, staff charged with quality assurance are able to check on the correctness of the implementation of the data model at an early stage in the software project.

A second reason is that the mere process of generating such a scenario enables quality assurance staff to check, at an early stage of the software project, that the data model is correct. The fact that sensible scenarios can be generated, and can be related back to the actions that occur in the application, provides a high degree of confidence that the data model is valid.

Tests corresponding to these scenarios will always be carried out formally; however, there is always the temptation to carry out them informally. By deriving scenarios early on in the project, the quality assurance staff set up the agenda for this form of testing and, as a by-product, check out the data model.

It is important to point out that the test scenarios will be processed at later stages in the project. After implementation of the entities is complete they should be at a sufficiently detailed level to enable a member of the development team to set up a test and execute it. For example, the second scenario above might be expanded into the following detailed test description:

> This test requires the use of the class *booking*. Create a booking for a specified period, within the allowable period in which bookings can be made, by means of a call on the function *book*. Check that the booking has been correctly entered by executing the function *view*. Then apply a series of calls of the function *modify_bookper*. Change the booking period each time, and use *view* to check that the correct data has been entered. Finally, call the function *cancel* and again use *view* to check that the data on the booking has been expunged.

What this extract describes is an implementation feature of C++ known as the *class*. In essence, this feature associates a series of functions with some stored data. In the case above, the stored data is the set of bookings. The instructions tell the tester to use a number of functions associated with the following classes: *book*, which places a booking into the data area that holds booking details; *view*, which retrieves and displays a particular booking; and *modify_bookper*, which carries out the modification of a particular booking period associated with a booking.

5.5 PROTOTYPING

In Chapter 3 I described some of the problems that occur with data modelling. First, that since system and acceptance test generation is left until a later stage of the project, some degree of validation is lost early on in a project that uses object-oriented techniques. Second, that it may prove difficult to get the customer—who, after all is used to thinking in terms of what a system should do—to check the rather abstract description that a data model represents. The first problem is one that is partially overcome by scenario generation. The second problem can be overcome by prototyping.

5.5.1 What is prototyping?

Prototyping is the process of developing a working model of a system early on in the project. Such a working model can then be shown to the customer, who suggests improvements. These improvements are incorporated in the prototype and it is shown again to the customer, and so on.

Prototyping is a valuable technique, both for the customer and the developer. All too often I have met customers, faced with an inadequate implementation, who have said during acceptance testing, 'If only you had shown me the system earlier in the project I could have told you exactly what I wanted'. Prototyping has a number of advantages:

- It enables the customer to get an early view of the system well before major development work starts.
- It enables the developers to know exactly what they need to deliver. Previously, developers have attempted to deliver the system that reflects the requirements specification. Unfortunately, since this specification is written in natural language there is always considerable scope for misunderstanding. By asking the customer to sign off the prototype, the developers are able to have an exact reference point to judge their implementation.
- It enables early customer training to take place. Such training is often rushed and inadequate. A prototype can be used to integrate training properly in the development project. It also has the allied advantage that it enables the developer to meet the staff who are actually going to use the prototype. A common circumstance in many software projects is of the customer representative who, perhaps, has rarely encountered or been part of the application that is to be developed and is, consequently, not the ideal person to talk to about system requirements.
- It can act as a test oracle during the later stages of system development. A test oracle is a version of a system that will always deliver the right results when executed. A prototype can be used as an oracle by feeding its output, together with the output of the final developed system, through a file comparator. This means that the tester has very little work to do when examining test output during system testing and acceptance testing. All that needs to be done is to examine the output of the file comparator in order to see whether the developed system has given a different result to the oracle.

5.5.2 Techniques to achieve prototyping

A number of techniques are available to the developer who wishes to produce an early version of a system. They range from rather simple techniques, such as showing the customer some sample screens, to using sophisticated programming languages which are capable of packing a lot of functionality punch into a small amount of program code. The main prototyping techniques are as follows:

- Relax the quality assurance standards of the project. Tolerate errors in the prototype in an attempt to get a rough working version of the system out quickly. This could mean a whole variety of tactics could be applied: skimping the requirements specification, omitting the system design stage, carrying out perfunctory system tests, and omitting many of the reviews that would normally be scheduled.

- Implement only those parts of a system whose requirements are felt to be ill-expressed or fuzzy. This might mean the developer deciding on an incremental development strategy with subsystems that have a high amount of risk attached to them being implemented first.
- Use a table-driven processor approach to development. This relies on a set of tools that are table-driven and have a clean interface between them. The ideal candidate for this approach is UNIX, which contains table-driven processors such as YACC that enable software to be produced very quickly.
- Employ a programming language that enables you to implement a large amount of functionality in a physically small amount of program code. Probably the best example of this type of programming language is the fourth-generation programming language. Such languages are usually interfaced to relational database systems, and allow very complex commercial data processing to be implemented in very short sections of program code. However, fourth-generation languages are not the only medium for this form of prototyping—programming languages such as PROLOG, SETL, LISP, and APL have all been successfully employed to produce prototypes.
- Use an application-oriented programming language. Such languages are aimed at one particular application area, and contain data types that are used continually in that area. For example, an application-oriented language for a warehousing application would use data types for warehouses, stock bins, and picking lists.

These, then, are some of the ways in which prototypes can be generated. Object-oriented programming languages are also an excellent medium for prototyping. Such languages contain a facility for defining the entities that were identified in the previous chapter using a facility known as a class. In Chapter 8 you will be told about some of the important features of classes, and how they are suited to the production of well-engineered software. In terms of prototyping an important facility of a class is inheritance. In order to explain what inheritance is, it is worth using an example: that of an invoice in a commercial data processing application.

Such an invoice will always contain the same details; irrespective of the application, it will contain the following information: the name of the supplier who has provided the services or goods that the invoice describes, the supplier's address, the name of the customer, the customer's address, a list of items supplied, their price, and the total price. In a purchasing application an invoice would, almost certainly, be the first entity that would be discovered by an analyst.

In the first application in which the software developer uses an invoice, it would be defined using a class description of the components of the invoice, together with the functions that manipulate the invoice, e.g. creating an invoice. The application would then be implemented, and the class stored in a company-wide library.

The next time an application is developed that requires an invoice, the designer responsible would look in the library for any classes that described an implementation of an invoice. Let us assume that the system requires a slightly different form of invoice from the one contained in the library, e.g. it might be for an overseas customer, where the tax deduction part of the invoice would be different.

The designer of the new system would define a new type of invoice which contained this new element but which was mostly made up of the invoice class stored in the project library.

This form of use is called *inheritance*—the new invoice class inherits many of the properties and operations of the stored invoice in the project library. This reduces the work required from the designer: all that has to be done is to write down the new components of the invoice and any new operations associated with this component and then bring in the invoice class from the project library.

If a developer has built up an extensive library of classes, then prototyping can be effectively carried out. All it involves is for the analyst or designer responsible to call down pre-written classes from a project library, and join them together with some processing code. This topic is dealt with in more detail in Chapter 8, which describes the properties of classes, and Chapter 12, which describes how to prototype using C++.

5.5.3 Models of prototyping

There are a number of ways of implementing prototyping. The choice is really dependent on the type of software that is being developed, and project-specific factors such as the duration and size of the project. There are three popular prototyping models: throw-away prototyping, evolutionary prototyping, and incremental prototyping.

Throw-away prototyping corresponds to the popular idea of prototyping: the developer produces a prototype and then initiates the iterative process of showing the prototype to the customer and modifying it in response to the customer's wishes. When the prototyping phase has finished the prototype is, in effect, thrown away: it is placed in an archive and conventional software development is started based on a requirements specification that has been written by examining the detailed functionality of the prototype.

Throw-away prototyping is effective for short projects of a few months duration. Unfortunately, for large projects it tends to be less than ideal. The reason, of course, is change. When conventional software development starts, the developer is almost invariably bombarded with changes of requirements from the customer. In the end, the conventional software part of a prototyping project can suffer from the same problems as a project that did not use prototyping.

Evolutionary prototyping is the complete antithesis to throw-away prototyping. Here, the developer aims to keep the prototype alive. The first stage of the evolutionary prototyping project involves the development of a prototype using the same activities and techniques that would be used for throw-away prototyping. However, after the customer has decided that everything is satisfactory, the developer then bases the remainder of the development work on the prototype that has been generated.

In the case of a prototype that has been generated using a fourth-generation programming language this involves a process of optimization, whereby the initial prototype is modified to make it run faster and use less memory and file space. The important point about this form of evolutionary prototyping—and evolutionary prototyping in general—is that throughout the project a working prototype that matches current customer requirements is always available.

The final form of prototyping is known as incremental prototyping. This can be used in a project where the requirements can be neatly partitioned into functionally separate areas. For example, developing a system for a chemical plant involves the following functional areas: monitoring, control, human–computer interface and management information. If one of these functional areas is fuzzy or the customer has difficulty expressing requirements, then a process of incremental development can be adopted. Here the system is developed as a series of small subsystems, each of which implements a subset of the functions. The earliest deliveries of the subsystem can then be used as prototypes.

This, then, is a brief discussion of prototyping. Chapter 12 describes how object-oriented techniques can be used in conjunction with prototyping—in particular in conjunction with evolutionary prototyping.

5.6 FURTHER READING

Pressman's software engineering book (Pressman, 1987) contains excellent descriptions of technical reviews, how they are organized, and how they are carried out. Ince and Hekmatpour (1988) contains a good description of the techniques that are available for prototyping. Connell (1989) is an excellent book which describes both the technical means and the management strategies required for evolutionary prototyping. The best detailed descriptions of reviews can be found in Fagan (1976, 1986)

BIBLIOGRAPHY

Connell, J. L. (1989) *Structured Rapid Prototyping*, Prentice-Hall, Englewood Cliffs, NJ.

Fagan, M. E. (1976) Design and code inspections to reduce errors in program development. *IBM Systems Journal*, **15**, 3, 182–211.

Fagan, M. E. (1986) Advances in software inspection. *IEEE Transactions on Software Engineering*, **12**, 7, 744–751.

Ince, D. C. and Hekmatpour, S. (1988) *Software Prototyping, Formal Methods and VDM*, Addison-Wesley, Reading, Mass.

Pressman, R. S. (1987) *Software Engineering—a Practitioner's Approach*, McGraw-Hill, New York.

6

ABSTRACT DATA TYPES

AIMS

- To describe the notion of an abstract data type.
- To describe the main categories of abstract data type.
- To outline the role that abstract data types play in object-oriented development.

6.1 INTRODUCTION

This chapter considers an important idea that forms the backbone of object-oriented software development: the abstract data type. The chapter first examines what is meant by the term *abstraction* and then shows how abstraction can be applied to the design of data. The chapter concludes with a description of the main types of abstract data types and how they can be combined. An understanding of this chapter is vital for accessing the remaining parts of this book. If you have any doubts about your perception of the main ideas presented here, then it is worth rereading the chapter.

6.2 THE NATURE OF ABSTRACTION

Consider what happens when a new car is designed. The designers usually sit down with staff from the marketing department and decide on an overall concept for the car: is it to be a tourer, a small family car, a large family car, or a sports car? In the initial discussion about the high-level features of the car there will be no discussion at all about other items such as the width of the suspension struts, the size of the tyres, or the circumference of the driving wheel. Such items are unimportant when discussing the high-level nature of the car that is being designed. When the design team get around to producing a drawing of what the car will look like, these items will not usually be highlighted in this drawing.

Items such as suspension struts are not unimportant. However, at this stage in the development of a new car, they are not relevant to the task in hand. What the designers of the car are carrying out is the process of *modelling*: ignoring those issues in an artefact that are not relevant to the task they are carrying out. The tool they use is *abstraction*: the process of representing an artefact in an ideal, lean form, for a task that is to be carried out on that artefact.

Modelling and abstraction occur everywhere in real life:

- The architect who produces a wooden model of a large building is modelling by producing an abstraction of the building that ignores many internal issues, such as the

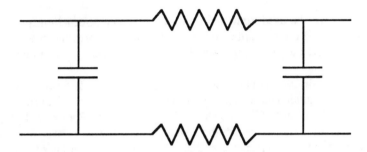

Figure 6.1 The design of an electrical circuit.

number of steps in a stairway and the size of the doors in rooms, and, indeed, the size of the building.

• The electronic engineer who produces a graphical circuit design, such as the one shown in Fig. 6.1, is modelling the circuits by means of an abstract representation that ignores issues irrelevant to the design process such as the colour of the resistors, the length of the wires joining the components together, and the size of the circuit board on which the circuit is to be implemented.

• The programmer who uses a high-level language such as Pascal or Ada is modelling the patterns of zeros and ones that represent the program being written. The program is an abstraction of issues such as the way floating-point numbers are represented in the computer.

These, then, are examples of abstraction. If you remain unconvinced about its value, then consider the problems that would occur if you attempted to navigate an underground railway system using a map that, as well as showing details about the stations and lines, showed all the streets above the tunnels, the position of litter bins and ticket machines, the location of the electricity supplies, the pattern of gas pipes and water pipes in the ground, and the location of the canteen where station staff take lunch. The map would be hopelessly complicated and virtually useless.

Happily, transport authorities provide simple maps that just contain enough detail necessary for the traveller: the stations, the links between stations, and those points where a traveller can transfer from one line to another. This map is, after all, just another abstraction of the whole jumble of detail that makes up an underground system. Needless to say, such a map would be useless for employees from a utilities company who are trying to find a gas leak, because it does not contain the detail necessary to locate a gas pipe—another map would be needed. This map would ignore all the details not required for gas workers to carry out their jobs, such as stations, lines, and the connections between lines. The gas workers' map is another model that uses abstraction; however, it is specifically aimed at helping them to carry out their own set of tasks.

Abstraction is a tool to reduce complexity and in that most complex of all subjects—software engineering—is used in virtually every task. For example, when high-level functions are expressed in a requirements specification, these are abstractions which ignore low-level details, and high-level programming languages are abstractions of the underlying fetch–execute cycle in the computer, and hide the messy underlying binary-based structure of programs and data.

In this book a major tool that will be used, time and time again, is data abstraction: the description of the underlying data and the operations on that data which ignores the actual implementation of the data—even if the data is implemented using a high-level programming language.

This book's obsession with data abstraction is rooted in two very practical concerns. The first is to do with change—both maintenance change, and the change that occurs during development. A large proportion of changes affect the stored data in a system. For example, during the system testing of a communications system the developer of that system may find that the response time is inadequate, a frequent response to this not-uncommon occurrence is to modify the system data structures, perhaps replacing the implementation of a queue by another, faster implementation. By developing a system in terms of an abstract description of the data, a developer is able to postpone any consideration of how data is stored until very late in the project, to a point near the end of the project where the actual time period in which such changes can occur is as short as possible.

Another reason for using data abstraction is that it enables a clearer view of the application to be gained by the designer. System designers do not want to be worried about arrays, linked lists, or any other implementation technique when they are worried about the gross properties of the data in a system.

Given that there is a need for some form of data abstraction in a system, how is it implemented? It is implemented using the concept of an *abstract data type*. This describes a data structure not by what it is, but by what is offers—via operations. This idea needs some explanation as it is an almost complete antithesis to the way we have taught about data in the past—certainly in non-commercial data processing courses. In the past we have concentrated on teaching the implementation of data: whole textbooks have been devoted to teaching topics such as how to implement linked lists via pointers or arrays. What abstract data types emphasize is the effect of operations on the stored data without worrying about implementations.

A concrete example of an abstract data type—if that is not a contradiction in terms—is the stack. Let us assume that a stack required for a particular application, say a programming language compiler application, has a number of operations associated with it. The operations are to place an item on the stack, remove an item from the stack, check whether the stack is empty, and count the number of items in a stack.

The definition of the stack together with the effect of adding an item *it* to a stack is shown opposite. The first line states that a stack data type will be a sequence of items, where items has been defined elsewhere. A sequence is a collection of objects where ordering is important. The next line is a data invariant, this is a condition that must be true for all stacks, the data invariant specified states that the contents of the stack will be limited to n items. The definition of *addstack* states that an item *it* will be added to the stack s at its top. The first line of the definition gives any parameters to the operation, the second line states that the stack s will be written to; this is indicated by the keyword WR.

The natural language description of the operation includes a precondition and a postcondition. The precondition gives the condition that must be true for the operation to be successful, while the postcondition states what is true after the operation has been executed. The precondition is that the stack must not be full, i.e. there are no more than $n - 1$ items already on the stack; the postcondition is that after the operation has been executed *it* will be added to the top of the stack. The remainder of the operations are shown below, the keyword RD indicates read access. The operations *empty* and *count* require no preconditions since they can be executed irrespective of the state of the stack.

stack = SEQ OF items

INVARIANT the stack will contain no more than n items.

OPERATION addstack(it:items)
WR s: stack
For this operation to be defined the stack s must contain no more than $n - l$ items. After the operation has completed *it* will be added to the top of s.

The specification for the other operations is shown below:

OPERATION removestack(it:items)
WR s: stack
For this operation to be defined the stack s must contain at least one item. After the operation has completed the top of the stack will be removed and placed in *it*.

OPERATION count(n:integer)
RD s: stack
After the operation has completed n will contain the number of items in the stack.

OPERATION empty(b:boolean)
RD s: stack
After the operation has completed b will be true if the stack s is empty and false otherwise.

These, then, are the operations that this particular stack offers to the outside world. My definition of the effect of the operations has been informal, at the end of this chapter I shall describe some mathematical ways of defining operations. However, for the time being I shall explore the notion of an abstract data type in informal terms but, at the same time, cautioning you to be very careful with natural language definitions.

6.3 SPECIFIC ABSTRACT DATA TYPES

The previous section discussed the notion of an abstract data type in terms of the operations that the data type offers the world. This section reinforces this message by describing a number of common abstract data types and the operations normally associated with them. However, before doing this, it is worth describing abstract data types in a little more detail and outline the vocabulary that is used to describe them.

6.3.1 Types and abstract data types

A type is a collection of values without duplicates. For example, when you write a declaration in Pascal to say that a particular variable is an integer, what you are saying is that the variable has an identifier, which labels an area of computer memory that will contain values taken from that set of integers currently allowable on your implementation of Pascal. Thus, a type is a collection, or set of elements. An abstract data type is a set of elements which are characterized by the operations that are implemented for that abstract data type. The individual items of the set will, in this book, be called *elements*.

6.3.2 Operations on abstract data types

The operations that an abstract data type is associated with can be partitioned into three classes: *constructor operations*, *selector operations*, and *iterator operations*.

A constructor operation alters the value of an element of a particular abstract data type. For example, an operation that removes the first element in a stack is an example of a constructor operation. The important feature of a constructor operation is that some overwriting takes place. This overwriting may affect one small part of a member of an abstract data type, or affect all the components of that member. For example, removing the top element of a stack is an operation that potentially affects a small part of a stack, but an operation that removes all the elements of the stack affects the whole of the stack.

A selector operation is one that evaluates an instance of an abstract data type. For example, an operation that returns with the second element in a stack without overwriting the stack is an example of a selector operation. Selector operations involve no overwriting, all that happens is that part of an element of an abstract data type is read. This could be a small part of the element or could be many parts.

Iterator operations are operations that allow a collection of objects in an abstract data type to be accessed. For example, iterator operations would be used in the stack example if the stack was to be traversed, say, when printing out the values in the stack. Typical iterator operations are an operation to set some pointer to the first element in an abstract data type, an operation to move the pointer to the next element in an abstract data type, and an operation to check that a pointer is pointing at the last item in an abstract data type.

SAQ What type of an operation is one that examines a stack in order to check whether there are any elements in it?

SOLUTION It is a selector operation. It will deliver a Boolean value that is calculated by examining the stack. Since this only involves a process of reading it is a selector operation. ❑

6.3.3 Basic types

In this chapter I shall assume that there are a series of basic types that cannot decomposed any further into any other type. Normally these types are automatically provided by a compiler. We can still regard these types as abstract data types because, in a sense, they ignore the detailed representation issues that a compiler hides away from the user.

The basic types which will be assumed in this chapter are natural numbers, characters, and real numbers. Also, all the standard operations on the basic types will also be assumed. For example, I shall assume that integers can be read, characters compared for lexicographic ordering, and real numbers converted into integers. The remainder of this section will describe many abstract data types that are not directly implemented in a high-level programming language. However, the first type that is described in the next subsection is normally found in such languages.

6.3.4 Records

A record is a collection of components whose values are taken from other types. For example, a record that contains details of each member of staff working for a company will have a number of components which represent information about the names of the members of staff, their annual salaries, their insurance numbers, and their addresses. All these components assume values from other types, e.g. the salary will assume values from the abstract data type: natural number.

Each component of a record is known as a *field*. Those fields that can be used to identify uniquely a record are known as *keys*. For example, in a personnel application, records for staff would contain a field that uniquely identifies each member of staff, this is usually a natural number that is assigned to the employee when he or she joins the company.

A key can be one field, or a series of fields. For example, the designer of a personnel system may decide that the records that describe staff will have two fields that represent the key: the first field, a department number, identifies the department in which a member of staff works; the second field, an employee number, is a natural number assigned to that member of staff by the department. Because two different departments may, inadvertently, allocate the same employee number to two different members of staff, the employee number field cannot be used as a key. However, the department number field, combined with the employee number field, would be a key—assuming, of course, that the department numbers are unique.

Records can have both selector and constructor operations associated with them. Typical operations would involve reading from and writing to fields of an element of a record type. A record is normally used as an abstract data type when items in a group of data are related to each other. For example, a record would be used to hold details of a reactor—reactor type, current temperature, and current pressure—in a chemical plant monitoring system.

An example of the notation used in this book to describe records is shown below:

```
Employee ::      nm:names
                 salary: integer
                 dept: department
```

This shows that the abstract data type *Employee* will consist of three components: *nm*, *salary*, and *dept*; *nm* is of type *names*, *salary* is of type integer, and *dept* is of type *department*.

6.3.5 Sets

A set is a collection of objects, each of which are unique. A collection of objects that have the set property are written in curly brackets. For example, the set of natural numbers 1, 4, 8, and 19 would be written as

{1,4,8,19}

The important property of a set is the uniqueness of its elements. Sets are used to model data that has this property. As an example of this consider a simple symbol table in a compiler. I shall make the simplifying assumption that this table only stores the current identifiers which are in scope in a program, and is used to check that identifiers encountered at a point in a program have been declared. In practice, a compiler symbol table will contain more information, e.g. the location of memory that the identifier represents, and the type of the identifier. However, let us assume that the only item in the symbol table will be the names of identifiers.

The symbol table can be modelled by means of a set because all its elements are unique: no identifier will occur twice. A typical list of operations for such a symbol table is shown below, the key-words SET OF indicate a set data type called *symbol_table*, the invariant specifies an upper limit to the table. In the definition of *addidentifier* the word *unioned* is used, this is a term from set theory which will be explained later in this chapter, all that needs saying about it is that it achieves the addition of *id* to the set *s*. In the definition of the operation *no_in_table*, the word *cardinality* is used, this again is a term from set theory, and it is used to describe the number of items in a set.

symbol_table = SET OF identifiers

INVARIANT the symbol table will contain no more than *n* items.

OPERATION addidentifier(id:identifiers)
WR s: symbol_table
For this operation to be defined the symbol table *s* must contain no more than $n - 1$ items. After the operation has completed *id* will be unioned with *s*.

OPERATION removeidentifier(id:identifiers)
WR s: symbol_table
For this operation to be defined the symbol table *s* must contain *id*. After the operation has completed the identifier *id* will be removed from the table *s*.

OPERATION no_in_table(n:integer)
RD s: symbol_table
After the operation has completed *n* will contain the cardinality of *s*.

A number of basic operations are associated with the set data type. The first is the set intersection operation. This takes two sets and forms a set which contains the common elements of the two sets. The second operator is the set union operator. This, again, takes two sets and forms a set by combining the two sets together. The action of these operators is shown in Fig. 6.2 where the union and intersection of the two sets {1,5,7,88} and {2,3,5,7,8,45,22} is formed. Notice that since a set contains unique elements, the union of the sets does not contain two occurrences of the natural numbers 5 and 7.

Before examining the next abstract data type—the map — it is worth saying something about combining data types. All the abstract data types that are discussed in this chapter can be combined together to form other abstract data types. Indeed, this is the norm: only the simplest software system would only use simple types such as the set. For example, a more realistic model of a symbol table would involve a composite abstract data type which would be a set of records that would contain three fields: a field holding the identifier, a field holding the memory location of the identifier, and a field that would contain the type of the identifier—whether it is an integer, a character, a string, and so on. Abstract data types that are made up of more atomic abstract data types are known as *composite abstract data types*.

SAQ Fig. 6.3 shows a collection of records used in a system for recording staff cars. Two of the records are for the member of staff Robytski, doesn't this violate the main property of a set that its elements should be unique?

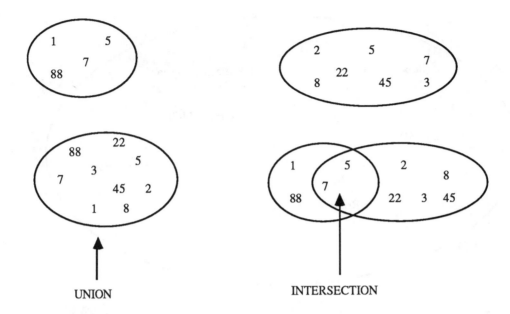

Figure 6.2 Union and intersection of two sets.

SOLUTION No, although the two fields containing the name are the same, the records differ in the remaining field. ❑

6.3.6 Maps

A map is an abstract data type that records a relationship between two other data types. As an example, consider a purchasing system that contains details of all the items kept in a warehouse by a supplier. These details include the item number (a unique natural number which identifies the item), a description of the item, its price, and the quantity of the item currently in stock. This could be modelled by a simple set of records. However, the system that will use this data will need to retrieve item details given the item number. In order for this relationship to be modelled, a map is used to relate the item number to the remaining details of the item. This is shown in Fig. 6.4.

Notice that a map consists of a collection of pairs, each pair being connected by an arrow and consisting of elements taken from some abstract data type. In the case shown in Fig. 6.4 the first item in a pair is taken from the product identifiers, and the second item is taken from the set of records that describe a product.

Maps are specified by means of the key-word MAP. The specification of the data type shown in Fig. 6.4 is detailed below:

```
stock_item ::      item: item_names
                   no_in_stock: integer
                   unit price: integer

Stock_details = MAP integer TO stock_item
```

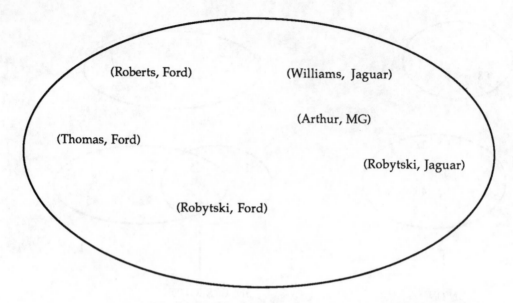

Figure 6.3 A set of staff records.

Here the record type is first defined as having a number of components: the name of the product that is stocked, the number in stock, and the price of each item. The next part of the specification then states that the data type *Stock_details* is a map which takes integers and maps them to stock items.

SAQ How would you model the following:
- The collection of chemical reactors in a chemical plant monitoring system.
- A complex number.
- The books in a computer system that administers the withdrawal and return of books.
- The data that describes the books borrowed by the users of a library system that administers the withdrawal and return of books.

SOLUTION The answer to this question will involve both simple abstract data types and composite data types. The four abstract data types are:

- A set of reactor names.
- A record with two integer fields, the first field containing the real part of the complex number, the second field containing the imaginary part.
- A set of records that contain book details.
- A map from registration numbers of books to the set of records that contain book details. The registration numbers would be integers that would uniquely identify a book.

Do not worry if you have given some wrong answers to the above: there will be plenty of practice in using abstract data types for modelling in the remainder of the chapter. ❏

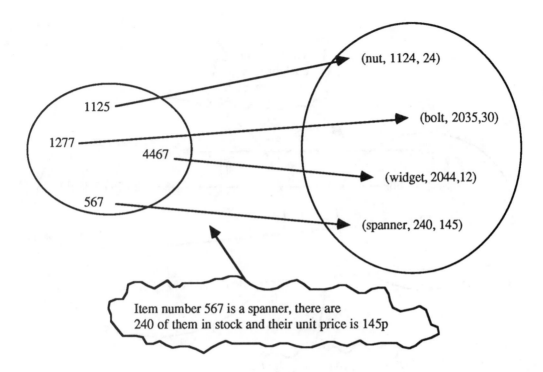

Figure 6.4 An example of a map.

A large number of operations are associated with maps: individual items can be inserted into a map, items can be removed from maps, the individual entries in a map can be modified, e.g. changing the first element of an entry or the second element of an entry, maps can be initialized, and they can also be overwritten with the contents of other maps.

6.3.7 Sequences

There will be a number of occasions when the data that is to be modelled has an inherent ordering relation associated with it. For example, a queue of orders awaiting processing in a purchasing system is often stored in the order of receipt of the orders, and the collection of files awaiting printing in an operating system is often stored in an order that is determined by some priority.

The important point about a sequence is that each element in the sequence is associated with a position. The position is a natural number which ranges from one to the number of items in the queue. A whole series of operations are associated with sequences: items can be extracted from a sequence, items can be added, a series of consecutive items can be removed, and sequences can be initialized. In order to illustrate some of these operations, consider the problem described over:

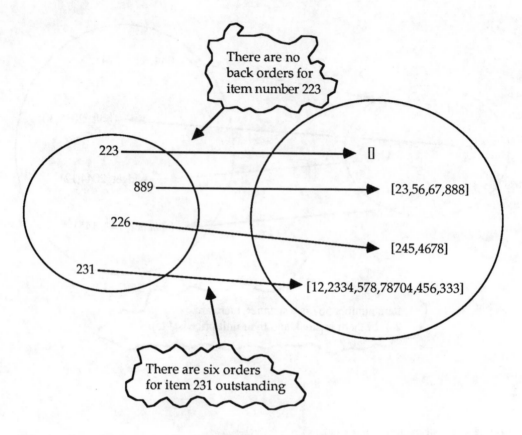

Figure 6.5 A composite data type for a purchasing system.

In a purchasing system there will often be occasions when a large number of orders are received for items that are stocked. When this happens, any orders received for an out of stock item are placed in a queue for that item. When a delivery of that item is received, orders which remain unsatisfied for that item are removed from the queue. For simplicity sake, orders consist of an order number.

SAQ Can you think what composite abstract data type would be used for this data?

SOLUTION The composite abstract data type would be a map that maps product identifiers into the sequences of orders for that item. An example of an instance of that map is shown in Fig. 6.5. Notice that elements of a sequence are enclosed in square brackets ❏

Given this data the abstract data type can now be defined; this contains a number of useful operations for the manipulation of queues:

Order_queues = SEQ OF order_numbers

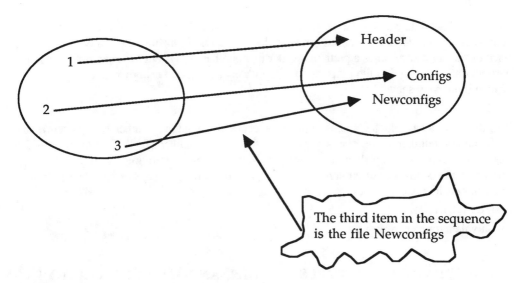

Figure 6.6 A sequence expressed as a map.

Order_details = MAP product_numbers TO Order_queues

INVARIANT Each queue must not contain duplicate order numbers

OPERATION AddtoQ (n:order_numbers, p: product_numbers)
WR dets: Order_details
For this operation to be defined there must not be an order on the queue associated with *p* in *dets* which is equal to *n*. After the operation has been completed, the queue associated with *p* will have the order *n* added to its end.

OPERATION RemfromQ (n:order_numbers, p:product_numbers)
WR dets: Order_details
For this operation to be defined the queue associated with *p* in *dets* must have at least one member. After the operation has been completed, the queue associated with *p* in *dets* will have its front element removed and placed into *n*.

OPERATION IsQempty (p:product_numbers, b:boolean)
RD dets: Order_details
After the operation has been completed, *b* will be false if the queue associated with *p* in *dets* has at least one element, otherwise *b* will be true.

In all the operations the product number *p* is used to identify the queue that needs to be processed.

SAQ Can you think of a connection between sequences and maps?

SOLUTION Yes, a sequence is just a special form of map. Each element of a sequence can be thought of as a pair. The first element of the pair will contain the position of the second element in the sequence. An example of this is shown in Fig. 6.6. This shows how a simple sequence of three computer files in an operating system can be thought of as a map which contains three elements. ❑

6.3.8 Bags

The set abstract data type has the property that no duplicate elements are allowed. Sometimes it is necessary to model data that does not have this property. For example, we may wish to keep track of the number of times a particular order in a purchasing system has been processed. The abstract data type that has the property that duplicates are allowed is known as a *bag*. Bags are written in the way shown below:

   [[1,4,1,4,88,1]]

This describes a bag which contains three occurrences of the natural number 1, two occurrences of the natural number 4, and one occurrence of the natural number 88. Typical operations that bags have associated with them are: adding an item to a bag, removing an item from a bag, removing all occurrences of an item from a bag, and initializing a bag to zero. The ordering of the elements in a bag is irrelevant. Thus, the bag

   [[1,1,88,4,1,4]]

is equivalent to the one above.

6.4 ABSTRACT DATA TYPES, DESIGN, AND IMPLEMENTATION

The previous section has described the main data types. Each of the data types has a property which should match the property of the stored data that it models. For example, in a purchasing system with a subsystem that checks that an order clerk has typed in a correct product identifier, the collection of valid identifiers in that subsystem would be modelled using a set: it is the uniqueness properties of the set that reflect the stored data.

In the design for a realistic system a number of abstract data types will be developed. As an example of this, consider the design of the purchasing system mentioned previously in this chapter. Normally, such a system will contain stock information which relates a product to the quantity in stock of that product; a queue of back orders whose elements will contain the identity of the company making the order; the product number that is ordered and the quantity ordered; and data that relates the identification of the company—say a natural number—to details of the company, such as its address. Also, the system will keep details of all the products that are sold, so that each order from a customer for a product can be checked for validity. Finally, the system will keep a queue of orders awaiting processing, this would be similar to the back orders queue, in that it would contain the same information.

In this system there are a number of abstract data types, e.g. the queue of back orders can be thought of as a composite data type that is a queue of records, each of which contains data about each purchase order.

SAQ What other abstract data types can you identify in the purchase order system?

SOLUTION Some of the abstract data types are:

- The queue of back orders which is a sequence.
- The collection of products that are sold which is a set.
- A map which relates product identifiers to natural numbers which represent the number in stock for a particular product.

- A map that relates the identities of a purchasing company to records that contain details of the company, such as its address.

This example is still something of a simplification: more data would need to be stored, e.g. products would need subsidiary data such as price and size. Nevertheless it gives a good idea of the spread of abstract data types that can be found in an industrial system.
❑

Before looking at some mathematical ways of specifying abstract data types, it is worth placing the material described in this chapter into context—to both the preceding chapters and the next chapters. Chapter 4 described how a statement of requirements can be analysed, and the entities in that document extracted and documented in terms of process entity life history diagrams for each entity. Also, it showed that once these diagrams have been drawn it is possible to extract the operations that are required on the data in the system. These operations correspond to the operations that this chapter has been describing. During requirements analysis these operations are sketched out. During design the abstract data types corresponding to entities are specified and the operations expanded out in terms of pre- and postconditions.

We now have a partial development method, one that covers some part of the software development process. It takes us from requirements analysis, where entities are discovered and operations identified, to design, where the data is designed in terms of abstract data types and operations on the data types that have been identified during requirements analysis.

The next stage is implementation. This is dealt with in the next three chapters. These describe how structured abstract data types can be implemented using a facility of the object-oriented programming language C++ known as a *class*. When implementing abstract data types the implementor will examine factors such as the memory required, the response time and the programming complexity; implementation of abstract data types tends to be a trade-off between these factors.

6.5 MATHEMATICAL SPECIFICATION

This is an optional section which describes how discrete mathematics can be used in specifying abstract data types. If your knowledge of this mathematics is poor, then this section can be skipped: the rest of the book does not depend on a knowledge of any mathematics.

In the previous section the abstract data types were specified informally: the operations associated with them were expressed in natural language. A number of problems can arise with this form of specification. These problems arise from the fact that natural language specifications are notoriously difficult to write accurately: natural language is an ideal medium for poems and novels, where the degree of ambiguity is regarded as a quality factor, but can give rise to poor specification documents, where accuracy is of major importance.

Because of the problems with natural language as a specification medium, there has been a considerable amount of research into using mathematics for this purpose. This has produced a number of development methods which have already achieved some success in industry. Descriptions of two of the most successful techniques can be found in Ince and Andrews (1991) and Jones (1989). These two works describe a method known as VDM, which provides facilities for specifying operations on abstract data types and methods for transforming such data types into program code, including methods for mathematically verifying that the transformations are correct.

In order to give you a flavour of how the operations are described in VDM, consider the problem of specifying a subsystem of a chemical plant control system that closes down and starts up the chemical reactors in the plant. Assume that three operations are required: an operation that starts up a reactor, an operation that closes down a reactor, and an operation that checks that a particular reactor is currently working. The system can be thought of as a composite abstract data type which consists of three sets: one containing the reactors that are currently working, one containing the reactors that are currently closed down, and the collection of all reactors. The specification of the abstract data type, together with the specification of the three operations, is shown below:

reactset = set of *reactors*

plant ::   *operating*: *reactset*
             shut_down: *reactset*
             all_reacts : *reactset*

where inv-*plant*(mk-*plant* (*op*, *sh*,*all*)) $\triangleq$ *op* $\cap$ *sh* = { } $\wedge$ *op* $\cup$ *sh* = *all*

pl_0 = mk-*plant*({ }, ALL_REACTORS, ALL_REACTORS)

CLOSE_DOWN (*reac*:*reactors*)
ext wr *operating*: *reactset*, *shut_down*:*reactset*
pre   *reac* $\in$ *operating*
post   *operating* = $\overleftarrow{operating}$– {*reac*}
              shut_down = $\overleftarrow{shut\_down}$ $\cup$ {*reac*}

START_UP(*reac*:*reactors*)
ext wr *operating*: *reactset*, *shut_down*:*reactset*
pre   *reac* $\in$ *shut_down*
post   *operating* = $\overleftarrow{operating}$ $\cup$ {*reac*}
              shut_down = $\overleftarrow{shut\_down}$ – {*reac*}

CHECK_CLOSED (*reac*:*reactors*) *closed*:$\mathbb{B}$
ext rd *shut_down: reactset*
pre T
post *closed* $\Leftrightarrow$ reac $\in$ *shut_down*

The first line of the specification states that that the abstract data type *reactset* will be a set containing reactors. The specification assumes that the definition of reactors occurs elsewhere. Lines 2–4 state that the abstract data type *plant* consists of three reactor sets: *operating*, *shut_down*, and *all_reacts*. The first set represents those reactors that are currently operating, the second set are those reactors that have been shut down, and the final set represents all the reactors in the system. Notice that the notation used is very similar to that adopted in this book— this is no coincidence!

The final part of the declaration is the data invariant. This specifies that for all values of *plant* the open set (*op*) and the shutdown set (*sh*) have no common members; this is achieved by means of set intersection. This is as it should be: a reactor cannot be both operating and shut down. The final component states that the union of the shutdown set and the operating set is the collection of all reactors (*all*). This just states that all the reactors in the system will either be operating or be closed down. The data invariant has what at first sight seems a strange structure. The invariant is a function that takes a plant as its parameter, the plant parameter above is formed by applying what is known as a *make function*, this creates a plant with an open component *op*, a closed down component *sh*, and an all-reactors component *all*. The final line states that the initial value of the system is formed from no operating reactors and a set of closed down reactors ALL_REACTORS.

The remainder of the specification is a definition of the three operations that occur. Each specification consists of a name, the parameters of the operation, details of the stored data that is affected by the operation, and two predicates: the precondition and the postcondition.

The first operation follows this form. The first line of the operation gives it a name CLOSE_DOWN and states that it will have one parameter *reac*, which will be a reactor. The next line states that the operation will write to variables *operating* and *shut_down*, which represent the state of the system, i.e. these variables will be changed in some way. The precondition is a statement that must be true for the operation to be executed. In the case of the CLOSE_DOWN operation, the precondition states that the operation is valid if the reactor that is to be shut down is contained in the operating set. This just states that the operation is valid if the reactor to be closed down is working. The final line is the postcondition. This is a predicate that must be true after the operation has completed its processing. It states that after CLOSE_DOWN has finished, the new value of the *operating* will be equal to the old value of the set minus the reactor *reac*, which will have been removed. It also states that after the operation, the reactor *reac* will be added to the set *shut_down*, which represents the set of working reactors. Notice the notational device used in the postcondition: a harpoon is placed over an identifier in order to designate it as the value of the identifier *before* the operation has been executed. In essence the postcondition of this operation just says that the parameter *reac* is closed down.

The next operation, START_UP, follows the same pattern. It is named, and its parameter *reac* identified as being a reactor. The state that it alters is the pair of sets representing the reactors that are operating and shut down, and these are written to. The precondition states that for the operation to be executed, *reac* must be in the set of shut-down reactors. The postcondition states that when the operation START_UP has completed its action, the set of shut-down reactors is reduced by removing *reac* from it and the set of operating reactors has *reac* added to it. The effect of this postcondition is to notify the system that the reactor *reac* has started operating.

The final operation, CHECK_CLOSED, is slightly different from the two preceding operations. The first line specifies a result parameter *closed*, which becomes true if the parameter *reac* is a reactor that is closed. The $\mathbb{B}$ symbol stands for the fact that this result parameter has a Boolean type. The next line uses the keyword *rd* to signify that the state is only to be read from and, hence, will not be altered. Only one component of the state *shut_down*, the set of reactors that are shut down, is actually specified in this line, since the operation does not require access to the other components. The precondition is equal to the Boolean constant *true* (T). This states that the operation is defined under all circumstances. The postcondition states that after the operation has been executed, the result parameter *closed* will be set equal to true if the parameter *reac* is contained in the set of shut down reactors, and false otherwise.

This, then, is a sample of one form of mathematical specification of an abstract data type. It has many advantages: it is exact, can be validated using mathematical proof methods, and does not contain any design and implementation directives.

VDM, the development method described above, is an example of what is known as a *model-based method* where the underlying state of a system is modelled by mathematical structures such as sets. This brief introduction has omitted many of the facilities of VDM, the interested reader can examine Andrews and Ince (1991), which provides a good introduction.

Before completing this chapter it is worth describing another type of mathematical specification technique, usually referred to as *algebraic specification* or, less frequently, as *axiomatic specification*. This form of specification involves the specifier or designer writing down the properties of a data type using a series of true statements that relate each of the operations on the data type to one other. An example of an algebraic specification of a stack is shown below. It contains four components types, which describe the abstract data type that is defined, and the types that are used in the definition; exceptions which are infrequently occurring events, such as stack underflow; signatures which define the type of objects manipulated by operations and produced by operations; and equations which specify the behaviour of the operations on the type that is being defined.

types

    stack

uses

    boolean, elem

exceptions

    underflow, undefined

signatures

    Push: stack x elem $\rightarrow$ stack

    Pop: stack $\rightarrow$ stack

    Top: stack $\rightarrow$ elem

    Empty: stack $\rightarrow$ boolean

    NewStack: $\rightarrow$ stack

equations

    Pop(NewStack) = underflow

    Pop(Push(s,e)) = s

    Top(NewStack) = undefined

    Empty(NewStack) = true

    Top(Push(s,e)) = e

    Empty(Push(s,e)) = false

The part of the specification labelled *types* gives the name of the type being defined, in this case *stack*, and *uses* gives the name of other pre-declared types being used in the definition—in the case of the stack these are *boolean* and *elem*. The next part of the definition states that there are two exceptions, stack *underflow* and *undefined*. In a later part of the specification you will see that the former is associated with an attempt to remove an element from an empty stack, while the latter is associated with reading the top element in an empty stack. The part labelled *signatures* gives the type of the objects that the operations process. For example, the operation *push*, which places an object on a stack, is a function that takes an *elem* and a stack and delivers a stack, and the operation *top*, which delivers the top element of a stack takes a stack and delivers an *elem*.

Finally, the part labelled *equations* gives a detailed specification of the axioms that define the action of the operations. For example, the first equation states that an attempt to pop an element off an empty stack will give rise to the underflow exception, and the second equation states that an attempt to push an element *e* onto a stack followed by the popping of the stack will result in the stack being unchanged.

6.6 SUMMARY

This chapter has described how data can be viewed more abstractly than has been done in the past: in terms of the operations that are associated with an abstract data type. Many of the common abstract data types have been described, together with their operations. The chapter has concluded by discussing how a more precise definition of the operations on an abstract data type can be characterized using discrete mathematics. In many ways this chapter forms the kernel of the book: much that follows revolves around the implementation of abstract data types using an object-oriented programming language. Therefore, if there is anything that you feel hazy about, it might be worth your while rereading this chapter.

6.7 FURTHER READING

Booch (1987) contains a good discussion of the operations that abstract data types can provide, it also contains a large amount of Ada program code which shows how operations on abstract data types can be implemented in the Ada programming language. Hoare (1972) contains the original, set-oriented view of abstract data types. Although this piece of work was written in the early seventies it still reads exceptionally well today. Lamb (1988) is an excellent book on software engineering which contains a sympathetic description of algebraic specification.

BIBLIOGRAPHY

Andrews, D. and Ince, D. C. (1991) *Practical Formal Methods with VDM*, McGraw-Hill, London.

Booch, G. (1987) *Software components with Ada*, Benjamin Cummings, New York.

Hoare, C. A. R. (1972) Notes on Data Structuring. In *Structured Programming*, Academic Press, New York.

Ince, D. C. (1988) *An Introduction to Discrete Mathematics and Formal System Specification*, Oxford University Press, Oxford.

Jones, C. B. (1989) *Systematic Software Development with VDM*, Prentice-Hall, Englewood Cliffs, NJ.

Lamb, D. A. (1988) *Software Engineering*, Prentice-Hall, Englewood Cliffs, NJ.

THE BASIC FACILITIES OF C++

AIMS

- To describe the basic programming facilities of the C++ programming language.
- To describe the data structuring facilities of C++.
- To describe the control facilities of C++.
- To describe the facilities for implementing functions in C++.

7.1 INTRODUCTION

The previous chapters have shown how requirements analysis, requirements specification, and design can be carried out using an object-oriented paradigm. This chapter is the first of two chapters which describe the programming language that will be used for implementing the systems that have been defined as entities and operations. C++ is a superset of the C programming language: the data typing, control flow, and subroutine facilities are all borrowed from C. This chapter describes these facilities. If you regard yourself as a C expert, then you can skimp reading this chapter and proceed to Chapter 8, which will contain a large amount of new material. Before proceeding with the description a warning is necessary. This section is a tutorial introduction to the facilities of C++, it only contains enough description of those facilities necessary for an understanding of later sections of the book. If you are interested in the minutiae of C++, then Stroustrup (1986) provides a comprehensive description.

7.2 SCALAR DATA TYPES AND OPERATORS

C++ offers a rich set of data types. The aim of this section is to describe them. The data types in C++ can be divided into scalar data types and aggregate data types.

7.2.1 Scalar data types

C++ contains eight different integer data types and two floating-point types, along with pointers and enumerated types, both of which will be described later. They constitute what is known as scalar types. All variables which are required by a program need to be declared. For example, the declarations

```
int j, k;
float a,b,c;
char x;
```

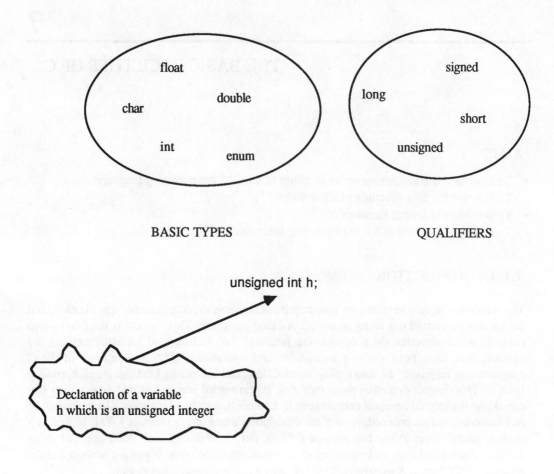

BASIC TYPES   QUALIFIERS

unsigned int h;

Declaration of a variable
h which is an unsigned integer

Figure 7.1 Basic types of C++.

declare two integer variables j and k together with three floating-point variables a, b, and c, and a character variable x. The different basic types are shown in Fig. 7.1. They are int, an integer, char, a character, float, a floating-point number, double, a double-length floating-point number, and enum, which is an enumerated type. Many of these basic types can be prefaced with the qualifiers short, unsigned, signed, and long.

int is the basic integer type and short int represents an integer that is stored in a smaller area of memory than an int—usually half the space. long int is an integer that is stored in more memory than an int— usually twice the number of bytes is used.

The declaration of a character results in a storage location being created that holds an integer equal to the internal integer value of the character. This variable can be treated just as an integer. For example, the program code shown below declares an integer x which is first assigned the character c and then the integer 44. The second integer represents the character whose internal value is 44. Depending on the implementation, the value will either be an ASCII value or an EBCDIC value.

```
char x;
x ='c';
x = 44;
```

The character stored in x by the second assignment will depend on the internal character code of the computer on which the C++ compiler is implemented. If it is ASCII, then the character corresponding to ASCII 44 will be stored.

Unsigned variables have positive values. Declaring a variable as unsigned ensures that the bit that is normally used for indicating whether the number is negative or positive can be used for the number. Thus, if the implementation of C++ that you are working with stores integers in 16 bits with 1 bit for the arithmetic sign, then a declaration of an unsigned integer will usually result in doubling the positive number range of the variable, with integer variables of up to 16 bits capable of being processed.

C++ also has facilities for defining variables that are stored as floating points. The keyword float declares a variable to be a normal floating-point variable, while the keyword double declares a variable to be a double-length floating-point variable. Thus, the declaration

```
float a, n, newone;
double k3, you;
```

declares three floating-point variables, a, n, newone, and two double-length floating-point variables k3 and you.

An enumerated type is one in which the variables can receive values from a discrete set of values. For example, if a program required a variable CurrentDept, which holds the name of a department in a company, and a variable CurrCount, which holds names of countries, then this might be declared as:

```
enum Dept   {sales, marketing, personnel} CurrentDept;
enum Country {Britain, USA, France, Germany} CurrCount;
```

The variable CurrentDept can only hold the values sales, marketing, and personnel, while the variable CurrCount can only hold the values Britain, USA, France, and Germany. Thus, the following assignments are legal

```
CurrentDept = personnel;
CurrentDept = sales;
CurrCount = France;
```

while the following assignments are illegal

```
CurrentDept = research;
CurrCount = Japan;
CurrCount = China;
```

because research is not one of the values that are specified for the CurrentDept variable and Japan and China are not values specified for the CurrCount variable.

The final type of variable that you can declare is the pointer variable. A pointer variable contains the address of a location, and is extensively used in array processing. In a later subsection of this chapter I shall describe the detailed use of pointer variables, however, for completeness sake it is worth describing how they are declared here. An example of some pointer declarations is shown below:

```
long int *p1;
char *p2;
int *p3;
```

The first line declares a variable p1, which is going to hold the address of long integers, the second line declares a variable p2, which is going to hold the address of characters, and, finally, the third line declares the variable p3, which holds the address of an integer. The important point to notice about this fragment of program code is that pointer variable declarations are distinguished by the use of an asterisk character in front of the variable name.

When variables are declared they can be given a value. These values, or literals, are expressed in a number of ways: integers are written as either octal constants, hexadecimal constants, or decimal constants. An octal constant is specified by writing a leading zero, a hexadecimal constant is specified by beginning the constant with the leading characters 0x, and decimal constants are just written using the digits 0 – 9, with an optional + or – preceding the constant. Thus, the following are examples of integer constants: 0777 (octal), 0xdd3 (hexadecimal) and 345 (decimal).

Floating-point constants are written as decimals only. Such constants contain both an integer part and a fractional part, along with an optional E or e which signifies that the figures following are to be raised to the power of 10. Thus, the following are examples of floating-point constants, with their values shown in parentheses following them: 8.4 (8.4), 3.4e2 (340) and 345.4E-2 (3.454). Such constants are regarded as being of type double.

Constant strings are written within double quotes. Sometimes escape characters are embedded in the strings, typical escape characters are \n, which stands for a newline, \b, which is a backspace, and \t, which stands for a horizontal tab. Thus, the string constant "This is a message\n" stands for the text *This is a message*, followed by a newline.

Character constants are surrounded by single quotation marks. For example, 'y' stands for the y character. Enumeration constants are written as they are declared. For example, the declarations

```
enum dept {Sales, Marketing} ad1, ad2;
enum country {France, USA, Britain} c1, c2;
```

would allow the following assignments to take place:

```
ad1 = Sales;
c1 = Britain;
```

where the constant Sales and Britain are assigned values to the variables ad1 and c1.

Variables can be assigned constant values in two ways: first, in the declaration of the variable by writing the variable followed by the equals sign and then the value, or in an assignment in the executable part of a C++ program. Thus, the following sections of program code are equivalent:

```
double a, b, c = 10.89;
char e, f, g, h = 'a';
e = 's';
g = 'h';
a = 23.456e4;
```

and

```
double a = 23.456e4, b, c;
char e = 's', f, g, h = 'a';
g = 'h';
c = 10.89;
```

Another assignment facility that is available in C++ is the ability to define constants. All that is required is for the keyword `const` to be written, followed by a constant name, an equals operator and the value of the constant. Thus, the declarations

```
const float pi = 3.142;
const int DEPSIZE = 2055;
```

declare two constants `pi`, a double constant and `DEPSIZE`, an integer constant. Such constants can be used anywhere in a C++ program, except on the left-hand side of an assignment.

So far, this chapter has used variables and named them, without explicitly giving the rule for what is, and what is not, a valid variable name. The rule is that identifiers are made up of letters of the alphabet, digits, and the underscore character _, with the proviso that a name cannot start with a digit. The case of the letters is significant, so, for example, the identifiers `Speed` and `speed` are taken to mean two different things.

Comments are also available in C++ . They can be written in two different ways. C++ uses the C convention that comments are enclosed within the symbols `/*` and `*/`. It also allows comments to be preceded by the characters `//` and terminated by a newline. Examples of the use of these comment facilities are shown below:

```
/* Initialize speed variables */
speed1 = 23;
speed2 = 34;
wind_speed = 900;
```

and

```
speed1 = 23;   // Initialize speed variables
speed2 = 34;
wind_speed = 900;
```

7.2.2 Operators

C++ provides a large number of operators for the manipulation of arithmetic types, pointers, and arrays. This section describes many of these operators. It is worth pointing out that there is a precedence with operators in C++, in the same way that operators in more conventional programming languages have a precedence. For example, in C++ the operators for arithmetic operations have a higher precedence than the logical operators. The full list of operators and their precedence in Zortech C++ is shown in Table 7.1.

The table shows the operators with the highest priority at the top, and those having the lowest priority at the bottom. A number of operators are duplicated in this table, e.g. the `&` operator appears a number of times, the reason for this is that these operators are used in a number of different contexts, and their priority depends on the context. At this stage do not

Table 7.1 List of C++ operators and their precedence.

1	()	.	[]	->	::	->*	&
2	*	&	new	delete	!	~	++
	-	.	-	sizeof			
3	*	/	%				
4	+	-					
5	<<	>>					
6	<	<=	>	>	>=		
7	==	!=					
8	&						
9	^						
10	|						
11	&&						
12	||						
13	?:						
14	=	+=	-=	*=	/=	%=	<<=
	>>=	&=	^=	|=			
15	,						

worry about the fact that you have not seen these operators in action. The remainder of this chapter will include descriptions of the functioning of most of these operators.

The arithmetic operators are + (addition), − (subtraction), * (multiplication), / (division), and % (modulus). All these operators are binary, i.e. they operate on two operands. However, + and − also have unary versions. The modulus operator returns the remainder on dividing its first operand by its second operand, e.g. 5%7 evaluates to 5; this operator cannot be applied to variables of type float or double. When integers are divided, the result of the division is truncated. Thus, 4/3 evaluates to 1.

C++ also contains a number of relational operators: < (less than), > (greater than), <= (less than or equal to), >= (greater than or equal to), == (equal to), and != (not equal to). An important point to make about these operators—something which programmers in other languages who learn C or C++ initially find difficult—is that a relational expression delivers either a 0 or a 1, depending on the truth of falsity of the expression. A 0 is delivered if the expression is false, and 1 is delivered if the expression is true. For example, the logical expression a < b will deliver 0 if a is greater than or equal to b, and 1 otherwise.

SAQ What is the result of the following assignment statement. If b contains 45 and c contains 77?

```
a = b < c
```

Examine Table 7.1 before you answer the question.

SOLUTION What happens is that since < has a higher precedence than =, the expression b < c is evaluated first, since b is less than c the value returned will be 1 and this will be assigned to the variable a. ❏

The previous self-assessment question is an example of an important point which holds for both C and C++, namely that in these languages it is important to know about the various priorities of the operators. Both these languages allow you to write much richer expressions than languages such as Pascal—expressions whose exact semantics is difficult to understand without a good knowledge of operator precedents.

C++ also provides a number of logical operators that operate on values of 0 and 1. The operators are && (and), || (or), and ! (not). The evaluation of an expression that contains these operators stops as soon as the eventual result of the expression has been determined. For example, the expression a && b && c && d would stop as soon as a or b or c is determined to be false.

SAQ What is the result of the following expression if a contains 1, b contains 0, and c contains 0?

```
(a + b && c)*a
```

Examine Table 7.1 before you answer the question.

SOLUTION Addition has a higher precedence than &&, so a and b are added together to give 1, this is anded with c to give zero, which is then multiplied by a to give zero. ❏

A useful pair of operators that are continually used in C++ programs are the increment operator and the decrement operators. These are written as ++ and --. They are unary operators and increment or decrement their operands by 1. Thus, if the value of the integer variable t was 5, then the result of t++ would be to assign the value 6 to t. The result of t-- would be to assign the value 4 to t.

It is important to point out that these operators deliver a result. For example, the program code

```
int t = 1, s;
s = ++t;
```

would increment the variable t by 1 and assign the resulting value (2) to the variable s. These operators can be written before or after the operand. If they are written before the operand, the new value of the operand is used in expressions; if the operators are written after an operand, the old value of the operand is used in expressions. For example, the program code

```
int s, p = 66;
```

```
s = ++p;
```

would assign the value 67 to the variable s, while

```
int s, p = 66;
s = p++;
```

would assign the value 66 to s.

C++ also provides a number of operators that operate at the bit level. These operators are useful when performing bit-level programming, e.g. when interfacing non-standard input/output devices, or when space is at a premium and words have to hold a number of fields.

These operators are & (bitwise and), | (bitwise inclusive or), ^ (bitwise exclusive or), << (left shift), >> (right shift) and ~ (ones complement). All these operators are binary, apart from ones complement which is unary. The bitwise *and* operator takes two operands and applies the *and* operator to each corresponding bit of the operands; the inclusive *or* operator takes each corresponding bit of the operands and applies the *or* operator to them; the exclusive *or* operator takes each corresponding bit of the operands and applies the exclusive *or* operator, this operator is similar to the *or* operator except that it returns zero if the corresponding bits are both 1; the left shift operator takes has two operands: the operand to be shifted and the number of shifts to the left that should occur; the right shift operator takes has two operands: the operand to be shifted and the number of shifts to the right that should occur; finally, the ones complement operator takes a single operand and reverses the values of the bits in the operand: a 1 is transformed to 0 and vice versa.

Thus, if the variable a contained the binary pattern 01011100, and the variable b contained the pattern 00001111, the results of the operators being applied to the these variables is shown below:

```
c = a & b;              // c becomes 00001100
c = a | b;              // c becomes 01011111
c = a ^ b;              // c becomes 01010011
c = ~b;                 // c becomes 11110000
```

C++ also provides a number of combined assignment operators. By writing an operator as =*operator*, C++ provides the facility for assignments that involve the same variable on the right-hand and left-hand sides to be written succinctly. For example, the assignments

```
y *= 2;
Bitflag &= nullf;
```

are equivalent to the assignments

```
y = y*2;
Bitflag = Bitflag & nullf;
```

The following operators can be used in this way:

```
+     –     *     /     %     <<     >>     &     ^     |
```

An important class of operators—one that often gives programmers new to C and C++ a large amount of trouble—are those concerned with addressing. There are two such operators: the address of operator & and the de-referencing operator *. The former operator yields the address of the variable to which it is applied. The latter is applied to a pointer variable, and yields the value contained in the memory location(s) whose address is contained in the variable. An example of the use of these operators is shown below:

```
int u, v, *w;            // declares 2 integer variables and
                         // an integer pointer variable

u = 4;                   // Sets u equal to 4
w = &u;                  // Sets w equal to the address of u
v = u;                   // Sets v equal to 4
u = 66;                  // Sets u equal to 66
v = *w;                  // Sets v to 66
```

The declaration informs the compiler that two integer variables and a pointer to an integer variable are to be used. The first assignment is a simple assignment of 4 to the variable u. The second assignment sets w to be the address of u. The third assignment sets v equal to the contents of u, which in this case is 4. The fourth assignment sets u to be 66. The final assignment sets v equal to the contents of the variable whose address is in w. Since the address of u has been already been placed in w the effect of this is to set v to 66.

An operator that is used in *for* statements is the comma operator, this has the effect of evaluating its operands from left to right and throwing away each result, until the last operand is encountered. It is the value of this operand that the comma operator then returns. For example, the effect of the program code

```
int p, i = 3;
i++, p = i, p <=3;
```

is to increment i by 1, set p equal to 4 and then deliver 0, which is the result of the logical expression 4 <= 3.

An important concept in both C and C++ is that of type conversions. Both these languages allow a very rich syntax for assignments. For example, they allow an integer variable on the left-hand side of an assignment and an expression that delivers a character on the right-hand side of the assignment. In order to define what happens in all the cases encountered, there are a whole set of rules which are used for type conversion. For example, with the operators + and *, if either of the operands are of type long double, the other operand is converted to long double before the operator is applied. Another example involves the assignment of an expression which delivers a character to a variable of type int. What happens here is that the int variable is given the internal value of the character, either ASCII or EBCDIC.

Before leaving this topic it is worth describing a way in which the programmer can influence the type conversions that occur in a C++ program. This facility is known as the *cast operator*. By preceding the name of a variable with a type name enclosed in parentheses, that variable is converted to the type specified. For example, consider the program fragment shown below:

```
int *j;
char *rem;
int k;

k = (int) rem;
k = (int) j;
```

The first assignment results in the character pointer variable `rem` being converted to an `int` and then being copied into `k`, the second assignment results in the integer pointer variable `j` being converted to an `int` and then being copied into `k`.

7.3 AGGREGATE DATA TYPES

The previous section has discussed simple data types. You will not be surprised to find that C++ also contains facilities for defining more complicated types; in particular, types that contain multiple values. If the values are all of the same type, then the data type so formed is known as an *array*; however, if the values are of differing types, then the data type is known as a *structure*. Arrays are declared in a similar way to simple data types. For example, the program code shown below declares two one-dimensional arrays of integers and a one-dimensional array of characters:

```
int a[10], b[15];
char name[30];
```

The integer array a has 10 elements and starts at a[0] and finishes at a[9], the integer array b has 15 elements and starts at b[0] and finishes at b[14]. The character array name has 30 elements and starts at name[0] and finishes at name[29].

Arrays can be initialized in their declaration by specifying their elements enclosed in curly brackets. For example, the initializations

```
int a[10] = {44,55,66,7,8,9,10,12,1,1};
char b[3] = {'a','b','c'};
```

initialize the array a to the list of 10 integers inside the curly brackets, and the character array b to the list of three characters. When the whole list of constants is not specified on the right-hand side, the uninitialized positions in the array are set to zero. For example, the declarations

```
int a[10] = {44,55,66,7,8,9,10};
int b[3] = {2};
```

sets the array a equal to the seven specified integers, and sets the remaining three locations, a[7] to a[9], to zero; similarly, the second declaration sets the first element of b to 2 and the remaining elements to zero.

An alternative form of initialization specifies no bounds in the array declaration. For example, the declarations

```
int a[] = {44,55,66,7,8,9,10,55,66};
int b[] = {2,4,1,1,18,8,9};
```

first set the array a equal to the nine integers on the right-hand side, and then set b equal to the seven integers on the right-hand side. The important difference between this form of initialization and the previous one, in which the bounds of the array were specified, is that this latter initialization sets the bounds of the array to the number of elements on the right-hand side. Thus, the declarations

```
int b[] = {2,4,1,1,18,8,9};
int b[9] = {2,4,1,1,18,8,9};
```

are not equivalent, since the first assignment sets the bound of the array to 7 while the second sets the bound to 9, filling in the unspecified values with zero.

Character arrays are treated in a similar way. However, such arrays can be initialized in a simpler way, namely by quoting the right-hand side of a declaration as a string. For example, the declarations

```
char a[] = "There";
char b[] = "is";
```

declare two character arrays containing the strings There and is.

It is important to point out that such declarations set the bound of the array to one more than the number of characters specified, and fill the last location of the array with a terminating character \0, which stands for the null character. This character is used in processing to check for the end of a string. Thus, the following two declarations are equivalent:

```
char a[] = {'a','b','n','k','\0'};
char a[] = "abnk";
```

It is important to point out that the declaration of an array is equivalent to the declaration of a pointer, which points at the first location of the array. For example, the program code

```
int y[3] = {1,2,4};
int *point;
point = y;
point++;
```

will declare an array of three integers y, then declare an integer pointer variable point, and then set point to contain the address of the first element of y and then the address of the second element of y.

SAQ What occurs when the following program code is executed?

```
int y[5] = {1,5,6,7,8};
int *p;
int s;
p = y;
p +=2;
s = *p;
```

SOLUTION First an array of integers y with five elements is declared and given the five values 1, 5, 6, 7, 8. Then an integer pointer p is declared together with an integer s. p is set to point at the first element of the array y in the first assignment statement, p is then incremented by 2. Finally, the contents of the location pointed at by p is placed into s. So the overall result is to place 6 into the variable s. ❑

Whenever pointers are changed, the units of change are such that they will point to a location in an array. For example, the incrementation of a pointer to an array by 1 will always point to the next element of the array—irrespective of the amount of storage used for each array element. Arrays can also contain pointers. A frequent use for such arrays is to hold a series of strings. The declaration:

```
char* dept[3] = {
  "alfred",
  "george",
  "david"
};
```

declares an array of character pointers called dept. This array is initialized to point at the first characters in the three strings on the right-hand side. The processing of such arrays is quite complicated, and is a topic that we will look at in the next section of this chapter. However, before doing this it is worth looking at another aggregate data type: the structure.

A structure is a collection of variables bound together by virtue of the fact that they are related to each other. An example of a structure is shown below:

```
struct addr{
  int day;
  char typos;
  char *startpos;
} nm;
```

This declares a variable nm of type addr which has three components: an integer day, a character typos, and a pointer to a character startpos.

The components of a structure can be referred to by writing the name of the structure, followed by a full stop and the name of the component. Thus, with the structure above, all the following are legal C++ statements:

```
nm.day = 23;
nm.typos = 's';
nm.day++;
```

Structures can be initialized in the same way as arrays; the declaration below specifies a structure with three components, all of which are integer:

```
struct date{
  int day;
  int month;
  int year;
} d
= {2,5,1989};
```

This form of declaration can be cumbersome when a large number of structures of the same type need to be declared in a program. In order to cope with this, C++ provides a facility known as the typedef facility. This enables a single word to stand for a complex data type declaration. An example of this is shown below:

```
typedef struct dateof{
          int day;
          int month;
          int year;
          } daydate;
```

This associates the name daydate with the structure definition. This means that wherever the structure definition can be written the name daydate can be written. For example, to declare three daydates and use them, all that is required is

```
daydate today, tomorrow, yesterday;
today.day = 12;
today.month = 11;
today.year = 1990;
tomorrow.day = 13;
yesterday.day = 11;
```

This facility is of most use when complex types are being used. However, there is no reason why it cannot be used for simpler types. For example

```
typedef int* pint;
typdef  char* pchar;
```

states that pointers to integers will be known as pints and pointers to characters are known as pchars. A structure can contain components of any type, including functions.

In C++ it is possible to define pointers to structures. For example, pointers to the daydate type can be declared as

```
daydate *el;
```

The components can be retrieved using the dereferencing operator *. For example, the program code below shows the declaration of a pointer to daydate and a daydate together with program code that accesses the daydate:

```
daydate today = {12,3,89}, *pdate;
pdate = &today;
(*pdate).day++;
```

The assignment statement first retrieves the variable pointed at by p, extracts the day field, and then increments it by 1.

SAQ Why could we have not written the above program code as

```
daydate today = {12,3,89}, *pdate;
pdate = &today;
*pdate.today++;
```

SOLUTION The reason is to do with operator precedence. If you examine Table 7.1 you will find that the . operator has a higher precedence than the * dereferencing operator. This means that the compiler will interpret the expression *pdate.today as a reference to the address of the today component of a pointer variable, a nonsense that the compiler will normally flag as an error. ❑

Structures can contain components of an arbitrary type; they can even be functions. This seemingly eccentric facility has major ramifications for program design, ramifications that are explored in detail in the next chapter. Before proceeding to that chapter it is worth looking at the control flow facilities and modularization facilities within C++. These correspond to the facilities found in many other programming languages.

7.4 CONTROL FLOW FACILITIES

So far this chapter has only looked at data types and operations; although some notion of what a C++ program is has, indirectly, been given, no details have been described. The purpose of this subsection is to look at how the various forms of control structure in C++ are implemented and the overall structure of C++ programs.

Statements in C++ can be either a null statement, i.e. nothing followed by a semi-colon; a declaration, many examples of which you have seen in the previous subsections of this chapter; an expression statement such as

```
s = k+1;
```

and compound statements, which are collections of statements surrounded by an opening curly bracket and a closing curly bracket. There are a number of facilities available in the language to control the flow of statements. An important point about C++ assignment statements and operators that involve an implied assignment such as ++ is that the assignment statement returns a value which may be used by other parts of a C++ program. For example, the assignment statement

```
s = 23 + p;
```

will assign the sum of 23 and p to the variable s and deliver the result. This result can then be used in any context when an integer can be written. For example, it is perfectly permissable to write

```
a=(s=23+p);
```

which will assign to a the sum of 23 and p, although I would not recommend it on stylistic grounds!

The first facility that we shall discuss uses the if/else notation. It has the form

```
if (expression)
   statementtrue
else
   statementfalse
```

The expression in parentheses is evaluated, and if it is true, then statementtrue is executed, otherwise statementfalse is executed. There are a number of points to make about this control construct. First, the expression that determines the flow of control will either evaluate to 0 or 1. Second, that the else part of the if construct is optional: if no processing is required when the expression is false it can be omitted. Third, statementtrue and statementfalse can be simple statements or compound statements.

Some examples of the use of this facility are shown below:

```
if (!flag) {
   a= 3;
   day = 12;
}
else {
   a=4;
   b=3;
};
```

Here, if the variable `flag` is false the first branch of the `if` construct is executed, otherwise the second branch is executed. Notice the way that the program code has been displayed with the curly brackets clearly delimiting the scope of the `if` construct. Another example of the `if` construct is shown below:

```
if (day = *p) {
a++;
b++;
};
```

Here the variables a and b are incremented if the integer pointer p points at a location which holds the same value as the variable `day`.

C++ also provides a multiway `if` facility. This is normally written as

```
if (expression1)
    statement1
else if (expression2)
    statement2
else if (expression 3)
    .
else if (expression n)
    statementn
else
    finalstatement
```

Execution of this will result in the statement corresponding to the first true expression being executed. If none of the expressions are true, then `finalstatement` will be executed. An example of the use of this facility is shown below:

```
if (!flag)
    z++;
else if (a=9)
    s = 12;
else if (b=9)
    y++;
else if (c=9)
    x++;
else
    flag = 1;
```

This form of multiway decision processing is a little cumbersome. Consequently, C++ provides an alternative form known as the `switch` statement. This has the form

```
switch (expression) {
    case constant_expression1:
        statement1_1;
        statement1_2;
        statement1_3;

        statement1_m;
        break;
```

```
        case constant_expression2:
            statement2_1;
            statement2_2;
            statement2_3;
                .
            statement2_n;
            break;
        case constant_expression3:
            statement3_1;
            statement3_2;
            statement3_3;
                .
            statement3_p;
            break;
                .
                .
                .
        default:
            statementd_1;
            statementd_2;
            statementd_3;
                .
            statementd_q;
            break;
    }
```

The execution of the switch statement depends on the value of expression. When the switch statement is executed, expression is evaluated and each constant expression is checked against the value of expression. If a match is found, then the statements associated with the constant expression are executed until the keyword break is encountered or until the closing curly bracket of the switch statements is encountered. If none of the constant expressions match, then the statements labelled with the keyword default are executed.

There are a number of points to be made about the switch statements. First, the constant expressions must be character constants, integer constants, character expressions, or integer expressions. Second, all the constant expressions must be different. Third, the branch of the switch statement headed by the keyword default can be omitted. If it is, then if none of the branches match the expression, execution is transferred to the first statement that follows the switch statement. Fourth, curly brackets are not required around the statements in each branch of the switch statement.

An example of a switch statement is shown below:

```
switch (transaction_type) {
    case 1:
        day++;
        month++;
        log_total++;
```

```
      break;
  case 2:
    day--;
    break;
  case 3:
    log_total = 0;
    break;
  default:
    day = 0;
    month =0;
    break;
};
```

If transaction_type is 1, then the day variable, month variable, and log_total variable are all incremented and processing of the switch statement terminates. If transaction_type is 2, then day is decremented and processing terminates. If transaction_type is 3, then the variable log_total is set to zero. If the transaction type does not lie between 1 and 3, then the default part of the switch statement is executed, and the day variable and the month variable are set to zero.

SAQ What is the result of the following processing if the integer variable a is equal to 99 and the integer variable b is equal to 19?

```
switch (a<b) {
    case (0):
        p=0;
        s=0;
    case (1):
        p--;
        s--;
};
```

SOLUTION Since the value of a is greater than b the result of the expression a<b will be false. This means that it will deliver a zero. Hence the first branch of the switch statement will be executed. Consequently p will be set to zero and s will be set to zero. However, since there is no break keyword, execution continues along the other branch of the switch statement and p is decremented by 1 and s is decremented by 1. This means that the result of the processing is to set p equal to –1 and also set s to –1.
❑

The next control facility is the while statement. This processes a section of program code while a condition is true. It has the form

```
while (expression)
    statement
```

While expression is true statement will be executed. An example of the use of this statement is shown below

```
p = a;
```

```
count = 0;
while (*p !='\0') {
   if ( *p == 'a') count++;
   p++;
};
```

What this statement does is to process an array a of characters. The first statement sets the character pointer p to the address of a. The while statement continually loops until the last character in a—the null character—has been encountered. Inside the loop is an if statement which increments the variable count by 1 if the character a is encountered. The function of this section of code is thus to count the number of occurrences of lower-case a in the array a.

Another repetitive statement is the do/while loop. Here, in contrast to the while loop, the condition that tests whether the loop should terminate its processing occurs at the end of the loop. The format of the do/while loop is

```
do
   statements
while (expression)
```

Here statements are executed while expression is true. An example of the use of this form of looping is shown below:

```
i=0;
do {
   sum += vals[i];
   i++;}
while (vals[i] != 0);
```

This examines the integer array vals, and finds the sum of all those integers in the array that are terminated by a zero.

SAQ Write a fragment of C++ program which examines the integer array values and sets the variable enough to true if more than half the contents of the array are zero. Assume that the array is terminated by an element that contains a negative number. Use a do/while statement

SOLUTION The fragment is shown below:

```
i=0;
sum = 0;
do{
   if (values[i] == 0)
      sum++;
   i++;}
while (vals[i] >=0);
enough = (sum > i/2);
```

❑

SAQ What does the loop

```
do
   statements
while(1);
```

represent?

SOLUTION It represents a loop that, theoretically, loops forever, the argument in the while part of the loop is 1, which stands for true. Normally the loop will contain processing that enables it to exit by means of a jump or a break. ❑

The final control structure facility is the `for` loop, this has the form

```
for (expression1; expression2; expression3)
   statement
```

This is equivalent to the `while` loop

```
expression1;
while (expression2) {
   statement;
   expression3;
};
```

`expression1` carries out some initialization, `expression2` represents the condition of the loop, and `expression3` contains the processing which often progresses the loop. An example of a `for` loop is shown below:

```
for (sum=0, i =0; i <=49; i:=i+1)
if (a[i] >10)
   sum:=sum+a[i];
```

This examines the first 50 elements of the array a, and if an element is greater than 10 will add it to the variable sum.

7.5 FUNCTIONS

The aim of this section is to describe the modularization facilities of C++. The facility in the C++ language that enables sections of code to be packaged up as single entities is known as the *function*.

A function declaration has the form

```
type name (argument list)
```

where `argument list` is the data that the function processes or returns. Some examples of the declaration of functions are shown below:

```
int retdate(int);
int* retloidate(int, int);
char* largearr(int, int, double, char*);
```

The first declaration states that the function `retdate` will take an integer argument and will return an integer, the second declaration states that the the function `retloidate` will take two integer parameters and will return a pointer to an integer, and the third declaration states that the function `largearr` will take four parameters—two integers, a double, and a pointer to a character—and will return a pointer to a character.

So far we have discussed how the form of functions is declared in C++. What has not been discussed is how the actions that a function carries out are described. Before doing so it is worth looking at a general structure of a C++ program. This is shown below:

```
includes
global declarations and classes
main()
{
declarations
processing
};
function definitions
```

The first line marked `includes` contains include statements. This brings in any library functions that are needed in a file. The format of the include statement is simple: it consists of a hash followed by the keyword `include` followed by the library required. For example, the include statement

```
#include <stdio.h>
```

directs the C++ compiler to use the the library `stdio.h` which contains input/output facilities. A whole series of includes can be written here if a number of libraries are required

The include statement is followed by the declaration of any global variables, classes, and functions—classes will be dealt with in the next chapter. The keyword `main` which, in essence, declares a function with no parameters and no results then follows. `main` is used by the operating system as an entry point. It can be regarded as a keyword that marks the beginning of the C++ program. In the example below `main` has no text included between its brackets. In some cases text is included. However, assume at this stage that the brackets are empty.

The keyword `main` is followed by the declarations of the constants and variables used in main. These declarations are then followed by the processing required. Finally, the functions are defined. A simple example of a C++ program is shown below:

```
#include <stdio.h>

// Function declaration
int addup(int,int);
main()
{
int i,j;
// code to read in values of i and j here
printf (" Value of i = %d, value of j = %d, value of addup =
       %d",i, j, addup(i,j));
};
```

```
//// Function definition

int addup (int a,int b)
{
if (a+b >20)
   return(a+b);
else
   return (a);
};
```

The first line of the program brings in the library `stdio.h` which provides input/output facilities, this is followed by the declaration of the type of the function `addup`. The part of the program following the `main` keyword declares two integer variables. The lines following the declarations are the calls on the library facilities. The line

```
printf (" Value of i = %d, value of j = %d, value of addup =
        %d",i, j, addup(i,j));
```

displays the result of calling the function `addup` with the arguments `i` and `j`. This function will return the sum of its arguments if it is greater than 20, and will return the first argument otherwise. `Printf` is a facility provided by the library `stdio.h`.

The structure of a function definition is

```
type name(arguments)
{
statements
};
```

where `type` is the type of the variable returned, `name` is the name of the function, `arguments` are the parameters of the functions, and `statements` are the programming statements that are invoked when the function is executed. These statements usually refer to the arguments of the function. An example of a function definition is shown below. It represents a function that calculates the sum of two integers.

```
int sumup(int a,b)
{
return (a+b);
};
```

The keyword `return` indicates the value returned from the function. The keyword `int` indicates that the function will return an integer value. All the conversion rules that apply in C++ apply to function calls and arguments. So far only functions that manipulate values and return values have been described. There is often a need for a function to place data at some location. For example, let us assume, artificially, that we require a function that, as well as adding up two values, places the sum that has been formed into a variable. The function definition for this is shown below:

```
void newaddupt(int* a, int b, c);
{
*a = b+c;
};
```

A number of new features are shown here. First, the keyword `void` indicates that the function does not return a value. Second, the parameter `a` is an integer pointer parameter. When the statement `*a = b+c` is executed, the sum of `b` and `c` is placed in the location pointed at by `a`. Notice that with a void function no return statement is required.

Variables can be defined inside a function definition. For example, the function `swap` shown below requires the use of an integer variable that temporarily holds data while the contents of two integer locations are interchanged:

```
void swap(int* a, int* b)
{
int t = *a;
*a = *b;
*b = t;
};
```

SAQ Write down the definition of a function that has three parameters. The first parameter is an address of a series of integers, the second parameter is an integer, and the third parameter is an integer variable. The function should sum up the stored integers and place the result in the third parameter. The second parameter contains the number of integers to be summed.

SOLUTION The function is shown below:

```
void sumseries( int* poi, int number, int* result)
{
int sum = 0, num = number;
while (num>0) {
    sum +=*poi;
    poi++;
    num--;
    };
*result = sum;
};
```

❑

The use of pointers can lead to error-prone processing and can be a little cumbersome, consequently C++ provides a facility that enables variable parameters to be defined. A parameter preceded by the `&` symbol, or whose type is followed by a `&`, is taken to be a variable. For example, the `newaddupt` function could have been written as

```
void newaddupt(int& a, int b, int c)
{
a = b+c;
}
```

The argument `a` is passed by reference while the other two arguments are passed by value. There is, hence, no need to use the dereferencing operator `*` in either case.

When arrays are passed, what is required is for the address of the array to be passed. Unfortunately the vast majority of processing of arrays requires knowledge of how many items there are in an array. There are a number of solutions to this dilemma. First, if the array is a string, then it will always be terminated by the null / 0 character. If the array contains items of a type other than character, then another solution is to terminate the array with a value that could not possibly be contained in it. For example, if the array was one of integers between 0 and 100, then the array could be terminated with a value of 101. Another solution is to pass two parameters: the array address, and the number of items in the array. Some examples of this strategy are shown below, where the function setcount examines an array and returns with the number of zero values in it.

```
// Two parameters

int setcount ( int* poi, int number) {
int total = 0;
while (number>0) {
   if *poi == 0
      total++;
   poi++;
   number--;
   };
return (total);
};
```

An example of setcount, where the array is terminated by a number that should not exist in the array, is shown below:

```
// Terminator is the integer 101

int setcount ( int* poi){
int total = 0;
while (*poi != 101){
   if (*poi == 0)
      total++;
   poi++;
   };
return (total);
};
```

SAQ Write down the definition of a function that has one argument—a pointer to a string—and returns the number of lower-case letters in the string.

SOLUTION The function is shown below:

```
int count_lc(char* poi){
int total = 0;
while (*poi != '\0') do{
```

```
        if ( *poi <= 'z' && *poi >= 'a')
            total++;
        poi++;
        };
    return (total);
    };
```

The address of the string is passed over to the function, which loops around, examining each character in the string, and terminates when the null character is encountered. ❏

Functions can also be provided with default arguments. This is implemented in the declaration of the function by means of an explicit assignment to one of the arguments. For example, the function declaration `set_it` below declares the function `set_it` to be an integer function with two parameters, a character pointer and a character; the default value for the character argument is the space character.

```
int set_it(char*, char = ' ');
```

This function can be called in a number of ways:

```
set_it(a, b);
set_it (newst, '*');
set_it (oldst);
```

The first call uses the contents of the character variable b, the second call uses the character constant *, and the final call assumes the character constant ' '; it is equivalent to the call

```
set_it(oldst, ' ');
```

Optional arguments are useful when a default occurs frequently. For example, a function that fills up a string with the same character may be needed, where almost always the character required will be a space, but sometimes it may be another character. The code for the function declaration and definition is shown below:

```
void setchars(char*, char = ' ');
.
.
.

void setchars ( char* stringpoi, char val){
while (*stringpoi != '\0'){
   *stringpoi = val;
   stringpoi++;
   };
};
```

This could be called in a number of ways:

```
.
setchars(st1, '*');    /fill with asterisks
.
setchars(st2);         /fill with spaces
.
```

```
setchars(st3,'k');        /fill with the character k
```

An important point to make about functions with default arguments is that only the trailing arguments can be given defaults. So the declarations

```
void f1 (int = 10, int, char);
int f2 (char, char ='0', int);
void f3 (char = '+', char*, int = 9, int =12);
```

are all illegal.

A useful facility provided by C++ enables the programmer to use the same function name for different functions. This is useful when the same action needs to be carried out on parameters of a different type. For example, a programmer may require two initialize functions, one to initialize an int to zero and the other to initialize a string to contain a whole list of zeros. This name clash is communicated to the C++ compiler by preceding the declarations of the functions by the keyword overload.

```
overload initialize;
initialize(int*);
initialize(char*);
```

A final example of a function-like facility in C++ is the macro. This works in a similar way to a function, but the underlying mechanism whereby the effect is achieved is radically different. A macro is a definition which says to the C++ compiler: whenever you see this text sequence in the program, replace it with another text sequence. An example of a macro is shown below:

```
#define incri i++
```

This states that when the compiler processes the text incri it is replaced by i++. For example, the function

```
int count_lc(char* poi){
int i = 0;
while (*poi != '\0') {
   if ( *poi <= 'z' && *poi >= 'a')
      i++;
   poi++;
   };
return (i);
};
```

could be implemented as

```
#define incri   i++

   .

   .
int count_lc(char* poi){
int i = 0;
while (*poi != '\0') {
   if ( *poi <= 'z' && *poi >= 'a')
      incri;
   poi++;
```

```
    };
  return (i);
  };
```

This is a simple and not too useful use of a macro. Better uses of macros can be made in conjunction with arguments. This is shown below with the definition `arraddset`:

```
  #define arraddset(a,b,c) a[b++] = c
```

What this macros states is that the text `arraddset` has three parameters `a`, `b`, and `c`. Whenever the text `arraddset` is encountered by the C++ compiler followed by three arguments, it is replaced by the text `a[b++] = c`. So, for example, the text extracts

```
  arraddset(i,j,p);
  arraddset(arr1, inc, val);
  arraddset(arr2, nmcount, 78);
```

will be converted into

```
  i[j++] = p;
  arr1[inc++] = val;
  arr2[nmcount++] = 78;
```

Macros should be used with care: the C++ macro-processor is a very simple macro-processor which really only implements text substitution and does not know about the detailed syntax of C++. Macros have very limited use. The two main uses are in implementing short sections of program code where the time overhead of a function call is too expensive, and in the implementation of general-purpose data structures.

Another form of macro facility provided by C++ is the inline function. If a function is preceded by the keyword `inline`, then whenever the function is called in the main function, its call is replaced by the processing code of the function. So, for example, if the function `incr` was defined as

```
  inline int incr( int* i){
  ++(*i);
  };
```

then a call `incr(k)` would result in the substitution `++(*k)` at the point of call.

7.6 SUMMARY

This chapter has described facilities of C++ that are normally found in other programming languages—facilities such as assignment statements, control structures, and subroutines. Many of these facilities are part of the C programming language, which C++ is a superset of. The next chapter describes the very powerful programming facilities that distinguish C++ from other programming languages such as Pascal, PL/1, and FORTRAN.

7.7 FURTHER READING

This book only really contains an introduction to the C++ programming language. The two C++ books which are my particular favourites are Berry (1989) and Stroustrup (1986). The former is a fairly gentle introduction, while the latter is really an excellent reference book.

BIBLIOGRAPHY

Berry, J. T. (1989) *The Waite Group's C++ Programming*, Howard Sam's and Co., Indianapolis, Indiana.

Stroustrup, B. (1986) *The C++ Programming Language*, Addison-Wesley, Reading, Mass.

8

OBJECT-ORIENTED PROGRAMMING IN C++

AIMS

- To describe the main concepts of object-oriented programming.
- To describe how the concepts of object-oriented programming are implemented in C++.
- To outline the relationship between object-oriented programming and abstract data types.
- To describe two small examples which contain many of the features of C++ necessary for object-oriented programming.

8.1 INTRODUCTION

The previous chapter described the basic facilities of C++. It should have convinced you that C++ looks very much like any other high-level, procedural language. However, you may now be worrying about what makes C++ so special. The aim of this chapter is to answer that worry. It will describe those facilities in C++ that can be used for object-oriented programming, and how the abstract data type descriptions of Chapter 6 can be converted into programming code. However, before doing this, it is worth looking at some of the main concepts that are associated with object-oriented programming.

8.2 OBJECT-ORIENTED PROGRAMMING

The main concept in object-oriented programming is the object. Object-oriented programming languages contain sophisticated facilities for implementing the abstract data types that were discussed in Chapter 6: they implement the description of the implementation of an object, together with a definition of all the operations associated with an object. A key idea which all object-oriented languages implement is that of information hiding.

8.2.1 Information hiding

Information hiding is a term used to describe the fact that the detailed representation of the data structures implemented in a system are hidden from the programmer. Information hiding is a very powerful device for ensuring that change—during both maintenance and development—is accommodated efficiently. In order to see how information hiding works, and how it enables change to be a smooth process, examine Fig. 8.1. This shows a system that is poorly structured because, throughout the system, there are references to the underlying data structure.

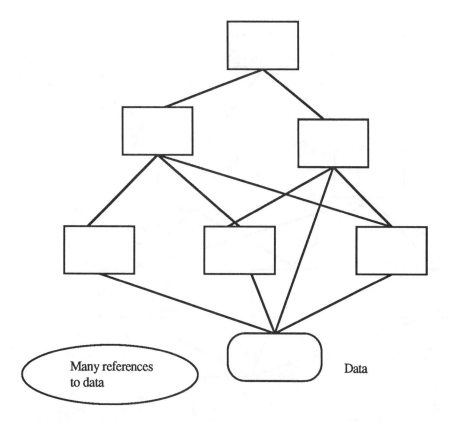

Figure 8.1 A poorly structured system.

For example, if the system was a communication system that manipulated message queues implemented as arrays, you would find that scattered throughout the system there would be array references.

If a maintenance change required the data structures in the system to be modified—in the communications system example, this might be a change from an array implementation to a linked list implementation—then the staff charged with this task would have a lot of work to do. They would have to examine every instance of the data structure, replace it with code that manipulated the new data structure, and check that the new code worked.

In order to see how information hiding helps, examine Fig. 8.2. Here the system has been structured in a particular way: the only access to the underlying data structures is by function call. Nowhere in the main program is there any reference to the underlying data structure. For example, in the communication system the code to add an item to a message queue would not be represented by

```
message_q[currpos] = mess;
currpos++;
```

which adds an item to a message queue at the position `currpos` and then increments `currpos`, but would be represented by a call to the function `addmess`

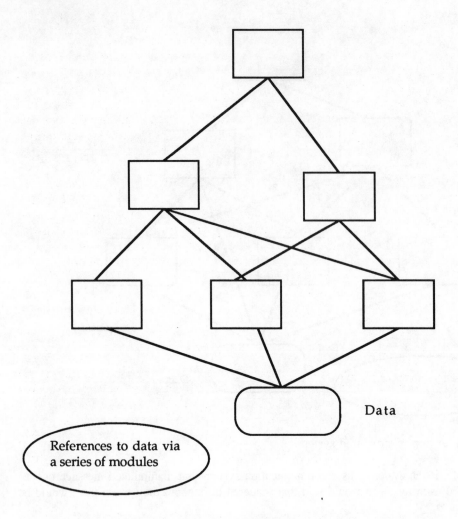

Figure 8.2 A system that exhibits information hiding.

```
addmess(message_q, mess);
```
where message_q would be of a type whose details would be hidden from the user.

   This means that when a maintenance or development change is raised—a change that almost invariably affects the stored data in an application—all that is required is for the developer to change the code in the functions that access the data structure that is changed. The functions act in many ways like a fire-wall. They provide facilities, but do not allow access to the underlying data.

   Information hiding can be employed in any programming language. However, with conventional programming languages there is no mechanism for enforcing the discipline of not referring directly to the underlying data structure. In object-oriented programming languages such a mechanism is available. Normally, when a programmer tries to access the underlying data structure the compiler flags this as an error. The facility in C++ that provides information hiding is known as the class, and is described in detail in Section 8.3.

Another feature associated with object-oriented programming languages is *polymorphism*. In order to explain the simple idea underlying such a terrifying word, consider the act of sorting a set of items. Sorting is a popular operation in all systems: integers are sorted, messages are sorted, strings are sorted, and so on. A wide variety of data types often need to be sorted. In a conventional programming language a sort function often has to be written anew for each data type that is required to be sorted, although a clever programmer will find the code of an already existing sort function, and edit in any changes required to convert it to a sort function for a data type for which no sort function is available.

Object-oriented programming languages allow a programmer to write one sort function and, with minimal change, use that sort function for any data type. This is one of the strengths of object-oriented programming. A developer who uses such a language can define general libraries of functions which carry out frequent operations such as sorting, and can then apply functions in such libraries to arbitrary data types. This is a feature of object-oriented programming languages that particularly suits them as a medium for reusable software.

Another feature of object-oriented programming languages that enables them to be an effective medium for software reuse is *inheritance*. This term is used to describe the fact that data types can be built up from other data types very easily and inherit many of the properties of the data types from which they are built. As an example of this consider retail systems.

A major entity in such systems is the invoice: a retailer issues an invoice when a product has been supplied to a customer; irrespective of the application, invoices contain common information: the name of the supplier, the name of the customer, the customer's address, the items supplied, the price of each item, and so on. Object-oriented programming languages allow you to define a general invoice data type that contains all these common details.

Now, in each retail application an invoice will differ in small ways from invoices used in other applications, e.g. the numbering system used for the invoice may be different, there may be special information on the invoice when the supplier is delivering dangerous chemicals, there may be a discount scheme, and so on. Object-oriented programming languages allow a developer to take a general data type and decorate it with specific properties which are only of interest to the application that the developer is computerizing.

Thus, the developer who uses object-oriented techniques and a programming language such as C++ is able to build up a library of data types which can then be brought into application programs, modified easily to take into account the local circumstances of the application, and then used. This facility of building up application-specific data types from more general data types is known as inheritance. In C++ the medium for inheritance is, again, the class.

8.3 IMPLEMENTING ABSTRACT DATA TYPES

In Chapter 6 abstract data types were described. The development of these abstract data types is analogous to conventional system design. A major aim of this chapter is to describe how such types can be implemented in an object-oriented programming language. However, before describing the details of implementation, it is worth examining the decisions that have to be made when an implementation is decided upon. A number of factors have to be taken into consideration when developing the program code for an abstract data type.

SAQ   Can you think of the factors that have to be taken into account when implementing abstract data types?

SOLUTION   There are three factors: speed, memory utilization, and programming complexity. ❑

In order to illustrate these factors it is worth looking at one particular implementation of an abstract data type. Assume that we are interested in implementing a set of names, say the names of account holders in a banking application. Also, assume the following operations have been identified by means of entity analysis: an operation to add an account holder to a set, an operation that deletes an account holder from a set, an operation that returns the number of items in a set, and an operation that checks if a particular item is in the set.

There are a number of possible implementations of the data structure used to represent the set. Let us concentrate on two: an unordered array of names and an ordered array of names. In order to examine the ramifications of this choice, consider each of the operations in turn.

The implementation of the insertion operation for an unordered array would be straightforward: all it would involve is keeping an integer variable which marked the end of the array. All that would then be required in the implementation would be for the item to be deposited at the end of the array, and the variable updated by incrementing it by 1. In an implementation using an ordered array what would be required would be to find the position that the item is to be placed in the array, and move all the items alphabetically later than the item one location further along the array. Hence, there is a need for more programming.

The operation to check that an item was in the unordered array requires a simple linear search starting at the first item. The search for an item in the ordered table would require a more complicated search in which the table was continually chopped in half, each time focusing in on the part of the array that contained the item. This search is very fast: since it splits the table into two approximately equal halves it has a speed proportional to $\log_2 n$, where n is the size of the array being searched, as compared to a speed proportional to n for the searching of the unordered array.

The operation for deleting an item in an unordered table requires that the operation for searching the array for a particular item was called first to find the position of the item in the array, if it existed. Then all the items in the array would be moved up one position in order to eliminate the item. The implementation of this operation for the ordered array would be similar: the operations for checking an item is in the array would be called, and then the items beyond the item to be deleted would be shifted up one position. The only difference in this case would be that checking the item is in the array is quicker.

Finally, the operation for finding the number of items in the array could be implemented simply, in both the ordered and unordered cases. A simple implementation would involve the maintenance of a variable which would be initialized to zero when the array was created, and incremented by 1 whenever an item was added to the array, and decremented by 1 when an item was removed from the array.

It is clear, then, from this example that there are a number of factors that have to be borne in mind when implementing an abstract data type: the amount of memory used, the response time of the operations, and the complexity of the programming involved. The text above described two implementations: an implementation where the amount of memory used for the data structure—the array—was the same, where the programming for the unordered array was relatively simple, and where the response time of some of the operations on the ordered array was very fast. In general, when you decide on an implementation there will be a trade-off between these factors. For example, in the set implementation example described later in this chapter, programming complexity is being traded-off against response time.

SAQ Normally an ordered array implementation would be chosen for a set. However, can you think of any circumstances when you would choose an unordered array implementation?

SOLUTION Yes, an unordered array implementation would be chosen when the maximum number of items in the set was relatively small, say less than 6. In this case the binary search operation on the ordered array would not be significantly faster than the simple linear search. ❑

It is these trade-offs that make the implementation of abstract data types a challenging process. The process of deciding on an implementation consists of looking at the operations that are necessary to support the operation and examining which of these operations are going to be called frequently. Once this has been done, an implementation is decided on. This implementation has to satisfy the memory requirements of the system, lead to a complexity that will not consume too much programmer resource, and optimize the execution speed of those operations that are carried out frequently.

SAQ After analysing an application that required an implementation of a set by means of an array data type it was found that retrieval was one of the most frequently executed operations. However, it was also found that only a comparatively few—about four—of the items in the array were retrieved frequently, out of an average number of items in the set of 30. Can you think of a possible implementation.

SOLUTION Yes, a good implementation would be to keep the items that are frequently accessed in a small array which could be searched linearly. The rest of the items could be kept in a larger array which could be searched using a binary search. When an item was to be retrieved the small array would be searched first. ❑

8.4 C++ AND OBJECT-ORIENTED PROGRAMMING

The aim of this chapter is to describe the main facility for object-oriented programming in C++: the class. In order to describe what classes are it is worth looking at an example of a particular class in action. Assume that we are developing a system to monitor and control the operation of a number of reactors in a chemical plant. Inside this system there is the need to keep status information. This status information includes the number of reactors that are currently functioning; the state of each reactor—whether it is functioning normally or whether it is switched off; and the current temperature and pressure of each reactor. Assume, also, that memory is short and this information has to be packed into fields in four integer locations. These locations I will refer to as the system status variable.

A number of operations on this variable will be required: an operation to notify the system that a particular reactor has been switched off, an operation to notify the system that a particular reactor is functioning normally, an operation that retrieves the temperature of a particular reactor, an operation to change the temperature of a particular reactor, an operation to read the pressure of a particular reactor, and an operation to change the pressure of a particular reactor.

The facility whereby these operations are associated with the memory locations that hold this information is known as the class. The class that describes the chemical reactor data and the operations that operate on this data are shown below:

```
class system_status{
   int* sys_poi;
public:
   void switch_on(char*);
   void switch_off(char*);
   void set_temp(char*, int);
   int read_temp(char*);
   void set_pressure(char*, int);
   int read_pressure(char*);
};
```

This is a typical example of a declaration of a class. It first contains the name of the class (system_status) followed by a list of items that the programmers who use the class are not allowed to use; this is known as the private part of the class. In the example above there is only one item that programmers are not allowed access to, and that is the pointer variable sys_poi, which points at the system status information.

Following the keyword public is a list of items that programmers are allowed access to. These can be variables, constants, or functions. Normally they will be functions as in the example above. There are six functions that programmers are allowed to use. The first two are void functions, switch_on and switch_off, which take the name of a reactor, and inform the system that the reactor is functioning normally or that it has shut down. The only argument to each of these functions is a pointer to the string that is the reactor name.

The next two functions are concerned with the temperatures of reactors. The first, set_temp, sets the temperature of a particular reactor to a value, and the second, read_temp, obtains the current temperature from a reactor. set_temp has two arguments, the first is a string that represents the name of a reactor, the second is the temperature to which the temperature is to be set. read_temp has one argument—the name of the reactor whose temperature is to be sensed—and returns one result: the current temperature of the reactor. The final two functions represent the operations of setting a pressure and reading a pressure, and are similar in their declarations to the functions that manipulate temperatures.

The important point to notice about a class is that it separates the items associated with a particular object into those that can be accessed by the programmer, and those that cannot be accessed; the keyword public indicates the former. This is a simple implementation of the information hiding principle that was discussed earlier in this chapter: the internal representation of the data in an application is shielded away from the programmer.

If, for example, a programmer had attempted to use the variable sys_poi in a program, the C++ compiler would have flagged it as an error. This implementation means that if circumstances change, say more reactors were commissioned, and a change in the underlying data was required, then the only items that would need to be changed would be the six functions referred to in the class, with the major bulk of the code remaining unchanged.

The discussion of classes has, so far, omitted to describe how the functions are defined. In fact, they are defined in the same way as any other function. The program listing shown below describes this:

```
/includes


class system_status{                       /declaration of class
   int* sys_poi;
public:
   void switch_on(char*);
   void switch_off(char*);
   void set_temp(char*, int);
   int read_temp(char*);
   void set_pressure(char*, int);
   int read_pressure(char*);
};
/ any other declarations of classes.




///////////////////////////////////
/ Class system status definitions  /
///////////////////////////////////

void system_status::switch_on( char* reac_name){
   .
   .
   }

void system_status::switch_off( char* reac_name){
   .
   .
   }

void system_status::set_temp( char* reac_name, int temp){
   .
   .
   }

int system_status::read_temp( char* reac_name){
```

```
   .
   .
   }

void system_status::set_pressure( char* reac_name, int temp){
   .
   .
   }

int system_status::read_pressure( char* reac_name){
   .
   .
   }

/ declarations of globals
/ main program using instances of the classes declared
```

This shows the structure of a program that uses classes, but does not show the actual processing code associated with the public functions. Notice one important point about the declaration of functions associated with a particular class: their declaration is preceded by the name of the class followed by two colons.

Given that we now know how classes are declared, the next question concerns how they are used. It is important to point out that the declaration of a class does not create any objects of that class. All it does is to specify the structure of the objects that are to be manipulated by a program, and the public and private components of the object, including the operations associated with the object. In order to introduce an instance of a class, all that is required is the analogue of the variable declaration. For example, to reserve space for an instance of the class system_status all that is required is the declaration

```
system_status sys_word;
```

which declares sys_word to be an instance of the class system_status. The programmer who has declared this instance can then use the functions associated with it, as shown in the following examples:

```
curr_temp = sys_word.read_temp(next_reactor);
curr_press = sys_word.read_pressure(main_reactor);
sys_word.switch_on(main_reactor);
sys_word.switch_off(reactor_3);
curr_press = sys_word.read_pressure(curr_reactor);
```

where all the reactors are of of type char*. It is important to point out again that if the programmer had written a statement such as

```
new_poi = sys_word.sys_poi;
```

it would have been flagged as an error by the compiler.

SAQ Write down a suitable class which describes the implementation of a set as an unordered array of integers. Four operations are required: one to add an item to the set, one to remove an item from a set, one to check that a particular item is contained in a set, and one to return the number of items in the set. Just write down the class declaration, do not bother with the definition of the functions which implement the operations.

SOLUTION The class declaration is shown below:

```
class set_int{                          /declaration of class
    int* set_arr;
    int no_in_set;
public:
    int check_in_set(int);
    void add_to_set(int);
    void remove_from_set(int);
    int no_in_set();
};
```

It shows that the set is implemented by an integer pointer `set_arr` which points to a series of locations holding integers, and an integer `no_in_set` which contains the number of items currently in the set. Both these items are private and hence cannot be used by a programmer. The four public functions are `check_in_set`, which takes one argument that is an integer and returns an integer which is 1 if the argument is in the set and 0 otherwise; `add_to_set`, which adds its argument to the set; `remove_from_set`, which removes its argument from the set; and `no_in_set`, which has no parameters and returns the current number of members in the set. ❑

A useful facility in C++ is the ability to include, in a class definition, functions that are invoked when a new instance of an object defined by a class is created, and a function that destroys the instance of the class when it is no longer needed. The former function is known as a *constructor*. It is included in the class declaration and signalled as a constructor by using the same name as the class. So, for example, a class constructor for the set implementation described in the previous SAQ would be defined as

```
class set_int{                          /declaration of class
    int* set_arr;
    int no_in_set;
public:
    set_int();
    int check_in_set(int);
    void add_to_set(int);
    void remove_from_set(int);
    int no_in_set();
};
```

Here `set_int` takes no parameters. The action that would be carried out when `set_int` is called is to initialize `no_in_set` to zero, and to make space for an array of integers. If 50 integers are to be stored in the array, then the body of the function `set_int` would look like

```
set_int::set_int (){
set_arr = new int[50];
no_in_set = 0;
}
```

This function is called automatically every time that an `set_int` is created, e.g. when a `set_int` is declared or when a new `set_int` is created by means of a call on `new`.

A constructor function can also have arguments. For example, the above definition of a set is rather restrictive in that it only allows sets of up to 50 integers, and we may require sets that contain many more numbers or many fewer members; what is needed is a way of changing the class declaration above to reflect this. The way to do this is to declare another private component of `set_int` which is an integer variable `max_no` that holds the maximum number of items in a set. The definition of the constructor function would also need to be changed in order to allow the size of the array to be specified when it is created. This would result in the declaration

```
class set_int{                          /declaration of class
   int* set_arr;
   int no_in_set;
   int max_no;
public:
   set_int(int);
   int check_in_set(int);
   void add_to_set(int);
   void remove_from_set(int);
   int no_in_set();
};
```

Notice the argument to the constructor `set_int`, which represents the value required for the maximum number of items in the set. The definition of the constructor `set_int` will now need to be changed to reflect this more flexible class:

```
set_int::set_int (int maxsize){
set_arr = new int[max_no = maxsize];
no_in_set = 0;
}
```

Sometimes the code associated with a public function in a class is so short that it can be written close to the declaration of the function. C++ allows the programmer to write the definition of a function next to its declaration. For example, the definition of the `set_int` class could have been written as

```
class set_int{                          /declaration of class
   int* set_arr;
   int no_in_set;
   int max_no;
public:
   set_int(int maxsize)   {
           set_arr = new int[max_no = maxsize];
           no_in_set = 0;}

   int check_in_set(int);
```

```
   void add_to_set(int);
   void remove_from_set(int);
   int no_in_set();
};
```

where the definition of the constructor function follows its declaration. The declarations of `check_in_set`, `add_to_set`, `remove_from_set`, and `no_in_set` would be declared separately further into the program. This course is not to be recommended for anything but the simplest functions whose actions can be defined in one or two lines. It tends to make the class definitions rather unreadable.

As well as containing facilities for constructing instances of a class, C++ also has facilities for destroying an instance of a class. These are functions called *destructors*. They are called when a class object goes out of scope, or when the delete function is called. They are written by preceding the class name with the character ~. An example of a class that has both constructor and destructor functions is shown below:

```
class arrint{
   int size, current;
   int* arr;
public:
   arrint(int ln){arr = new int[size=ln]; current = 0;}
   ~arrint() {delete arr;}
   void searr(int);
   void cleararr();
};
```

Here a class `arrint` is defined as two integer variables, `size` and `current`, together with an integer pointer, `arr`. The class has four public functions, one of which is a constructor, and another a destructor. The constructor reserves space for an integer array of size `ln`, sets `arr` to point at the first element of the array, sets `size` equal to `ln`, and initializes `current` to become zero. The destructor `~arrint` deletes the space occupied by the array pointed at by `arr`. The definitions for `searr` and `cleararr` would be found in a later part of the text of the `main` function, after the processing statements of this function.

Often in a class you will find that many of the functions provided as public are very small—often just one or two lines of program code. It is worth declaring them as inline functions. When a function is declared as inline, any call on that function will be converted into the code of the function very much like the macro facility provided by the define facility described in the previous section. For example, a common form of processing in the access to classes based on arrays and found as a single statement in functions associated with arrays is the statement ++i or i++. A function that just carries out this incrementing can be easily implemented as an inline function

```
void inline incr(){
+ii;
}
```

8.5 AN EXAMPLE OF A CLASS

We have now learnt enough about classes to be able to implement some useful examples. The aim of this section is to describe the implementation of two simple classes: that of a set of integers and that of a queue of integers.

Let us first concentrate on developing a simple instance of a set containing integers with a finite limit to the number of integers that can be stored, in this case 10. I shall assume that the number of integers is so small that an implementation using an array and linear search would provide an adequate response time. I shall also assume that the following operations are required: `insert_set`, which inserts a particular member into a set; `del_set`, which deletes a particular member from a set; `empty`, which returns true if a set is empty; `check_in`, which checks if a particular item is in a set; and `number_in`, which returns the number of items in a set.

The declaration of the class is shown below. It is worth stressing again the point that this declaration does not create any objects, it just specifies a particular template which describes all members of a class.

```
class set {
   int no_in_set;
   int poiset[10];
public:
   inline set(){ no_in_set = 0;};
   void insert_set(int);
   void del_set(int);
   inline int empty() { return(no_in_set = 0);};
   inline int number_in() { return no_in_set;};
   int check_in(int);
};
```

The private part of the class consists of two variables: `no_in_set`, which contains the number of items currently stored in a set; and `poiset`, which is an array variable that points at the first location of the array that is used to implement the set. Notice that three of the functions, including the constructor and destructor functions, have been defined as inline. They contain only one line of program code and hence are perfect candidates for inline functions. The remaining functions can be defined relatively easily. You may be worried by the fact that the array has one more member than required, this extra location is used in the program code for `check_in`, `insert_set`, and `delete_set` and saves a little program complexity. The function `del_set` is shown below:

```
void set::del_set(int member){
int offset = 0;
poiset[no_in_set] = member;
while (poiset[offset] != member)
   offset++;
if (offset == no_in_set)
   printf( "delete error\n");
else
   while (offset < no_in_set-1){
```

```
      poiset[offset] = poiset[offset+1];
      offset++;
   };
   no_in_set--;
  }
 }
```

The function first deposits member—the integer to be inserted in the no_in_set+1th location of the array. This item is known as a *sentinel*. It then scans the array an item at a time for member. If the member that it has encountered is the sentinel, then an error has occurred. However, if the sentinel was not encountered, then the item to be deleted is contained in the array at the position marked by offset. The final part of the function moves all the elements of the array one location forward, starting at the position where member was found. Finally, the number of elements in the set is decremented by 1. The function insert is shown below. It first checks that the array is not full.

```
void set::insert_set(int mem){
int offset = 0;
if (no_in_set == 10)
   printf("error set is full\n");
else {
   poiset[no_in_set] = mem;
   while (poiset[offset] != mem)
     offset++;
   if offset < no_in_set
     printf("error in insert -- duplicate insertion\n");
   else
     no_in_set++;
  }
 }
```

The function then checks whether the element mem is in the array by depositing the sentinel and then examining each element of the array for one containing mem. If the element is at the end of the array, then it is the sentinel and it does not occur in the array—in which case a suitable error message is displayed. Finally, if the element mem is not in the array, then it is added to the array at the end and the number of elements in the array incremented by 1.

SAQ Write down the definition of the function check_in which returns true if its argument is in the set defined by set. Use a sentinel.

SOLUTION The function definition is shown below:

```
     int set::check_in(int mem){
     int offset = 0;
     poiset[no_in_set] = mem;
     while (poiset[offset] != mem)
       offset++;
     return(offset != no_in_set);
     }
```

The sentinel is first placed at the end of the array. The while loop then continually scans the array looking for the argument mem and terminates when it is encountered. Finally, the function returns `offset != no_in_set`, i.e. it returns true if the item was encountered in the array and not at the sentinel position. □

In order to gain further practice in the definition of classes and the declaration of class components, let us look at the implementation of a queue. Queues are used in many computer applications, e.g. in operating systems, telecommunication systems, and in commercial data processing systems.

Let us assume that we wish to implement a queue of integers that has a maximum number of items associated with it, in an array. Also, assume that the implementation of queues will be via a pointer that marks the beginning of the queue and variables that hold information about the queue. The queue is capable of wrapping around when an item is added to the end of the array used to hold queue items.

Assume that a number of operations are required, namely to add an item from the queue, to delete an item from the queue, and to check whether a queue is empty. The class definition is shown below:

```
class queue {
   int   queue_head, queue_tail, no_in_queue, q_size;
   int* quearr;
   void nextitem (int&);
public:
   queue(int);
   inline ~queue() {delete quearr;};
   inline int q_empty () {return(no_in_queue =0);}
   void insert_q(int);
   int remove_q ();
}
```

The four private parts of the class are `no_in_queue`, which holds the total number of items currently in the queue; `queue_head`, which contains an integer that represents the position of the head of the queue and which will be initialized to zero; `queue_tail`, which represents the position of the next item which is available for filling in the queue; `q_size`, which is the maximum number of items that can be inserted into a queue; `queuearr`, which holds the address of the first item in the array used to implement the queue; and a void function `nextitem`.

This function takes an array index i and sets i equal to its next value. Normally this value will be i+1; however, since items in the queue will be wrapped around, it will set i to zero when i currently points at the last item in the array. The code for this function is shown below:

```
int nextitem (int poi){
if (poi ==q_size -1)
   poi=0;
else
   poi++;
}
```

The code for the constructor function is shown below:

```
queue::queue(int size) {
queue_head = 0; no_in_queue = 0;
quearr = new int[q_size=size];
queue_tail = 0;
}
```

All this does is to allocate enough space for the array that holds the queue items; initializes queue_head and queue_tail; and sets the number of items in the queue to zero. All that is now required is to define the program code for the functions insert_q and remove_q. The first function has to check that the queue is full, if it is not, then the item to be inserted is placed at the location designated by tail.

```
void queue::insert_q(int mem){
if (no_in_queue = q_size)
   printf("error in insert --- queue is full\n");
else{
   *(queuearr+queue_tail) = mem;
   tail++
   nextitem(queue_tail);
   no_in_queue++;
   }
}
```

Notice that nextitem is used to get the next value of the tail variable.

SAQ Write down the definition of the function remove_q.

SOLUTION The function definition is shown below:

```
int queue::remove_q(){
int headofq
if (no_in_queue = 0)
   printf("error in remove --- queue is empty\n");
else{
   headofq= queue_head;
   nextitem(queue_head);
   no_in_queue--;
   return (*(queuearr+headofq));
   }
}
```

remove_q first checks to see if the queue is empty; if there is an item on the queue, then the variable headofq is set to the head of the queue, head is moved to point at the next item in the queue, and the number of items in the queue is decremented. Finally, the value of the head of the queue is returned. ❑

It is worth pointing out two things at this stage. First, errors are handled very simply in the class functions that have been described: all that happens is that when an error is discovered, such as an insertion occurring into a full queue, an error message is displayed.

The second thing to point out is that the functions that have been developed as the public part of a class have been limited, I have assumed that the application in which the class was required only required these functions—and no others. In general, a class written for a real application would require more public functions than have been declared above.

8.6 INHERITANCE

Inheritance is one of the most powerful facilities in an object-oriented programming language. It allows the developer to build up a library of reusable objects and operations. In order to explain what exactly inheritance is all about, consider an example: that of a personnel system which administers staff for a company. Such systems keep track of information such as salary, job grade, and the current department of the staff member whose record is stored.

However, some members of staff may require further information on their records, e.g. the sales staff may have on record details of the commission that has been received over the last year. Many applications are similar to the personnel example: they contain data that all the instances of a particular entity share but certain categories of entity differ slightly in that extra information is required.

C++ contains facilities for defining objects and operations and then creating new objects and operations derived from those already in existence. As an example of this concept, consider an implementation of a set as an ordered array. Assume that the class for this entity is

```
class set{
    int* setrep;
    int  no_in_set, size_of_set;
public:
    set (int size)
            {setrep = new int[size]; size_of_set = size;}
    ~set(){delete setrep;}
    int total_in_set() {return no_in_set;}
    void add_to_set(int );
    void remove_from_set(int );
    int check_in_set(int);
};
```

It contains four public functions which return the total number of items in a set, add an item to a set, delete an item from a set, and check whether a specific item is in a set using a binary search.

Now this class is quite general: it does not take into account any specific circumstances in the applications in which it is used. Let us look at one particular circumstance, in which the average size of the set to be searched is around 1000 items but that three of the items, which will always be in the set, are checked for 95 per cent of the time. It would seem rather wasteful to use such an implementation of a set considering that we know that three of the items are going to be examined frequently.

Also, if we had an implementation based on a linear search this method would be rather wasteful, since 5 per cent of the searches would involve a lengthy item-by-item search of the array used to implement the set. In order to cope with this, C++ allows us to define a new class which takes many of the properties of the class set above. This is written as

```
class newset:set{
int stata,statb,statc;
public:
    newset (int i,int j,int k, int size):(size){stata =
            i;statb=j;statc=k;}
    int total_in_set();
    int check_in_set(int);
    set::add_to_set;
    set::remove_from_set;
};
```

What this declaration does is to define a new class called newset. This new set is based on the class set. It will contain all the private members of set together with the three new private members, stata, statb, and statc. These are the integers that will always be in the array used to implement the new set and are frequently accessed. The constructor function for newset takes the three integers and places them into stata, statb, and statc. Normally when a new class is constructed by augmenting an old class, the public members of the old class become private to the new class. However, in the example described here two of them, add_to_set and remove_from_set, need to be public since they will be used by the software that employs this class. In order to make them public all that is required is for them to be listed in the public part of this new class with their names preceded by the class name and two colons.

In the constructor for newset the parameter size appears. This is used to communicate to the set class the size of the array to be used when the constructor for this class is called. Details of this mechanism follow later. Hence to declare an object a of type newset which has three constant members 1,4,6 and a size of array 50 all that is needed is

```
newset (1,4,6,50);
```

You can see in the definition of newset that this means that the functions add_to_set and remove_from_set become public in newset. A new function which checks that an element is in the set is introduced in this class definition. The definition of this function is shown below:

```
newset::check_in_set(int member){
if(member == stata||member ==statb|| member==statc)
return 1;
else
return set::check_in_set(member);
}
```

Here the possible member of the set is checked against the three static members of the set and then check_in_set, which forms part of the class set, is used to ensure member is in the ordered set. Notice that the call on check_in_set is preceded by the name of its class set and two colons, this is to distinguish it from the function check_in_set which we are defining. If this was not used, then a call on `check_in_set` would result in an infinite recursion occurring.

The declaration of the function that returns the number of items in the set is shown below:

```
newset::total_in_set(){
return(set::total_in_set()+3);
}
```

Here the function uses the function `total_in_set` associated with the class `set`. It adds 3 to the value returned by this function to cater for the three items that will always be in the new set. A class based on an existing class is known as a *base class*; a class formed from a base class is known as a *derived class*. Thus, in the simple example, above `set` is the base class and `newset` is the derived class.

In general, if `base` is the base class and `derived` is the derived class, the definition of a derived class has the form

```
class derived: base{
   private elements
public:
   public elements
}
```

This states that a new class `derived` is formed from `base`, which has a series of private components and public components. The private components of the base class cannot be used in the derived class, furthermore in this declaration the public components of the base class cannot be provided to any user of the derived class, but can be used inside the derived class. If the public elements of a base class are required to be provided to a user of the derived class, then there are two options. The first is to write the keyword `public` in front of the base class name, thus

```
class derived: public base{
   private elements
public:
   public elements
}
```

This results in all the public components of the base class being made available. However, in some circumstances only a subset of the public components of a base class are required to be made available. This occurs in the set example above. In this case all that is required is that the items in the public part of the base class are declared in the public part of the derived class. These items are distinguished by writing the base class name followed by two colons and the name of the public item of the base class.

A problem with derived classes is connected with constructors and destructors. What if a base class has a constructor, how are its initial values communicated to it when the constructor of the derived class is called? Also, in what order are the destructors called: is the base class destructor called before the derived class destructor?

The rule with destructors is very simple: the derived class destructor is called before the base class destructor. The problem with constructors is more complicated. Often, the constructor for the base class will require initial values and a mechanism is required whereby these values are communicated to the base class from the constructor of the inherited class. C++ provides a facility where this can be achieved. The header line of the constructor function of a derived class contains the values needed to initialize an instance of the base class. For example, the function header shown below describes a constructor for the derived class `triple`, this derived class is based on the base class `pair` which requires two integer values for its constructor.

```
triple(int a,b,c):(a,b)
```

Here the triple class constructor requires three integers, `a`, `b`, and `c`, in order to initialize an instance of the class. The arguments for the constructor of the base class `pair` are written after the declaration of these arguments. In the definition of `pair` is a function

```
pair(int x, y);
```

which will be invoked when the triple constructor is called and will pass to it the first two arguments of its call. So, for example, if a declaration of

```
triple a(1,45,89);
```

occurs in a program, this will result in the constructor of `pair` being called with arguments 1 and 45. This use of arguments occurs in the set example previously described.

8.7 SUMMARY

This chapter has described a major facility of C++ known as a class. This enables the structure of objects to be specified, and implements the information hiding idea that was described early in this book. The chapter also described how classes can be derived from other classes, enabling a high degree of reusability to take place. This chapter has been an introduction to classes, the following chapter shows them in action and describes a number of further facilities that are used with classes.

9

IMPLEMENTING OBJECTS

AIMS

- To describe how operators are implemented in C++.
- To describe the concept of virtual functions.
- To reinforce the teaching of derived classes in Chapter 8.
- To show how polymorphism can be implemented in C++.
- To describe how unit testing and class integration testing can be carried out.

9.1 INTRODUCTION

The previous chapter has described how classes are implemented. In reading that chapter you may have felt some frustration: although the detailed syntax and semantics of classes had been described, there were no solid examples of the concept in action. This chapter remedies this. Two case studies are presented, one of which increasingly becomes more complex. The case studies involve classes but, more importantly, also introduce a number of new concepts that increase the power of the class concept.

The first case study introduces the idea of an operator, in the context of implementing a class which describes complex numbers. The second case study introduces the idea of polymorphism: a concept that enables a class to be defined for a particular type and then reused for different types.

9.2 COMPLEX NUMBERS

C++ does not contain a facility for complex numbers. Ideally, we would like to manipulate complex numbers in as natural a way as possible. The ultimate aim would be to write C++ programs such as

```
complex a(2+3i), b(8+9i), c;
c=a+b;
cout<< c;
```

A number of facilities within C++ allow us to come close to this ideal, although not quite reaching it. It is worth pointing out that complex numbers can be implemented almost directly using the facilities of C++ that have already been described. For example, a class of pairs could be defined, and a number of public functions provided with this class which carry out complex number operations such as addition and subtraction. For example,

```
class complex {
   double realpart, imagpart;
public:
   add(complex, complex, complex&);
   subtract(complex, complex, complex&);
   .
   .
   .
};
```

This class could be used in a program in statements such as

```
complex a,b,c,d;
add(b,c,a);
subtract(b,c,a);
```

Unfortunately, more complex arithmetic operations such as a+b−c+d would require continual calls on the public functions add and subtract, and would lead to unreadable program code. What is required is a facility of declaring operators such as +, −, and * which directly operate on complex numbers.

C++ offers facilities for defining operators in the same way that functions are defined. An example is shown below for the class complex which implements complex numbers:

```
class complex{
    double real, imaginary;
public:
   complex(int real =0, int imaginary = 0 );
   complex(char* );
   complex operator+(complex&);
   complex operator-(complex&);
   void display_complex();
};
```

The class contains two private floating-point numbers, real and imaginary, which represent the real and imaginary parts of a complex number. There are two constructor functions. The first constructor takes two integer arguments and forms the complex number from these arguments; if no arguments are specified, then the complex number is initialized to zero. The second constructor function takes a character string which represents the complex number, and sets the real and imaginary parts of the class equal to this number. This constructor allows the programmer to write declarations such as

```
complex y("3+12.9i")
```

which declares the complex number y equal to 3 + 12i. The next two functions implement the addition and subtraction operators. The syntax of these operator definitions is similar to that of function definitions. All that is required is the replacement of the function name by the keyword operator followed by the operator symbol(s). Functions that declare the following operators are allowed in C++:

+	−	*	/	%	^	&	~	!
=	<	>	+=	−=	*=	/=	%=	^=
&=	|	|=	<<	>>	>>=	<<=	==	!=

```
<=      >=      &&      ||      ++      --      []      ()      new
delete
```

In the example of the `complex` class the operators that are defined are + and −. It is important to point out that when operators are defined, the original use of the operators is not lost. For example, the fact that the complex class has defined + to operate on complex numbers does not mean that this operator cannot be used to add integers, doubles, and other numbers together—the compiler for C++ is clever enough to discover which meaning of an operator is required when it encounters the operator in a program. The facility whereby operators can be redefined is known as *overloading*.

Let us return to the class declaration of `complex`. The declaration of + and − uses only one parameter. When operators are declared in this way it is assumed that the other argument to the operator will be the private values maintained by the class, and we will see this in action when the operators are declared.

The final public component of the complex class is a function that displays a complex number.

The definition of the first constructor function is shown below:

```
complex::complex( int r, int i){
real = r;
imaginary = i;
}
```

The definition of the + operator is shown below:

```
complex complex::operator+(complex& cnum){
complex rtemp;
rtemp.real = real +cnum.real;
rtemp.imaginary = imaginary + cnum.imaginary;
return rtemp;
}
```

An instance of the complex class known as `rtemp` is created. Its real part is then assigned the sum of the real part of the class and the real part of the single argument to the operator. Its imaginary part is then assigned the sum of the imaginary part of the class and the imaginary part of the single argument to the operator. It is important to point out that the declaration does not require a second argument to represent an operand of the + operator: it assumes that one of the operands is provided by the class in which it is declared.

SAQ Write down the definition of the − operator.

SOLUTION The definition is shown below:

```
complex complex::operator-(complex& cnum){
complex rtemp;
rtemp.real = real - cnum.real;
rtemp.imaginary = imaginary -cnum.imaginary;
return rtemp; }
```

This is very similar to the definition of the + operator. ❑

The final definition is of the function `display_complex`.

```
void complex::display_complex(){
if( imaginary >0)
   printf( "%f+%fi",real, imaginary);
else if(imaginary == 0)
   printf("%f",real);
else if (imaginary <0)
   printf("%f-%fi",real, -imaginary);
  }
```

This function uses the library function `printf` to carry out the printing.

9.3 THE POLYMORPHIC SET

The previous chapter discussed the implementation of a class that represented the set abstract data type where the elements of the set were integers. The definition of the class that represents a set of integers is shown below:

```
class set {
   int no_in_set;
   int poiset[10];
public:
   inline set(){no_in_set=0;};
   void insert_set(int);
   void del_set(int);
   inline int empty() { return(no_in_set = 0);};
   inline int number_in() { return no_in_set;};
   int check_in(int);
}

void set::del_set(int member){
int offset = 0;
poiset[no_in_set] = member;
while (poiset[offset] != member)
   offset++;
   if (offset == no_in_set)
     printf( "delete error\n");
   else
     while (offset < no_in_set-1){
       poiset[offset] = poiset[offset+1];
       offset++;
     }
     no_in_set--;
   }
};
```

```
void set::insert(int mem){
int offset = 0;
if (no_in_set == 10)
  printf("error set is full\n");
else {
  poiset[no_in_set] = mem;
  while (poiset[offset] != mem)
    offset++;
  if offset < no_in_set
    printf("error in insert -- duplicate insertion\n");
  else
    no_in_set++;
  }
};

int set::check_in(int mem){
int offset = 0;
poiset[no_in_set] = mem;
while (poiset[offset] != mem)
  offset++;
return(offset != no_in_set);
};
```

This definition of the class, together with the implementation of the public functions, could be made much more general. Ideally, we need the class to be capable of defining a set of objects of any type: integers, reals, characters, character strings, or a user-defined type. This section describes how this can be achieved.

The ability to declare data types that can be parameterized over other data types is known as *polymorphism*. In order to develop a polymorphic set, a new type definition is required, as shown below:

```
typedef void* entity;
```

This defines a type `entity` to be a pointer to `void`. Normally, you have met `void` as a keyword which indicates that a function returns no value. However, you have not met `void*` before: a pointer to nothing! Happily this type has the property that a pointer to any type can be assigned to it—a property that makes it ideal for implementing polymorphic data types. In order to make the `set` class polymorphic, the occurrences of `int` need to be changed to occurrences of `entity`.

Thus, the class definition needs to be changed to

```
class set {
  int no_in_set;
  entity item[10];
  char* key[10];
public:
  inline set(){no_in_set=0;}
  void insert_set(entity,char*);
  void del_set(char*);
```

```
inline int empty() { return(no_in_set = 0);}
inline int number_in() { return no_in_set;}
int check_in(char*);
}
```

There are a number of changes in the class definition that need explaining. The major change arises from the fact that the set can now handle a wide variety of data types. The first part of each object in the data type will be a string key which serves to identify the object, the rest of the object can be anything, remember that it is set to a pointer to void at the moment. Since items in the set will be identified by a string key, the parameter lists of `insert_set`, `del_set`, and `check_in` have been changed to cope with this fact. Also the objects stored in the set will be stored in two arrays: `key`, which contains the key value; and `item`, which contains the remainder of the object. Thus, the key part of object `i` can be found in `key[i]` and the remainder of the object can be found in `item[i]`.

The definition of the functions now needs to be changed to cater for this new generality:

```
void set::del_set(char* keyval){
int offset = 0;
key[no_in_set] = keyval;
while (strcmp(key[offset],keyval) != 0)
  offset++;
  if (offset == no_in_set)
    printf( "delete error\n");
  else{while (offset < no_in_set-1){
      key[offset] = key[offset+1];
      item[offset] = item[offset+1];
      offset++;
    }
    no_in_set--;
  }
};


void set::insert_set(entity mem, char* keyval){
int offset = 0;
if (no_in_set == 10)
  printf("error set is full\n");
else {
  key[no_in_set] = keyval; item[no_in_set] = mem;
  while (strcmp(key[offset],keyval) !=0)
    offset++;
  if (offset < no_in_set) then
    printf("error in insert -- duplicate insertion\n");
  else
    no_in_set++;
  }
}
```

```
int set::check_in(char* keyval){
int offset = 0;
poiset[no_in_set] = keyval;
while (strcmp(key[offset],keyval)!=0)
  offset++;
return(offset != no_in_set);
}
```

The function `strcmp` is contained in the C library and compares two strings for equality: if they are equal, then it returns zero. The class can now be used with a number of data types. For example, to implement a class that represents a set of employee records containing a name and an address and uniquely identified by their name, all that is required is

```
class empset: set{
public:
void insert_set (char* n,char* a) { set::insert_set(n,a);};
void delete_set (char* n) {set::del_set(n);};
int check_in(char* a) {return(set::check_in(a)};
empset()   { };
}
```

The functions `insert_set`, `delete_set`, and `check_in` are defined in terms of the functions `set::insert`, `set::delete`, and `set::checkin`. Since objects of type `*void` can be assigned to a pointer of any type, the latter functions work correctly.

If a programmer wishes to use the function `insert_set` from the class `empset` in order to insert an employee and the employee's address, then all that is required is

```
s.insert_set(addressp,namep);
```

where `namep` is a pointer to a string containing the name of the employee and `addressp` is a pointer to a string containing the address. This of course assumes that the name is a key. It is important to point out that any class derived from the base class `set` provides functions that take parameters that are pointers to objects of the type contained in the sets.

An important concept which is used frequently with inheritance is that of a virtual function. Virtual functions are a vitally important concept in C++: they allow a uniform approach to the data that is manipulated in an application.

For example, consider a commercial data processing system that processes a number of classes: `manager`, `managing_director`, `supervisor`, and `worker`, which are all derived classes based on the class `worker`. Let us assume that each of these classes contains different information, but much of the information is common and can be based on a base type `worker`. For example, the manager may inherit the properties and data of worker, but also have details about his or her current company car, the worker type may have information about the department he or she works in, and so on. Let us assume that the base class is

```
class worker{
private:
  type1 first_data;
  type2 second_data;
```

```
       .
       .
public:
   virtual void print_work();
       .
       .

       .
```

Let us also assume that there is a need for details for each employee to be printed out, e.g. in response to a query from the personnel department, this is carried out using the function `print_work`. The fact that this function is virtual is indicated by the `virtual` keyword. Now if there was a class `manager`, this might inherit many of the properties of the base class via

```
class manager: worker{
private:
   newtype1 new_first_data;
   newtype2 new_second_data;
       .
       .
       .
public:
       .
       .

       .
   void print_work();
```

However, there would be a print function associated with this class which would overwrite the original virtual function and carry out the printing associated with the manager. This would be defined in the normal way that a member of the `manager` class would be defined:

```
void manager:: print_work(){
       .
       .

   };
```

Hence, in the program that manipulates different categories of employees there might appear the statements

```
mandir1.print_work();
markman.print_work();
emp[num].print_work();
```

where `print_work` is the function that carries out the display of the object and where each object would have a different type. The use of virtual functions leads to the implementation of heterogeneous data types where the components of the data type would be of a variety of data types, e.g. it allows the definition of a set of objects of differing types.

Virtual functions are also important in error handling where a class would include as a component a virtual error function which could be capable of being overridden when a new class is derived by inheritance from the class in which the error function is contained.

9.4 UNIT TESTING

So far I have said nothing about the verification of the components of a class. A programmer will normally be given the type of abstract data type specification shown in Chapter 6 and asked to develop the class that is described by the specification. This entails deciding on the representation of the data type, and detailed processing embedded in the algorithms used in the functions which access the representation. Once these decisions have been made, and the result committed to program code, a number of testing activities need to be carried out. The first is unit testing: the testing of individual functions to ensure that they implement the abstract data type operation that is required. The first aim of this section is to describe a number of strategies for this task.

The first strategy is very simple, all it involves is writing down a tabular representation of the individual data items and deriving tests based on combinations of these data items. As a simple example, consider the testing of a function which forms part of a class which implements a map. Assume that the map associates an integer key that lies between 1000 and 2000 with an employee record. The aim of the function is to check that a particular employee with a particular key is in the table. If a key is given that lies outside the range, then an error is displayed. Table 9.1 shows the different outcomes.

Here the various conditions that affect the function are displayed and all the possible conditions of conditions are combined. For example, the third row states that when a valid key is provided, and the key is not in the map, then it will not be found. The first and second rows of the table contain a blank, this is a 'don't care' condition for which it is irrelevant whether the key is in the map; indeed we can be certain that it is not in the map since the key for these two rows will be out of the range of the map.

Table 9.2 gives another example. It represents the tests for a function which has two arguments: `arr` an array of integers which contains up to a maximum of `maxint` items; and an integer n. The function sorts the first n items in the array. The first column of Table 9.2 details the values of n and the second column details the outcome that occurs.

Such tables are useful for exploring combinations of data values and are normally used to develop an initial data set. There are, however, two further strategies for deriving data that tend to be more revealing when it comes to discovering errors.

The first strategy is known as *error guessing*. Here the tester derives test data which supposedly is an error. For example, in the sorting example above, error guessing data for n would be a negative integer, zero, and an integer greater than `maxint`.

The second strategy is based on a technique known as *equivalence partitioning*. In order to understand this technique, consider Fig. 9.1. This shows the data space for a particular function. This represents all the possible data values that can be processed by a function or a program. The data space is partitioned into three subspaces. Each subspace represents data that is processed in the same way by the function or program, e.g. one of the subspaces may represent the processing of a particular type of error data.

Test data generation based on equivalence partitioning involves the tester generating test data that either lies on, or is close to, the boundary of the subspaces. Test data generated in this way is capable of detecting common programming errors such as a loop that executes one too many times, or one too few times, or a condition in which a < operator has been written rather than a ≤ operator. As you will recognize, these are all common errors committed by programmers.

Table 9.1 A tabular representation of data values.

Key value	Key in map	Result
<1000		error message
>2000		error message
valid key	no	not found
valid key	yes	found

Table 9.2 Test data for a sort problem.

n	Result
1	sorted
maxint/2	sorted
maxint	sorted

Table 9.3 The initial test set.

ar	n	num	Result
num in table	n = maxint		found
num not in table	n = maxint		not found
num in table	n = maxint/2		found
num not in table	n < maxint/2		not found
num in table	n = 1		found
num not in table	n = 1		not found

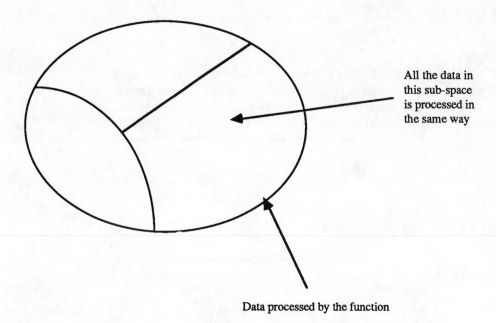

All the data in
this sub-space
is processed in
the same way

Data processed by the function

Figure 9.1 A data space and subspaces.

As an example of the three techniques in action, consider the testing of a function that has three arguments: the first, arr, is an array of integers which contains no more than maxint integers; the second, n, is an integer; and the third, num, is another integer. The function searches for num in the first n locations of arr. If it is contained there, then a 1 is returned, otherwise a 0 is returned. The initial test set might look like Table 9.3.

This is quite a good test set as it explores the behaviour of the table over its full size. Notice that the value of num has been marked as 'don't care'. A number of further tests can be generated from error guessing. The table can now be supplemented with this data which represents an empty array and an over-large array, as shown in Table 9.4.

The table can be further supplemented by data generated from equivalence partitioning. A number of tests can be generated. The first would involve the data being sought positioned at location n+1, just off the boundary of the array. The next would involve the data being positioned at location n, just on the boundary of the array. The final test would involve the data being positioned at location n-1, just within the array. Table 9.5 shows the final result of this delection of data.

To summarize, the initial test set is first formed by looking at all the possible conditions that can occur in the table. This is then supplemented by means of boundary data and error guessed data.

Table 9.4 The initial test set supplemented with error guessed test data.

arr	n	num	Result
num in table	n = maxint		found
num not in table	n = maxint		not found
num in table	n = maxint/2		found
num not in table	n < maxint/2		not found
num in table	n = 1		found
num not in table	n = 1		not found
	n = 0		error
	n>maxint		error

Table 9.5 The test set from Table 9.4 supplemented with boundary data.

arr	n	num	Result
num in table	n = maxint		found
num not in table	n = maxint		not found
num in table	n = maxint/2		found
num not in table	n < maxint/2		not found
num in table	n = 1		found
num not in table	n = 1		not found
	n = 0		error
	n>maxint		error
num at position n+1	n≤maxint		not found
num at position n	n≤maxint		found
num at position n-1	n≤maxint		found

9.5 CLASS INTEGRATION

Once the functional components of a class have been tested individually, they should be integrated and tested, both inside the class in which they are contained and with other classes that make use of them. As an example of the first category of test consider a class for a sequence which contains functions that add an item to a sequence, remove an item from a sequence, check if a sequence is empty, return with the number of items in a sequence, construct a sequence, and delete a sequence. One strategy for developing the members of this class, integrating them, and testing them in combination with each other is as follows:

- Implement the function that checks for an empty sequence, the program code for this function should be relatively simple and therefore it will not prove necessary to thoroughly test it. Compiling it until it is free of syntax errors would suffice.
- Implement the constructor function. Again this function will probably not be complex. It can be clean compiled. An integration test can then be carried out in conjunction with the previous function: the constructor function is called and the check function is then called to check that an empty sequence has been constructed.
- Implement the addition function and unit test it thoroughly. Carry out a further check of this function by repeatedly executing it and calling the function that checks for the empty sequence. This function should inform the tester that the the sequence is not empty.
- Implement the removal function and unit test it thoroughly. Carry out a further check on this function by repeatedly calling the addition function followed by the removal function, and then calling a function that checks that the sequence has remained unaltered after each set of calls. This test will require the use of a function that checks for the equality of two sequences. This function would almost certainly not form part of the delivered class, but is useful piece of subsidiary software which helps in checking the functionality of a class.
- Implement the function that calculates the number of items in a sequence and unit test it thoroughly. Then check it by repeatedly calling the addition function followed by the function in order to check whether the number of items in the sequence increases by one each time.
- Implement the destructor function. This can be quite a difficult function to test since it removes all trace of the sequence object it operates on, usually by employing a delete function. The best way to check this function is repeatedly to execute it a large number of times in conjunction with the constructor function. If there are any problems in storage items not being de-allocated properly, then the compiler will eventually display an error message.

This, then, is how to carry out an integration test on a single class. An important point to be made about this form of testing is that it often needs subsidiary functions in the class in order to help with the testing process. Typically, these might include a function for displaying the data part of the class or checking that two objects are equal. Often these functions are not required in a final delivered system. However, it is a good strategy to plan to develop these functions from the start. No programmer is perfect and, almost invariably, they will be required when errors start occurring. This strategy of unit testing and then testing functions in conjunction with each other can be extended to the situation where there is a class hierarchy; where one class uses facilities provided by some other classes, which in turn use facilities provided by other subsidiary classes, and so on. An example is shown in Fig. 9.2.

A good strategy to employ is to implement and thoroughly test the low-level classes first (C4, C5, C6), then implement the next level of classes (C2 and C3), again using the techniques described above, finally ending up with the test of the top-level class (C1). The alternative is to perform a top-down test starting with C1. Unfortunately this suffers from the

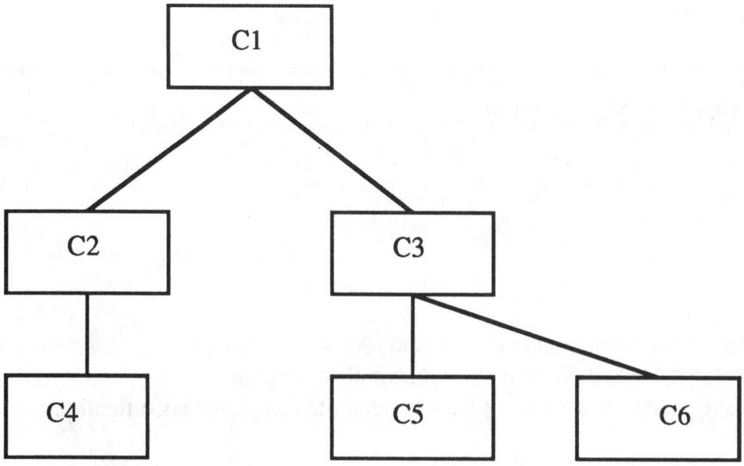

Figure 9.2 A class hierarchy.

disadvantage that dummy classes have to be implemented for any lower-level classes. Often these dummy classes require quite a large amount of program code, which has to be thrown away when their 'real' code is inserted.

9.6 SUMMARY

This chapter has completed the study of classes. Two important concepts were described: the virtual function, which enables different objects to be treated uniformly; and facilities that allow the programmer to define binary and unary operators. The chapter concluded by describing how individual functions can be tested, and how the whole of a class hierarchy can be tested and integrated together.

10

SPECIFYING FUNCTIONALITY

AIMS

- To describe how the functional components of a system can be specified.
- To describe one functional specification notation: the data flow diagram.
- To outline the relationship between objects, operations, and the functional specification.

10.1 INTRODUCTION

In the early chapters of this book much stress was placed on the fact that object-oriented design and programming enabled the developer to concentrate on the data aspects of a system at an early stage, and delay considerations of what a system does to a much later stage in the software project. The advantage claimed was that it enabled the most volatile part of the system—the functional specification—to be available only for a short time towards the end of a project. This has two effects.

First, when the functional specification is constructed it will represent functional requirements at a time n months after the start of a project and will, consequently, be a much more up-to-date representation of requirements than a functional specification generated m months after the project start, where m is very much less than n. Second, it means that the functional specification is only visible for a short time in the project with the effect that few changes will impact on it.

That is the theory. Practice is a little different. Using the development technique described in this book could, theoretically, mean that the functional specification would be generated after all the operations and objects have been implemented. However, there are a number of pressures on a development team that result in the functional specification being generated in some form at an earlier stage. For example, it is important that early in a software project a project manager estimates the resources required for the project. A major input into the resource estimating process is the functional specification. Consequently, it is a good idea to develop an outline functional specification early on that can be used for a rough costing.

Another way in which reality deviates from the theory presented in this book is that when carrying out analysis the developer will be asking hard questions about what a system does, and what functions are initiated by the users of a system: it is impossible to discover what objects make up a system without looking at the surface manifestations of operations on those objects. For example, in a hotel booking system, a reservation object might only be discovered after asking hotel staff exactly what they do.

Even though the examples above indicate that the simple development model of producing the functional specification after implementation of objects and operations has occurred has some exceptions, the main principle holds: object-oriented development allows the developer to

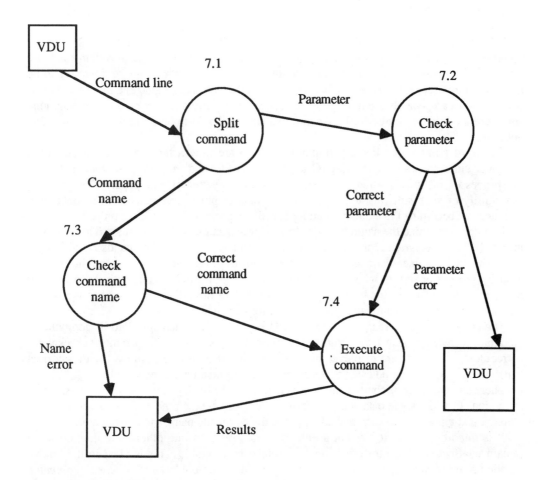

Figure 10.1 A sample data flow diagram.

delay considerations of detailed functionality until late in a project. A full-scale functional specification can be produced rather late in the development process, even though an outline may exist for costing purposes, and rough notes for analysis purposes. The full specification can be delayed until as much as 60 per cent of project resources have been committed.

10.2 A NOTATION FOR FUNCTIONAL SPECIFICATION

Given that there is a need for a functional specification, the next question is: how is that specification written down? Before answering this question it is worth reiterating a point that was made earlier, namely that the functional specification is only part of a whole requirements specification document which will contain other information such as hardware requirements and training requirements. However, in this book I shall concentrate on how functions are expressed. I shall also assume that by the time the functional specification is completed the developer will have identified and specified all the objects and operations that are required for a system.

The notation I shall use to describe functionality is the data flow diagram. This is a very popular graphical notation which describes the flow of data through a system, and the transformations that occur on that data. The reasons for its popularity are various: it can be understood by users and customers; it is more exact than natural language; a large number of software tools are available to help the analyst produce, modify and check data flow diagrams; and there are a large number of books and manuals available to help the developer use this notation.

The third point is particularly important. There are now a large number of so-called computer-aided software engineering (CASE) tools for PCs and workstations, which automate the processes of specification previously supported by pencil and paper. The growing availability of such software tools has ensured that graphical notations such as data flow diagrams are becoming the main medium for functional specification on large projects.

In order to examine the nature of data flow diagrams an example is in order. This is shown in Fig. 10.1. The diagram represents part of a system that processes commands typed in by a user, with each command containing a parameter; for example, the commands might be those used by process operators who monitor the action of a chemical plant, with the parameter being the name of a reactor in the plant. What the data flow diagram describes is a set of functions that process a command typed in by a user from a VDU.

The command is first read in from the VDU keyboard, it is then split into its components (command name, parameter), the command is checked for correctness, the parameter checked for correctness, any errors are displayed at the VDU, and if a correct command with a correct parameter has been communicated to the system, then the command is executed.

There are a number of components to this diagram. The bubbles represent processes. These are actions that take some data and transform it. For example the process *Split command* takes a line of text typed in by a user, and splits it into the command name and a parameter.

It is important to point out that a bubble transforms data into other data; data does not remain unaffected by a transformation represented by a bubble. This is clear in the bubble labelled *Split command*; however, it is less clear with the bubble labelled *Check command name*. Here a command name is input to the process represented by the bubble, and it is transformed into a correct command name and a possible error message. The implementation of the system could be that the process is represented by a module that just passes the command name forward. In this case you might be tempted to say that the command name has remained unaffected and violated the rule that a process transforms data. However, the important point to bear in mind with data flow diagrams is that they represent a high-level view or logical view of what goes on in a system and should not represent implementation details. The bubble *Check command name* has transformed a command into a different entity *Correct command name*, even though the implementation might treat them as the same object.

There are other components to a data flow diagram as well as processes represented by bubbles. Sinks and sources are represented by square boxes. A source is a producer of data and is represented by a box from which a data line emerges. A source could be a person, a piece of equipment such as a VDU or a thermocouple, or it could even be another existing computer system which has already been developed. In Fig. 10.1 the source that is represented is the VDU operated by the user who issues commands. There is no reason why this source could not be replaced by a box marked *User*.

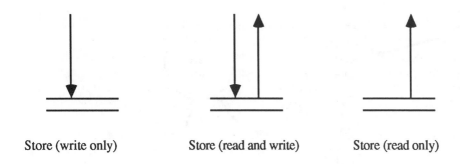

Store (write only)   Store (read and write)   Store (read only)

Figure 10.2 Various types of store.

Sinks are consumers of data. Data passes into a sink and does not emerge again. Typical sinks are a VDU, or more strictly the VDU screen, an actuator, an archive, or a tape punch. In Fig. 10.1 the VDU acts both as a sink and a source. The final component of a data flow diagram, not shown in Fig. 10.1, is a store. A store is something that holds data and can be read from and written to. Examples of the use of stores are shown in Fig. 10.2.

Stores can represent both computer-oriented and application-oriented storage media. For example, a store can represent a computer file, a data structure held in main memory, a filing cabinet, or a pile of papers on a desk.

Another point that ought to be made about data flow diagrams is that each bubble should be uniquely numbered. For example, in Fig. 10.1 each bubble is labelled by the integer 7 followed by another number. We shall not discuss the exact form of the numbering at this stage, the important point is that each bubble should have a unique number.

There are a number of rules about the construction of data flow diagrams that are worth listing at this stage; as the chapter proceeds, and more detail is added to how they are produced, further rules will be presented.

- A store can be read, written to, or read and written to.
- A sink can only consume data.
- A source can only produce data.
- A bubble will always transform the data that is input to it, into data that is logically different from the input data.

SAQ A simple chemical plant system is to be developed that reads a command from a user operating a VDU. The user types in the name of a chemical reactor and the system will then say whether the reactor is on-line or off-line. The format of the reactor names has been specified, and if the user does not type in a reactor that conforms to this format, then an error message should be displayed. Assume that a store is used to keep information about which reactors are on-line and off-line. Write down a data flow diagram that describes this system. Do not bother with the labelling of processes (bubbles) at this stage.

SOLUTION The data flow diagram is shown in Fig. 10.3. The user provides a reactor name. The reactor name is checked for correctness. If it is incorrect, then an error is dis-

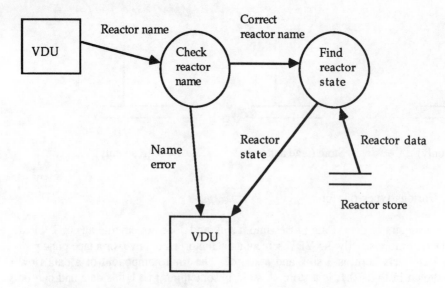

Figure 10.3 The solution to the SAQ.

-played. If it is not in error, then data on the current functioning of the reactor is retrieved from the store where it is held and then displayed. ❑

So far the data flow diagrams that have been presented have been small, consisting of only a few bubbles. A realistic system will usually contain thousands of these bubbles, so how can we organize a specification to reflect this?

One approach would be to draw all the bubbles on one continuous length of paper. This is clearly impractical: it would give rise to a specification that is virtually impossible to read and understand. The solution adopted is to represent the data flow diagram as a hierarchy of levels, with each level representing an expansion of a bubble in a higher-level data flow diagram. For example, the data flow diagram shown in Fig. 10.1 might have been the expansion of a bubble shown in Fig. 10.4. This is known as a context diagram.

This represents the high-level view of the data flow diagram shown in Fig. 10.1. Notice that the bubble has been given a unique labelling: the number 7 and the data flow diagram that represents an expansion of this bubble will contain bubbles prefixed with this number.

A data flow diagram, then, consists of bubbles that are expanded into further data flow diagrams, whose bubbles may be further expanded, and so on. In order to describe this process a small example will be presented.

10.3 AN EXAMPLE OF A FULL DATA FLOW DIAGRAM DEVELOPMENT

Assume that the document below represents an informal customer statement of requirements for a part of a system that is concerned with processing orders for goods sold by a wholesaler.

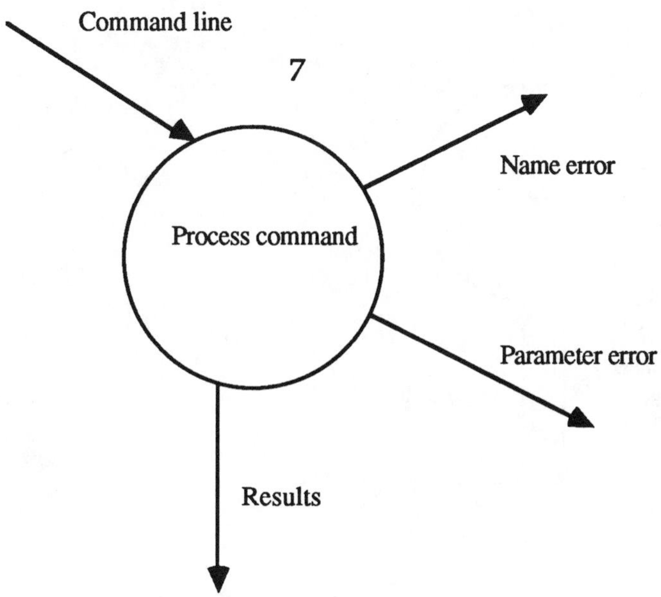

Figure 10.4 A bubble to be expanded.

ACME Warehouses Inc.

ACME are a high technology company who sell electronic components to the manufacturers of domestic appliances. Orders are received by an order clerk and communicated to the warehouse for dispatch to the company who have made a particular order. Sometimes the items that are ordered cannot be found in the warehouse, usually because we have exhausted the stock. When this happens the order is placed in a queue of orders which are scanned when a new delivery of components is received. A number of facilities should be provided for staff who maintain this queue:

QUEUELIST

This should display all the orders in the queue in the order in which they are stored.

QUEULISTCUST

This should display all the orders in a queue for a particular customer in the order in which they are stored in the queue.

QUEUESTATE

This should display how many items are on the queue.

QUEUEMOVE

This should move a particular order in the queue to another place in the queue. The order to be moved is identified by its unique order number, its new position is identified by an integer which represents the position in the queue to which it is moved. For example, if the integer 7 was quoted, then the order would be moved to the seventh position in the queue.

All the commands that implement the facilities should provide rigorous error checking.

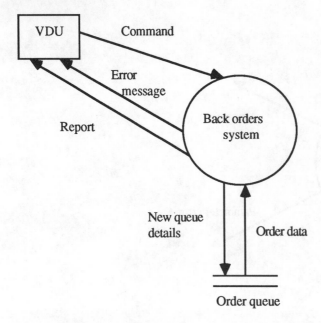

Figure 10.5 The context diagram.

This, then, is the user statement of requirements. In order to develop a data flow diagram an initial data flow diagram is constructed. This diagram, known as a *context diagram*, shows the global flows of data in the system, and acts as a starting point for the subsequent development of the rest of the data flow diagrams. The context diagram for the example above is shown in Fig. 10.5.

The context diagram shows that a command is to be processed by the system, error messages are to be produced, reports are to be produced on the VDU screen, and the unsatisfied order queue is to be accessed and updated. This represents the high-level view of the system. Notice that this context diagram does not have its bubble labelled. This is the only exception to the rule that data flow bubbles should be labelled uniquely.

The next stage is to expand this diagram into a more detailed data flow diagram which represents the next level of processing. This next level will involve a line being read from the VDU, the particular command decoded, and the parameters extracted. This data flow diagram is shown as Fig. 10.6.

This data flow diagram shows that a VDU issues a command line. The line is then split into the command and its parameters. The command is then checked for correctness—the user might have mistyped the command and the bubble would detect this. The correct command name, together with the parameters, are then passed to the bubble *Execute command*, which carries out the processing. There may be errors in the parameters and so this process emits error messages as well as a report from the execution of the command.

There are a number of important points to be made about this diagram. First, the bubbles have now been numbered; there is no particular ordering of the numbers, the important point is that unique numbers are used. The second point to be made is that the overall flows into or out

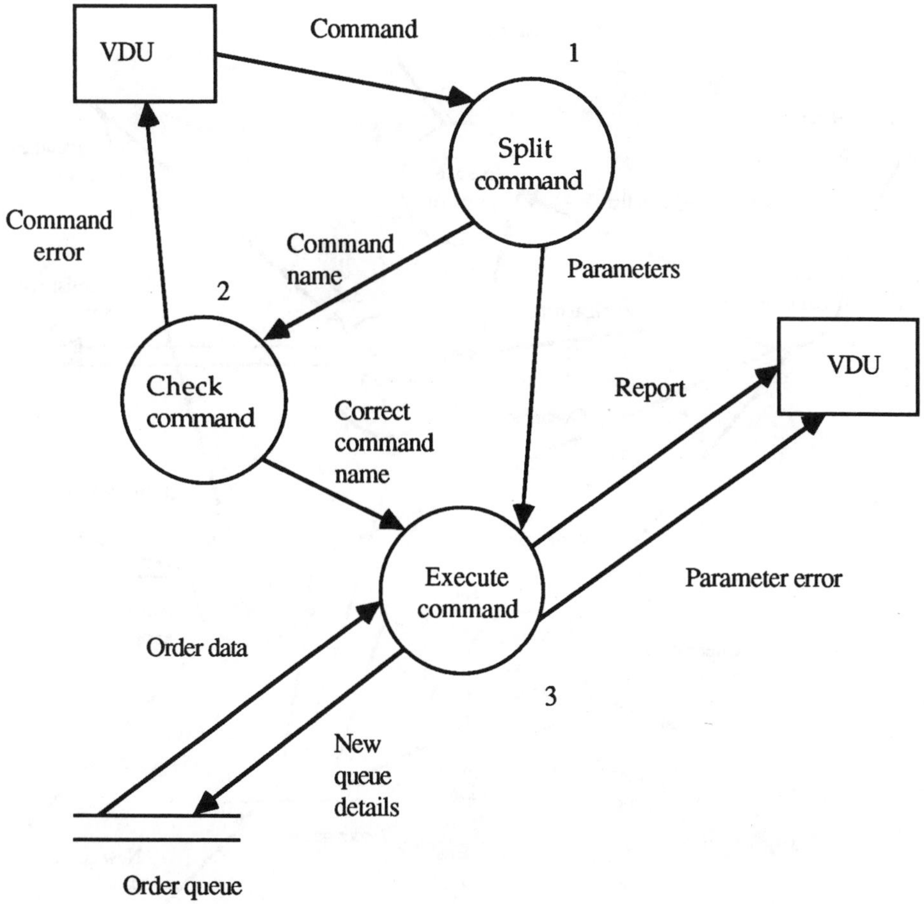

Figure 10.6 Refinement of the context diagram.

of the diagram must match those in the bubble from which the diagram has been expanded. For example, the context diagram contains an input command which is shown on the refinement of the context diagram. Also, the context diagram has an output called *Error message* and this is represented by the two errors *Command error* and *Parameter error* in Fig. 10.6. This is an important point as continuity of data is an important check that the analyst, or a CASE tool, can make in order to ensure correctness. Another point that should be made about data flow diagrams is that there should be an upper limit to the number of bubbles in such a diagram. The limit most often advised is seven. Above that, data flow diagrams become difficult to draw neatly, and are difficult to understand.

The next stage in the specification is to expand the data flow diagram shown in Fig. 10.6. To do this each bubble is examined and the analyst asks whether there is more functionality hidden by the bubble. Bubbles 1 and 2 do not require further expansion: there are rules for what

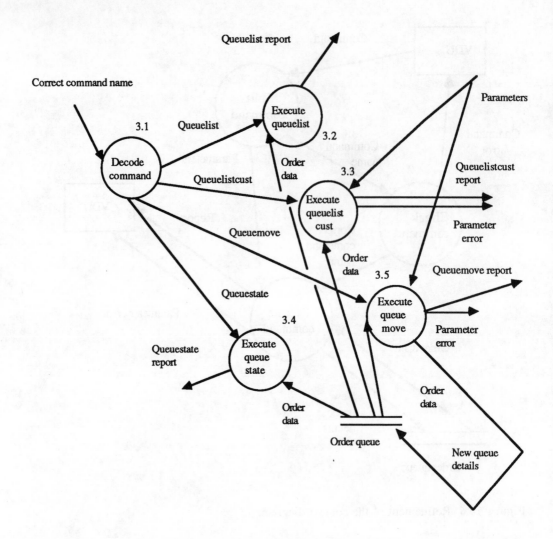

Figure 10.7 Expansion of bubble 3.

is and what is not a valid command, and furthermore the action of splitting up a command into the command name and its parameters is simple and really an implementation issue.

However, bubble 3, which executes a command, requires further expansion. The data flow diagram that represents this expansion is shown in Figure 10.7. It shows that a command is processed, decoded, the command identified, and executed. Each command execution is represented by a bubble. Bubble 3.2 is the execution of the *Queuelist* command; this requires no parameters and produces a report. Bubble 3.3 corresponds to the execution of the *Queuelistcust* command and requires the name of the customer whose orders are to be displayed.

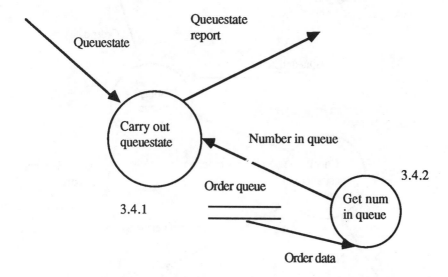

Figure 10.8 The execution of Queuestate.

Bubble 3.5 corresponds to the *Queuemove* command, and requires the number of the purchase order and the new position of the purchase order in the queue. This command can produce either a report or errors when its parameters are incorrect. Finally, bubble 3.4 corresponds to the execution of the *Queuestate* command; it requires no parameters and just displays the number of items on the queue.

Again notice the numbering convention: since the data flow diagram represents the expansion of bubble 3, all the bubbles are prefixed with the number 3.

SAQ Can the data flow diagram shown in Fig. 10.7 be expanded any further? If so, which bubbles need expanding?

SOLUTION The answer is, of course, yes. Each of the bubbles corresponding to the execution of a command need to be expanded further in order to indicate functions such as those corresponding to error processing. ❑

The expansion of bubble 3.4 is shown as Fig. 10.8. All this data flow diagram describes is the retrieval of queue data from the orders queue, and the calculation of the number of items in the queue. The expansion of bubble 3.3 is shown in Fig. 10.9.

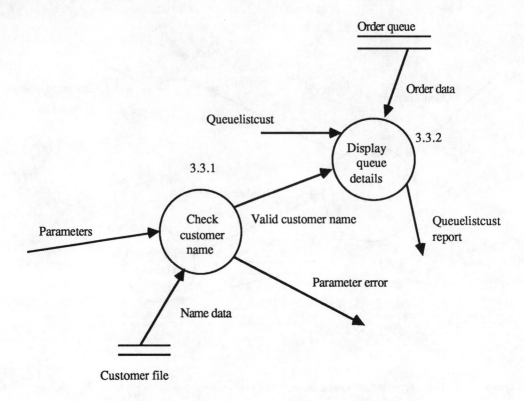

Figure 10.9 The expansion of bubble 3.3.

The parameter to the command is first checked to see if a valid customer identifier has been input. In order for this processing to take place, access is needed to a store which holds customer details. If the customer name is not in this store, then an error is displayed. However, if the customer is valid, then the queue details corresponding to orders placed by this customer are retrieved and displayed.

SAQ Draw the data flow diagram corresponding to the expansion of bubble 3.5 in Fig. 10.7.

SOLUTION The diagram is shown as Fig 10.10. The parameters are extracted from the list of parameters presented to the command. In this case there are two parameters: the order number of the purchase order which is to be moved, and the new position in the queue of the purchase order. These parameters are checked: the purchase order number is checked to see whether an order corresponding to it is in the queue, the new queue position is checked to see if, in fact, there is a position specified by the integer, for example the position 7 may have been specified and the queue only contained four items. If the parameters are not correct then error messages are displayed, if they are correct then the movement of the purchase order in the queue takes place. ❑

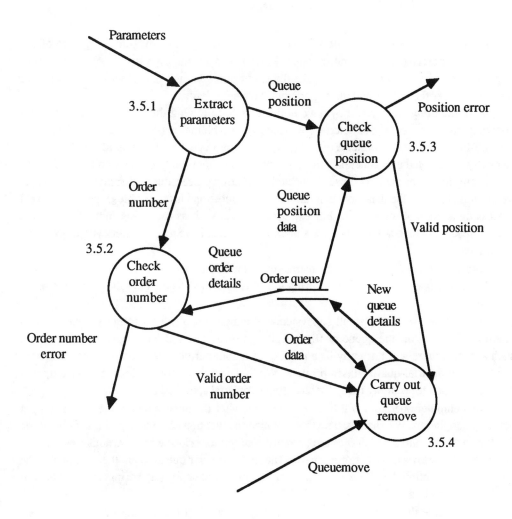

Figure 10.10 The answer to the previous SAQ.

The remaining bubble expansion is left as an exercise.

At this stage it is worth writing down some more rules for the construction of data flow diagrams:

- A data flow diagram should contain no more than seven bubbles.
- The data flowing into and out of a data flow diagram should be consistent with the data flowing out of and into the data flow bubble that it refines.
- The number of a bubble in a data flow diagram should reflect the number used in the bubble from which it is refined, apart from the context diagram where the only bubble is unlabelled.

10.4 DATA FLOW DIAGRAMS AND OBJECTS

So far, nothing has been said about where objects fit into data flow diagrams. The aim of this section is to describe how operation specifications can be incorporated into the data flow diagrams. In order to do this I shall make the assumption that the data flow diagram is being constructed after the objects and their operations have been defined.

One of the things that you may have noticed when following this chapter is that the data flow diagrams that were constructed were expressed as a hierarchy of functions, sub-functions, sub-sub-functions, and so one. You may also have noticed that bubbles at the top of the hierarchy represented user functions: those functions that represent the external manifestation of the system, functions such as those connected with error processing or displaying results. As we progress lower in the data flow diagram hierarchy, more and more bubbles represent internal processing actions of the system. For example, actions such as retrieving items from a data store or reading data to a data store. It is these bubbles that have a connection with objects and operations.

In order to show this, and to demonstrate the relationship between data flow diagrams and the objects and operations identified during the early analysis stages, the following example is presented.

The example involves a small subsystem—a component of an operating system—which monitors and controls the queue of files awaiting processing in a large operating system. In such a system there will normally be a number of output peripherals, ranging from slow line-printers to industrial-quality laser printers. When a user asks for a file to be printed, it is normally queued for printing ready for an output peripheral specified by the user.

Also, computer operators will have the ability to alter the queues and redirect some output between peripherals. We shall assume that a number of functions are required for the operators: a function that enquires which files are currently waiting for printing by a particular peripheral, a function that allows an operator to move a file in a particular queue to another position in the queue, and a function that allows the operators to take a queue for one peripheral and attach it to another peripheral.

I shall assume that a number of operations have been identified during the early stages of analysis. First, an operation *start(peripheral, first)*, which returns a record *first* containing the file name and owner name of the first file in a queue for *peripheral*; *move(peripheral, user, name, new_position)*, which moves a file *name* belonging to *user* in the queue associated with *peripheral* to a new position *new_position*; an operation *check(name, user, peripheral)*, which checks that a particular file *name* owned by *user* is in the queue associated with *peripheral*; an operation *remove(peripheral, head)*, which removes the head of the queue of print files associated with *peripheral*; an operation *add(user, name, peripheral)*, which adds a file *name* associated with *user* to the queue associated with *peripheral*; and an operation *move(peripheral1, peripheral2)*, which moves all the files in the queue associated with *peripheral1* to the queue associated with *peripheral2*.

The top-level data flow diagram is shown as Fig. 10.11.

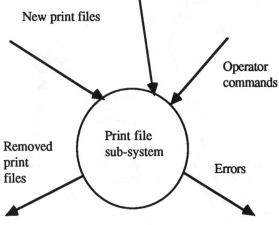

Print requests

New print files

Operator commands

Print file sub-system

Removed print files

Errors

Figure 10.11 The top-level data flow diagram for the print queue application.

There are three inputs: new files to be attached to a queue ready for printing; requests from the operating system for files to be removed for printing; and commands typed in by the computer operators. The two outputs are any errors made by operators, and any print files removed for printing in response to a request from the operating system. The next level of the data flow diagram is shown as figure 10.12.

Bubble 1 takes a request from the operating system for the next file on a peripheral queue to be printed. This bubble discovers which peripheral is required, and passes it forward to bubble 2. This finds the address of the file on some backing storage device, then removes details of the file and passes the operating system details of which file is to be printed. Bubble 3 takes details of a new print file to be added to a queue and then adds this file to the queue to which it is meant to be added. Finally, bubble 4 takes operator commands, and checks them for correctness: if they are incorrect, it flags them as errors; if correct, it carries out the operation specified with a consequent updating of the queue.

The next stage in the process is to refine these bubbles further.

SAQ Which bubbles in Fig. 10.12 require further refinement?

SOLUTION Bubbles 2, 3, and 4. ❑

The refinement of bubble 2 is shown as Fig. 10.13.

The first thing to notice about this data flow diagram is that bubble 2.1 is different in form to the bubbles that have been drawn before: it contains a horizontal line. This indicates that this bubble uses an operation which has been identified during analysis and will occur in an entity diagram. The operation in this case is *REMOVE*, which removes the head of the queue associated with a particular peripheral.

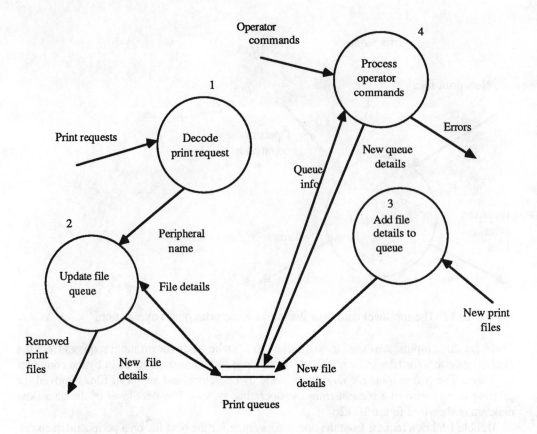

Figure 10.12 The next level of data flow diagram for the print file subsystem.

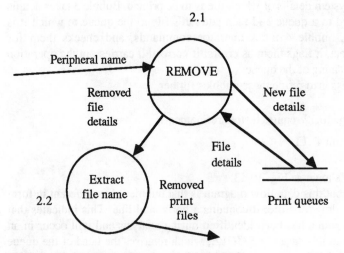

Figure 10.13 The refinement of bubble 2.

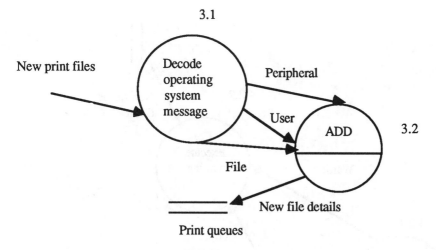

Figure 10.14 The expansion of bubble 3.

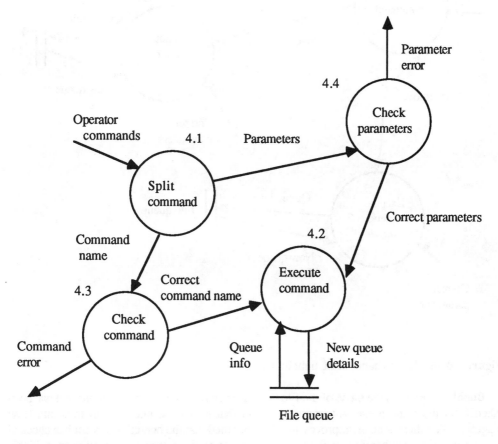

Figure 10.15 The expansion of bubble 4.

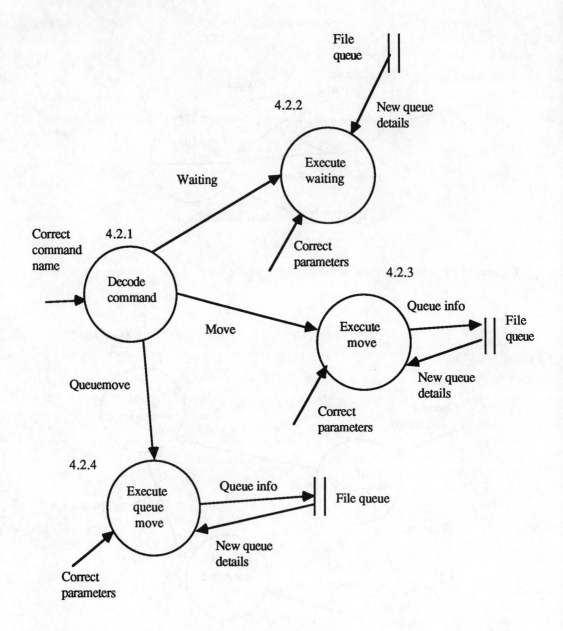

Figure 10.16 The refinement of bubble 4.2.

Bubble 2.2 extracts the name of the file that has been removed from the record that has been taken from the print queue. An important point that should be made about this data flow diagram is that there is no error processing: it is assumed that the operating system has checked that a particular peripheral is available and has a non-empty queue associated with it. If this checking had not been carried out, then the data flow diagram would need to contain some extra bubbles for this.

The next data flow diagram to refine is bubble 3.

SAQ Refine bubble 3.

SOLUTION The solution is shown as Fig.10.14. Bubble 3.1 discovers what peripheral and what file form the message from the operating system, decodes these components, and passes them on to bubble 3.2, which then uses the operation *ADD* to add the file to the queue associated with the peripheral. ❑

The next stage is to expand out bubble 4, which deals with operator commands. This bubble takes a command, extracts the name of the command and the parameters, checks that the command is correct, and then executes the command. The data flow diagram is shown in Fig. 10.15.

This needs to be expanded further in order to specify the processing that occurs. Bubble 4.2 requires further refinement. The next level of 4.2 is shown in Fig. 10.16.

All this data flow diagram does is to describe the decoding of a command—the process whereby the name of the command is discovered—and the execution of each type of command. The commands are referred to as *waiting*, the command that checks which files are waiting for printing by a particular peripheral; *move*, which moves the position of a file in a specified queue associated with a particular peripheral; and *move queue*, which moves a whole peripheral queue to another peripheral queue. The data flow diagram shows *file queue* three times, this has only been done to improve readability.

Each of the bubbles 4.2.2, 4.2.3, and 4.2.4 now need to be expanded further. We shall only show the expansion of one of these bubbles, bubble 4.2.4, which implements the *move queue* command. The data flow diagram for this command is shown as Fig. 10.17. This data flow diagram describes the fact that the system will split the parameters presented into two parameters: *peripheral1*, which is the peripheral whose files are to be transferred; and *peripheral2*, which is the peripheral to which the files are to be transferred. There are a number of checks that need to be carried out.

First, the system checks that both peripheral names typed in by the operator are valid, i.e. that they represent peripherals that are connected to the computer and switched on. Second the queue attached to *peripheral1* is checked to see whether it is empty. If it is, then an error message is displayed. The last part of the data flow diagram uses the operation *move* to move the file queues from *peripheral1* to *peripheral 2*.

10.5 SYSTEM TESTING

Once a requirements specification has been completed, the next task for the developer is the generation of the system tests. These tests are intended to check that those functions visible to the user have been implemented correctly. Given a data flow diagram, the process of generating these tests is relatively straightforward. It involves looking at each bubble and asking the question: is the function described by this bubble of direct interest to the user, or does it represent some form of internal processing? If it is the former, a system test should be generated for the bubble; if the latter, no system test should be developed.

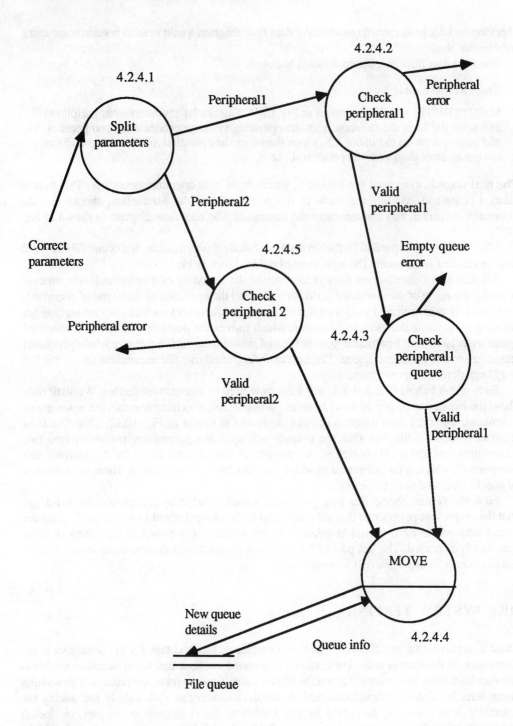

Figure 10.17 The expansion of bubble 4.2.4.

As an example of this process consider the data flow diagram developed for the subsystem described in Section 10.4. The top-level data flow diagram shown as Fig. 10.11 does not give rise to any system tests: it is at too high a level of abstraction. Now consider the next level of data flow diagram, the one shown in Fig. 10.12. Bubble 1 does not give rise to a system test because it represents some form of internal processing. Bubble 2 represents a functional system test in that it carries out the process of updating the file queue when the operating system requests a file to be taken from the print queue. Bubble 3 also requires a system test. This bubble represents the processing that occurs when a new file is added to the file queue. Finally, bubble 4 does not yet require a system test since it is at too high a level of abstraction. The system tests for this data flow diagram are as follows:

System test 2.

This test takes a series of print request messages from the operating system and checks that the file queue has been correctly updated.

System test 3.

This test takes a series of requests from the operating system to add print files to the queue of print files and checks that the print queue has been correctly updated.

There are a number of points to make about this list of system tests. First, they are at a high level of abstraction: the remainder of the project would involve these tests being further refined until they correspond to test procedures—step-by-step instructions for carrying out a test. Second, the tests are numbered according to which data flow bubble they are checking.

There are no system tests corresponding to the data flow diagram shown in Fig. 10.13, which represents the expansion of bubble 2. This data flow diagram just corresponds to some internal processing that occurs in the system. Similarly the data flow diagram shown as Fig. 10.14, which represents the expansion of data flow bubble 3, requires no system tests.

The data flow diagram shown in Fig. 10.15, which represents the expansion of bubble 4, has two bubbles that require testing.

SAQ Which bubbles in Fig. 10.15 give rise to a system test?

SOLUTION Bubbles 4.3 and 4.4. ❑

The tests for bubble 4.3 and bubble 4.4 are shown below.

System test 4.3

This checks that when an incorrect command is typed in by the computer operator, a suitable error message is provided by the system.

System test 4.4

This checks that when an incorrect parameter to a command has been typed in by the computer operator, a suitable error message is provided by the system.

The data flow diagram shown as Fig 10.16 requires three system tests, one for each command. The data flow diagram in Fig. 10.17 generates system tests that check for invalid peripherals.

The remaining commands would also have system tests associated with them. The next step with these tests will be to expand them so that they are expressed in a little more detail, and become test procedures. This is detailed in the next chapter.

10.6 SUMMARY

This chapter has described how the functional specification is constructed using data flow diagrams. The natural functional hierarchy in a system is expressed as a series of levelled diagrams which represent more and more detailed functions until the lowest level of divisible function is encountered. The chapter concluded with a discussion of how outline system tests could be extracted from such a functional specification.

10.7 FURTHER READING

There are many books that deal with data flow diagrams and graphical notations for specification. Page-Jones (1988) is probably the best exposition of data flow diagram-driven software development. Holloway (1989) describes a number of modern software development methodologies that rely on graphical specification notations.

BIBLIOGRAPHY

Holloway, S. (1989) *Methodology Handbook for Information Managers*, Gower Press, London.

Page-Jones, M. (1988) *Practical Guide to Structured Systems Analysis*, Prentice-Hall, Englewood Cliffs, NJ.

PUTTING IT ALL TOGETHER

AIMS

- To describe how functional decomposition enables the final program code of a system to be derived.
- To outline the relationship between data flow diagrams and functional decomposition.
- To describe how outline system tests are converted into test procedures.

11.1 INTRODUCTION

So far in this book little has been said about implementation. At a particular point in the software project all the objects and operations will have been tested and implemented using classes, the requirements specification will be complete, and a set of outline system tests will have been generated from this specification. The question that this chapter is intended to answer is: what happens next?

This chapter describes how the final implementation of a system can be achieved using a technique known as *functional decomposition*. This final implementation involves the designer developing the top-level program code which controls the operations identified during requirements analysis. Functional decomposition is an example of a divide and conquer paradigm, where the designer looks at the high-level functions of a system and then gradually decomposes these functions into sub-functions, sub-sub-functions, and so on, until a level of detail is achieved when program coding can occur.

The chapter first details this technique and then describes how a functional decomposition can be guided by the data flow diagrams generated during requirements specification. It concludes with a description of how the type of outline system tests discussed in the previous chapter can be processed, so that they can be applied directly to a completed system.

11.2 FUNCTIONAL DECOMPOSITION

Functional decomposition is not a new technique. It has been one of the weapons in the armoury of the software engineer for about fifteen years. It relies on the designer first specifying a high-level view of what a system does, and then refining it into increasingly more detailed views. In many ways this process mirrors the process of developing a data flow diagram, where the levels in the data flow diagram represent a more and more detailed view of what a system is to do. The only difference between data flow diagrams and what is described in this chapter is that this chapter concentrates on *how* a system is to be constructed.

The functional decomposition process also mirrors many engineering processes where high-level concerns are dealt with first, followed by low-level concerns. For example, in developing a car an auto-engineer is not concerned with details such as the width of the springs in the upholstery or the material used to construct the steering wheel. The engineer's first concern is to develop some conceptual ideas, such as what type of car is being built, followed by slightly more detailed concerns such as engine sizes, the physical dimensions of the car, and the overall structure of the electrical system. Only in the later stages of the design process do small concerns intrude into the design process.

As an example of the functional decomposition process, consider a non-computing example: the construction of a robot to produce an omelette. While this is not a product that has a huge commercial potential, its design can be used to demonstrate the processes involved in functional decomposition. A top-level description of the design of this product in terms of functionality is

Make an omelette

This is a very high-level description of what the omelette-making machine is to do. It can be broken down into a series of sub-functions. In order to make an omelette the ingredients need to be found, a frying pan needs to be obtained, the contents mixed, the contents added to the pan, and the omelette cooked. This can be described as

1   Obtain ingredients
2   Obtain frying pan
3   Pour ingredients into bowl
4   Mix ingredients in bowl
5   Pour ingredients into frying pan
6   Cook ingredients
7   Tip omelette out of frying pan

The design matches exactly what the omelette machine is to do. Each statement is at a lower level of detail and is uniquely numbered. This design can now form the basis of the next level of refinement. First, statement 1 can be refined. Let us assume that the ingredients are eggs, milk, and a little water. The design of step 1 hence becomes

1.1   Obtain three eggs
1.2   Obtain some milk
1.3   Obtain a small amount of water

Step 3 can be further refined to

3.1   Crack three eggs into bowl
3.2   Pour milk into bowl
3.3   Pour water into bowl

This leads to the design

1.1   Obtain three eggs
1.2   Obtain some milk
1.3   Obtain a small amount of water

2   Obtain frying pan
3.1   Crack three eggs into bowl
3.2   Pour milk into bowl
3.3   Pour water into bowl
4   Mix ingredients in bowl
5   Pour ingredients into frying pan
6   Cook ingredients
7   Tip omelette out of frying pan

Notice the numbering convention, where each refinement contains the number of the statement from which it was refined. An important question to ask now is: can this design be refined any further? The answer depends on whether the machine we are constructing can directly execute the statements in the design. For example, if the machine had a mechanism for extracting eggs from some large reservoir of eggs, then there is no need for further refinement of step 1.1. Let us assume that all the statements in the design correspond to actions carried out by the omelette-making machine except step 3.1. Let us also assume that the machine has a mechanism for cracking one egg. Consequently, step 3.1 needs to be further refined. One way to refine it would be

3.1.1   Crack an egg into bowl
3.1.2   Crack an egg into bowl
3.1.3   Crack an egg into bowl

A more elegant way would be to use a loop structure

3.1.1   For i from 1 to 3 do
3.1.2   Add the ith egg

This shows a for loop controlling the processing in step 3.1.2. Rather than using begins or ends or curly brackets to denote the scope of the loop, indentation is used.

When applied to the design of a software system this notation is known as a *program design language*. It consists of statements that describe some processing—usually written in natural language or some restricted form of natural language—and control constructs similar to those found in programming languages.

As an example of the development of a simple computer program using the functional decomposition technique and a program design language, consider the simple problem of reading in a series of integers from a file, and then finding the sum, average, largest integer, and smallest integer. The top-level design is as follows:

1   Set up files and initialize variables
2   Calculate sum, maximum, minimum, and number of integers
3   Compute average as being sum divided by number of integers
4   Display sum, maximum, minimum, average

This is at a high level of abstraction and needs to be further refined. Step 1 can be refined to

1.1   Initialize file of integers

1.2   Initialize variables

Step 2 can, of course, be refined further, what is required is a loop that reads in each integer from the file, adds it to a variable which keeps a running total of the integers that have been processed, and checks each integer against the largest and smallest integers so far processed. The refinement for this is shown below:

2.1	While there is an integer to process
2.2	Read an integer
2.3	Add the integer to a sum
2.4	Check for current maximum
2.5	Check for current minimum
2.6	Increment total number of integers by 1

This still needs further refinement. In particular steps 2.4 and 2.5 need to be specified in more detail. Step 2.4 checks that the integer that has been read is greater than the largest maximum so far encountered in the file. If it is not, then no processing takes place. However, if it is, then the current maximum is replaced by the integer that is read in.

Step 2.5 is similar: it checks that the integer that has been read in is less than the smallest minimum so far encountered in the file. If it is not, then no processing takes place. However, if it is, then the current minimum is replaced by the integer that is read in. The refinement of step 2.4 then becomes

2.4.1	If the integer is greater than the maximum integer then
2.4.2	Set maximum integer to the integer read

and step 2.5 then becomes

2.5.1	If the integer is less than than the minimum integer then
2.5.2	Set minimum integer to the integer read

The refinement of these steps and step 2 now means that we can refine step 1.2 further by specifically initializing the variables. The variables that contain the current maximum and minimum can be initialized by setting them equal to the first value in the file of integers. The value of the running total can be set to the first integer in the file and the number of integers can be set equal to 1. The refinement is then

1.2.1	Read first integer from file
1.2.2	Set maximum to this integer
1.2.3	Set minimum to this integer
1.2.4	Set sum to this integer
1.2.5	Set number of integers to 1

The final design then becomes

1.1	Initialize file of integers
1.2.1	Read first integer from file

1.2.2	Set maximum to this integer
1.2.3	Set minimum to this integer
1.2.4	Set sum to this integer
1.2.5	Set number of integers to 1
2.1	While there is an integer to process
2.2	Read an integer
2.3	Add the integer to a sum
2.4.1	If the integer is greater than the maximum integer then
2.4.2	Set maximum integer to the integer read
2.5.1	If the integer is less than than the minimum integer then
2.5.2	Set minimum integer to the integer read
2.6	Increment total number of integers by 1
3	Compute average as being sum divided by number of integers
4	Display sum, maximum, minimum, average

There are a number of important points to make about this example and functional decomposition in general. First, the example above has been refined to the point where the design can be coded. You will remember that in the omelette example the design stopped when we were confident that the omelette-making machine had some mechanism whereby it could directly implement the statements in the design. Second, the example above contains another control statement—the while statement—which repeatedly executes part of a design *while* a certain condition holds. Third, that so far no mention has been made of objects and operations, a later section will describe how objects and operations can be accommodated in this form of design. Fourth, the control constructs that have been used, and which will be described later, bear little relationship to the concrete syntax of any programming language, although they can be hand-translated very easily into control statements in any language. This was a deliberate decision. A company that develops software will often use a number of programming languages, ranging from languages such as C^{++} to assembler languages; rather than have a program design language for each of these programming languages, and a bulky quality assurance standard for each one, a developer often tries to use a program design language that abstracts from the facilities found in all programming languages, and includes a set of control structures that can easily be translated into any reasonable high-level language or even low-level language.

Before looking at the control facilities available in our program design language, it is worth describing another example. Many of you will be new to the idea of functional decomposition and will, initially, find some difficulty in writing statements at the required level of abstraction. This example, which requires you to do some work, will reinforce the ideas that have previously been discussed.

The example involves the development of a system for a small library. The library stocks a number of books, and has a number of borrowers who are allowed to borrow up to ten books. When a book is borrowed, the borrower turns up at the library, and shows the library assistant an identification card that displays the borrower's unique number. The library assistant then types in the number of the borrower, together with the number of the book that is to be borrowed.

When a borrower returns a book, all the library assistant does is to type in the number of the book, and place the book on a trolley ready for it to be returned to the library shelves. For the sake of this small and unrealistic example let us assume that only a small number of errors occur: first, when a book is borrowed the library assistant could mistype the book number or the number of the borrower, also a borrower may already have ten books on loan. Second, when a borrower returns a book, the library assistant could mistype the book number. Other less likely errors, such as a borrower bringing back a book that somebody else has already borrowed, will be ignored; however, it is worth stressing that such errors would have to be checked in any practical system.

The top-level design of the system is as follows:

1   Read in library files
2   While the last transaction has not been encountered do
3   Process a transaction
4   Close down library files

This shows the initialization of the files that contain both book, user, and loans information, followed by a continual process of processing a transaction.

Step 3 begs the question: what exactly is a transaction? Well, two have already been identified: the borrowing of a book and the return of a book. I shall also assume that there is another transaction which the library assistant uses, and which informs the system that it is to be shut down. This will normally only be invoked once a day when the library closes. This means that step 2 can be further refined to

2 While the closedown command has not been initiated

The next step to be refined is step 3, which reads in a transaction from a library assistant, decodes the transaction, and then processes one of the three transactions that could have occurred. The design for step 3 is shown below

3.1   Read the transaction type
3.2   Decode the transaction
3.3   Case transaction type of
3.4   Borrow: process borrow transaction
3.5   Return: process return transaction
3.6   Terminate: process system termination transaction

This shows a new construct that is the analogue of the case statement in a programming language. This construct is a multi-way decision which processes each labelled branch depending on the variable specified in its first line. So, for example, in the above refinement each transaction is invoked depending on the transaction type.

The design has now been transformed to the following:

1   Read in library files
2   While the closedown command has not been initiated
3.1   Read the transaction type
3.2   Decode the transaction
3.3   Case transaction type of
3.4   Borrow: process borrow transaction
3.5   Return: process return transaction
3.6   Terminate: process system termination transaction
4   Close down library files

SAQ Does this design require any further refinement? If so, which steps need further work?

SOLUTION There is still not much detail about the processing associated with each transaction. Thus, steps 3.4, 3.5, and 3.6 require further refinement. ❑

The refinement of step 3.4 is shown below. It shows that the borrower number is read, the book number read, each of these numbers checked, and if they are valid the book is marked as being borrowed by the borrower. A check is also made on the number of books that the borrower currently has on loan.

3.4.1 Borrow:
3.4.2   Read the borrower number
3.4.3   If the borrower number is valid then
3.4.4   Read the book number
3.4.5   If the book number is valid then
3.4.6   Retrieve the number of books currently borrowed by borrower
3.4.7   If borrowed books equals 10 then
3.4.8   Issue an error message that too many books have been borrowed
3.4.9   else
3.4.10   Mark the book as being borrowed by the borrower
3.4.11   else
3.4.12   Issue an invalid book error message
3.4.13   else
3.4.14   Issue an invalid borrower error message

This example shows another control construct, the if statement, which is a two-way decision; the else branch of this construct is optional.

SAQ Write down the refinement of step 3.5.

SOLUTION The refinement is shown below. It only checks for one error, namely that the book number has been input correctly by the library assistant. ❑

3.5.1 Return:
3.5.2   Read the book number
3.5.3   If the book number is invalid then
3.5.4   Issue an invalid book number error
3.5.5   else
3.5.6   Mark the book as being returned

The final refinement in the loop is that of step 3.6. All that is required here is to set some end of processing flag which can be sensed by the loop that controls the transaction processing:

3.6.1 Terminate:

3.6.2 Set an end of processing flag

This means that step 2 can be further refined to refer to the flag and to initialize the flag to be false:

2.1   Set end of processing flag to false
2.2   While the end of processing flag is not set to true do

The design now looks like the following:

1   Read in library files
2.1   Set end of processing flag to false
2.2   While the end of processing flag is not set to true do
3.1   Read the transaction type
3.2   Decode the transaction
3.3   Case transaction type of

3.4.1   Borrow:
3.4.2   Read the borrower number
3.4.3   If the borrower number is valid then
3.4.4   Read the book number
3.4.5   If the book number is valid then
3.4.6   Retrieve the number of books currently borrowed by borrower
3.4.7   If borrowed books equals 10 then
3.4.8   Issue an error message
3.4.9   else
3.4.10   Mark the book as being borrowed by the borrower
3.4.11   else
3.4.12   Issue an invalid book error message
3.4.13   else
3.4.14   Issue an invalid borrower error message

3.5.1   Return:
3.5.2   Read the book number
3.5.3   If the book number is invalid then
3.5.4   Issue an invalid book number error
3.5.5   else
3.5.6   Mark the book as being returned

3.6.1   Terminate:
3.6.2   Set an end of processing flag

4   Close down library files

Line spacing has been used to improve readability. It is important to point out that a number of the steps above could be refined further. For example, step 3.4.10 could, perhaps, require further expansion. However, such steps often coincide with operations on objects that have already been defined. For example, step 3.4.10 would, almost certainly, correspond to the exercise of an operation that updates a book object. This aspect of the functional decomposition process will be discussed in Section 11.4

11.3 THE CONTROL STRUCTURES AND SUBROUTINE FACILITIES

The aim of this section is to outline the control structures that are available in the program design language used in this book. You will have already met three in the previous section. The first is the case statement, this has the form

Case identifier of

    Value1:
       Statements 1

    Value2:
       Statements 2
    •
    •
    •
    Valuen
       Statements n

This represents a multi-way branch which executes *statements i* when *valuei* is equal to *identifier*. For example, the fragment

3.2   Check whether temperature is normal over the limit or under the limit
3.3   Case temperature status of

3.4   Normal:
3.5   Process normal temperature

3.6   Over:
3.7   Process over limit temperature
3.8
3.9   Under:
3.10   Process under limit temperature

has three branches corresponding to three states that a temperature may be in. The program design language also contains facilities for iteration. These are shown in outline below:

Repeat
   statements
Until condition

While condition do
   statements

For variable from start to finish {in steps of increment} do
    statements

These all match corresponding facilities in many high-level programming languages. The only item of note in the description above is the part in curly brackets in the *for* construct, which indicates that the step is optional.

Subroutines are provided by writing the name of the subroutine with a list of its parameters, followed by indented code which represents the actions that the subroutine is to carry out. For example, the fragment shown below represents a subroutine that finds the sum of *n* integers held in an array *a*.

```
7.1    FindSum(a,n,sum)
7.2        Set sum to zero
7.3        For i from 1 to n do
7.4        Add a[i] to sum
```

An *if* statement is implemented very simply. Its structure is shown below:

```
If condition then
    statements1
{else
    statements2}
```

where *statements1* are executed when *condition* is true, otherwise *statements2* are executed.

These, then, are the control, looping, and subroutine facilities of the program design language. While they are not as precise as those facilities found in a programming language—they are not meant to be—they represent a detailed design notation that can be easily translated into the vast majority of high-level programming languages.

11.4   OBJECTS, OPERATIONS, AND FUNCTIONAL DECOMPOSITION

The aim of this section is to demonstrate the relationship between the functional decomposition process and the operations and objects that have been identified during the analysis stage of the software project. In order to do this the design of part of the computer operator system described in the previous chapter will be developed

I shall assume that a number of operations and objects have been identified during the early stages of analysis. Two objects have been discovered: peripherals and peripheral queues. There are a number of peripheral queue operations: *start(peripheral, first)*, which returns a record containing the file details of the first file *first* in a queue for *peripheral*; *move(peripheral, user, name, new_position)*, which moves a file *name* belonging to *user* in the queue associated with *peripheral* to a new position *new_position*; *check(name, user, peripheral)*, which checks that a particular file *name* owned by *user* is in the queue associated with *peripheral*; *remove(peripheral, head)*, which removes the head of the queue of print files associated with *peripheral*; *add(user, name, peripheral)*, which adds a file *name* associated with *user* to the queue associated with *peripheral*; *movenext(current, next)*, which given the queue element *current*, returns with the next element of the file queue *next*; *last(current)*, which is true if the file element in the queue is the null element; *numbinqueue(peripheral)*, which gives the number of items in a queue for a peripheral; and *moveq(peripheral1, peripheral2)*, which moves all the files in the queue associated with *peripheral2* to the queue associated with *peripheral1*.

I shall also assume that there are also some operations on peripherals. The two that are important for us in this example are the operations *availableperiph(peripheral)*, which checks that a peripheral is available for printing to, and *validperiphname(peripheral)* which checks that peripheral is a valid name.

The top-level design of the subsystem is

1   Initialize any variables
2   Repeat
3   Read in a print queue command
4   Execute the print queue command
5   Until the print queue subsystem is shut down

The subsystem continually reads in a command from the computer operators, and then executes the command. Inside step 4 will also be a specification of the error processing that is to occur. There are three commands: a command that prints out all the elements of a queue, a command that moves a particular element in a queue to a new position, and a function that moves a queue for a particular peripheral to the queue for another peripheral.

The next level of refinement is shown below. Here, step 4 has been further refined to reflect the commands that need to be executed. Notice that the command *terminate* has been included. This is a command that the operator types to terminate the operation of the print queue system.

4.1   If command is valid then
4.2   Decode command
4.3   Case command type of

4.4   Terminate:
4.5   Process terminate command

4.6   Move queue:
4.7   Process move queue command

4.8   Move file:
4.9   Process move file command

4.10   Print queue:
4.11   Process the print queue command
4.12   else
4.13   Display an invalid command error message

The next level of refinement involves the expansion of the four commands. Step 4.5 is straightforward. All it involves is the setting of a flag which terminates the loop that continually processes commands.

4.5.1   Set terminate flag to true

This means that step 5 can be refined to

5.1   Until terminate flag

which means that step 1 can be further refined to

1.1   Set terminate flag to false

The remaining steps need much more refinement. For example, step 4.7 needs to prompt the operator for two peripheral names: a peripheral whose queue is to be moved, and a peripheral whose queue is to be increased by the addition of the queue associated with the first peripheral. These peripherals need to be checked for validity and then the first peripheral needs to be checked to see if there are any empty items in its queue.

4.7.1	Prompt the operator for two peripherals p1 and p2
4.7.2	If validperiphname(p1) then
4.7.3	If validperiphname(p2) then
4.7.4	If availableperiph(p1) then
4.7.5	If availableperiph(p2) then
4.7.6	If numbinqueue(p1) is greater than zero then
4.7.7	Moveq(p2,p1)
4.7.8	else
4.7.9	Display an empty queue error
4.7.10	else
4.7.11	Display an unavailable second peripheral error
4.7.12	else
4.7.12	Display an unavailable first peripheral error
4.7.13	else
4.7.14	Display an invalid second peripheral error
4.7.15	else
4.7.16	Display an invalid first peripheral error

A major point to notice in this decomposition is that some of the steps are underlined. These steps represent operations that have been identified and may even have been implemented; although these operations are at a high-level of abstraction, there is no need to refine them further.

The refinement of step 4.9 is very similar to that of step 4.7: first, the operator is prompted for a peripheral name, a file name, a user name, and a new position. The peripheral name is checked to see if it is valid and available. Next the queue attached to the peripheral is scanned in order to detect whether the file belonging to the user is in fact in the queue, the new position is then checked against the number of items in the queue to see if it is valid. If all these checks are positive, then the queue element is moved; if any are invalid, then a suitable error message is displayed.

SAQ Write down the refinement of step 4.9. Do not forget to use the operations that have been defined previously.

SOLUTION The refinement is shown following the the SAQ. ❑

4.9.1   Prompt the operator for the peripheral name p1, the file name fl, the user name us and the new position in the queue pos.

4.9.2   If <u>validperiphname(p1)</u> then

4.9.3   If <u>availableperiph(p1)</u> then

4.9.4.   If <u>check(fl, us, p1)</u> then

4.9.5   If <u>numbinqueue(p1)</u> ≥ pos and pos is positive then

4.9.6   <u>move(p1,us,fl,pos)</u>

4.9.7   else

4.9.8   Display a queue position error message

4.9.9   else

4.9.10   Display a file not found error message

4.9.11   else

4.9.12   Display an unavailable peripheral error message

4.9.13   else

4.9.14   Display an invalid peripheral name error message

Again notice how the operations that have already been identified have been underlined.

The next refinement is that of step 4.11. The operator has to be prompted for a peripheral name. This name is checked to see if it is valid, and then it is checked to discover whether it represents an available peripheral. If both checks succeed, then the queue associated with the peripheral is traversed until the end of the queue is reached. Each time a queue element is encountered the file name and the user name are extracted and displayed

SAQ Write down the refinement of step 4.11 Do not forget to use the operations that have been defined previously.

SOLUTION The refinement is shown below, after the SAQ. ❑

4.11.1   Prompt the operator for the peripheral name p1

4.11.2   If <u>validperiphname(p1)</u> then

4.11.3   If <u>availableperiph(p1)</u> then

4.11.4   <u>start(p1, el)</u>

4.11.5   While not <u>last(el)</u> do

4.11.6   Extract the user name and the file name from el

4.11.7   Display the user name and the file name

4.11.8   <u>movenext(el,el)</u>

4.11.12   else display an unavailable peripheral error

4.11.13   else display an invalid peripheral error

Here the traversal of the print queue is achieved by means of the iterators *start*, *last*, and *movenext*.

The process of functional decomposition, then, is a process of lowering the level of abstraction and allowing more and more detail to intrude. The process stops when either of two

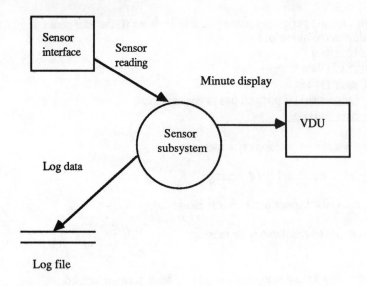

Figure 11.1 Top-level data flow diagram of the sensor subsystem.

conditions occur: a statement has been refined to the point where it can be implemented using a programming language; or a statement represents an operation that has been identified during the early part of the project and may even have already been implemented.

11.5 FUNCTIONAL DECOMPOSITION AND DATA FLOW DIAGRAMS

So far this chapter has treated the functional decomposition process in isolation: as a technique that conjures each level of refinement out of thin air. This often gives the student who is new to the technique many problems. However, there is a close relationship between data flow diagrams and the eventual product of the functional decomposition process. This enables a reading of a data flow diagram requirements specification to guide the functional decomposition process.

In order to illustrate this, consider a small system that processes readings from a set of remote sensors attached to an aircraft wing in a wind tunnel. Each reading consists of a sensor number and an integer which represents the pressure on that part of the wing. Sometimes a sensor will malfunction; this can give rise to an invalid sensor number or a zero reading. The function of the system is to take a sequence of these readings and display the average pressure for each sensor over the last minute of operation, together with the number of malfunctions for each sensor over the minute. Each time that a sensor malfunctions a message is sent to a log file, which is processed by another system in order to detect which sensors need attention. The context diagram for the system is shown as Fig. 11.1.

Sensor readings are processed and produce data, which is written to the log, and a report of the last minute's data. The program design language fragment corresponding to this is

   Carry out sensor functions

The next level of the data flow diagram is shown as Fig. 11.2.

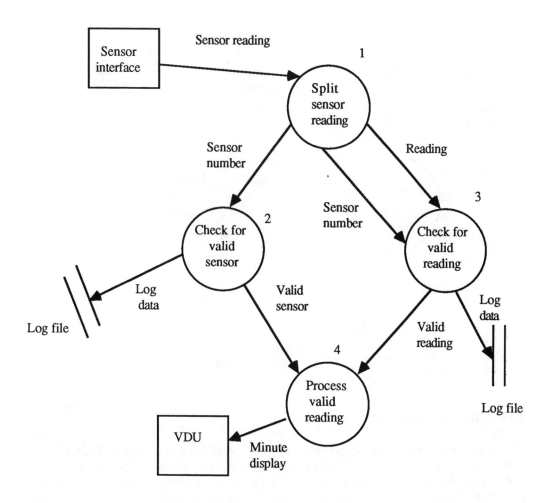

Figure 11.2 The refinement of the data flow diagrams in Fig. 11.1

The next level of the functional decomposition is

1	Repeat
2	Obtain a reading from the sensor interface
3	Split the reading into sensor number s and reading rd
4	If s is an invalid sensor reading then
5	Write log file data to the log file
6	else
7	If rd is an invalid reading then
8	Write log file data to the log file
9	else
10	Process the valid reading
11	Until the wind tunnel experiment has ended

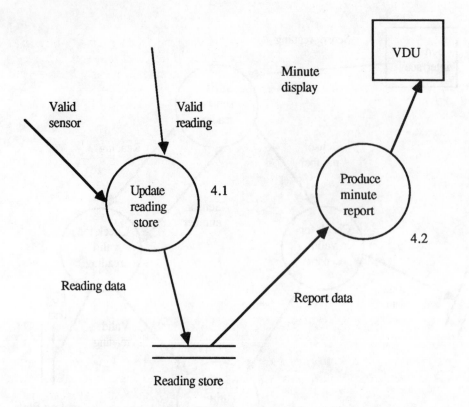

Figure 11.3 The refinement of bubble 4.

The functional decomposition differs from the data flow diagram. The main difference is that control flow details have intruded. One of the major rules in developing a data flow diagram is that this type of sequencing information should not be included, hence the difference. However, the data flow diagram does give the designer carrying out the functional decomposition a good idea of many of the sub-steps that have to be generated from a particular step in a data flow diagram. For example, all the bubbles in the data flow diagram appear as functions in the functional decomposition.

The expansion of bubble 4 is shown in Fig. 11.3. Here a valid reading and a valid sensor number are processed with, eventually, a minute report being produced.

The program design language fragment for this part of the data flow diagram is shown below:

10.1   For i from 1 to 60 do
10.2   Deposit the valid reading and valid sensor data into reading store
10.3   Produce a minute report

This process will continue with each data flow diagram being augmented by control flow facilities until, eventually, the final design is produced with operations on objects in the data flow diagram being replaced by calls on subroutines.

11.6 REFINING THE SYSTEM TESTS

During the process of design refinement and final coding of the top-level design of a system, the early system tests that exist in outline should be expanded further, and converted into test procedures. As an example of this, consider a test for the computer operator file query subsystem which forms part of an operating system.

> System test 4.2.4.2
>
> This test checks that if the move command is typed in with an invalid peripheral name for the peripheral whose queue is to be transferred then a suitable error message is displayed.

The first expansion of this test would perhaps involve specifying what is a correct peripheral name. Let us assume that it is a four-character string with the first two characters being letters and the last two characters being digits, e.g. LP01 would be a valid name. The second expansion might involve the specification of what error message is to be displayed.

> System test 4.2.4.2
>
> This test checks that if the move command is typed in with an invalid peripheral name for the peripheral whose queue is to be transferred then a suitable error message is displayed. A selection of peripheral names that do not contain two initial letter characters followed by two numeric characters should be chosen. The test should check that the message
>
> *** Invalid peripheral name — should be two letters followed by two digits.
>
> is displayed at the operator console.

This test can then be expanded to become a test procedure in which the instructions for carrying out the test are specified. Normally a test procedure will contain details of prompts, messages which are to be displayed by the software under test, where to find the software under test, where to find files of test data, and where to store test outcomes. The test procedure for the test above is shown below:

> Test procedure 4.2.4.2
>
> This test procedure checks that the file queue subsystem of the OXS operating system responds correctly to invalid peripheral names. The subsystem will be found in file OPQ.TST. Execute this file and you will be prompted by the > character. Type in the string MOVE followed by an invalid peripheral name (A valid peripheral name is two letters followed by two digits). The system should produce the error message
>
> *** Invalid peripheral name — should be two letters followed by two digits.
>
> followed by the prompt > again. Carry out this test a number of times, checking that the error message is displayed. Ensure that the software tool Playback is installed during the test session and that you write its output to the file TST4/2/4/2.INT after the test session is terminated.

The description of the test is self-explanatory except the part of it dealing with the software tool Playback. This is a software tool that captures all the keystrokes initiated by the tester, and allows the test input to be saved in a file. This input file would be invaluable if this part of the system is retested—either during subsequent development or during maintenance.

11.7 SUMMARY

This chapter has described how the top-level program code of a system can be designed by means of functional decomposition: a design technique that relies on a divide and conquer paradigm for its operation. This technique allows the developer gradually to refine a design expressed in a program design language, until the bottom level of its components are reached. In the case where an object-oriented programming language is used, the bottom-level components are the operations that have been identified during analysis, or program code that carries out the flow of control in the top level of the system.

The chapter also described how a designer is able to get a lot of help during the functional decomposition process by an examination of the data flow diagram that represents the functional decomposition of a system. Finally, the process of refining outline system tests so that they become test procedures was described. I have now completed the description of all the tools, methods and tactics required to carry out object-oriented software engineering. Chapter 14 will describe a case study showing all these components in action together. However, before this, the important topic of prototyping will be discussed.

SOFTWARE PROTOTYPING

AIMS

- To describe the rationale behind software prototyping.
- To describe how object-oriented techniques are able to support prototyping.
- To outline the different forms of prototyping.
- To describe how a prototyping project using object-oriented methods is organized and managed.

12.1 INTRODUCTION

In this book I have concentrated on describing a form of software engineering which, although different from conventional, phase-oriented software engineering, still has many similarities: for example, many of the software tasks are the same, and much of the management that is required is indistinguishable from that employed on normal software projects.

This chapter describes a more radical departure from the model presented in the book. It describes a technique known as prototyping which enables a working model of a system to be delivered early and demonstrated to the customer. Object-oriented programming allows a form of prototyping that relies on software reusability, and this chapter describes how this can be taken advantage of in producing a early version of a software system.

12.2 WHAT IS PROTOTYPING?

One of the common *cris de coeur* heard from software developers is: 'if only you had shown me the system at the beginning of the project'. This *cri de coeur* arises late in the project—normally during system or acceptance testing—when the customer discovers that the system that has been built does not satisfy user requirements. Prototyping is an attempt to deliver such an early system. Three forms of prototyping have been identified: throw-away prototyping, incremental prototyping and evolutionary prototyping.

Throw-away prototyping involves the developer constructing an early version of a system, and checking it with the user. When the user indicates that the prototype matches requirements, conventional software development starts, based on a requirements specification that has been constructed from a study of the prototype. The term *throw-away prototyping* arises from the fact that once a prototype has been agreed with the customer it is not used in the subsequent development that follows the prototyping process.

Incremental prototyping is really a euphemism for staged delivery. What this entails is the developer partitioning a software system to be delivered into sets of non-overlapping functions, with each delivered version of the system implementing a new subset of the functions. For example, a chemical plant control system would normally have four non-overlapping sets of functions: monitoring functions, control functions, user interface functions, and optimization and management information functions. The latter are used by chemical engineers who need to know about the detailed functioning of the system in the past, in order to optimize the operation of the plant in the future.

Incremental development is always a good idea. It leads to the establishment of small teams with little of the communicational overhead that bedevils large projects and soaks up valuable development effort—some large projects have had so much communicational overhead that adding staff to the project when the delivery date was becoming compromised has actually made the project later. As well as being a good idea in project management terms, it can also be used as a prototyping strategy. For example, a developer could decide on a delivery plan whereby those functions that were fuzzy or ill-expressed were delivered in the earliest versions of the system.

Evolutionary prototyping is in complete antithesis to the previous two approaches. In this form of rapid development a prototype is first constructed, agreed with the user, and then forms the basis for subsequent development. For example, a form of evolutionary development used in commercial data processing involves the developer producing a slow prototype and then devoting much of the rest of the project to the process of improving its running time.

Evolutionary prototyping is the most promising of the three approaches described here. It is an attempt to cater for change on the software project. Already, from this book, and maybe from your own experiences, you will have discovered that changes in requirements afflict software projects throughout their life and also during the maintenance of the subsequent system that is produced. Evolutionary prototyping provides a framework, and a number of mechanisms, whereby change can be easily accommodated almost right up to delivery. This will be discussed in further detail in Section 12.4. However, before proceeding to that section it is worth reviewing some of the techniques that can be used for software prototyping.

12.3 TECHNIQUES FOR SOFTWARE PROTOTYPING.

A wide variety of techniques are available for producing an early version of a system. They range from very low-tech solutions, to much more sophisticated tool-based techniques. A selection are described in this section.

- *Relaxing the quality assurance practices*—if any—of the software developer. Here the developer attempts to hack out a system, or more likely part of a system, by ignoring many of the developmental and managerial standards that would normally be obeyed. This might include producing only an outline requirements specification, skimping on unit testing, not carrying out reviews, or not producing a design.

- *Employing a very high-level language.* Such programming languages usually have a high-level data type which enables a massive reduction in code size to take place. Typically, a very high-level programming language enables a programmer to code a system in five to ten times less text than a conventional programming language such as Pascal or COBOL. Typical very high-level languages include APL, which has the array as its basic data type; SETL, which has the set as it data type; and LISP, which has the linked list as its data type.

- *Using a tool set.* Such tool sets contain a number of table-driven processors which are able to be driven by the contents of tables written by the user, together with a smooth interface facility which enables the software that is produced to be glued together effectively. Almost certainly the archetypal tool set for prototyping is UNIX. It contains a number of processors such as YACC, LEX and AWK which enable software to be developed quickly, together with the pipe facility which enables each chunk of software developed using the processors to be effectively integrated together.

- *Employing an execution specification system.* Such systems take a requirements specification produced by a developer, and then execute it. This is a very attractive technique since the requirements specification has to be developed, and if it can be executed no extra work is required for prototyping. There is only one problem with this technique: the specification notation that is used has to be exact—artificial intelligence techniques have not advanced to the point where a requirements specification notation containing natural language can be executed. The requirements specification notation that needs to be executed has to be written using discrete mathematics.

- *Implementing only a subset of a system.* This is a strategy that forms the basis of incremental prototyping. Here the developer identifies which parts of a system are at most risk; usually these are those parts where the technology is new, the requirements are fuzzy, or the user is unfamiliar with the functionality. This part of the system is implemented first and shown to the user, and techniques such as information hiding are used to enable modification to be carried out relatively easily if there are any problems with this early delivery.

- *Using a fourth-generation language.* A fourth-generation language is a programming language used for commercial data processing applications. It provides a large degree of saving in terms of program size. Fourth-generation programming languages often offer a saving of ten to one in terms of textual program size over other commercial data processing languages such as COBOL or RPG2. They achieve this by a number of means. First, they provide very high-level facilities for report generation, which is probably the most frequent operation in commercial data processing. Second, if they interface with a relational database management system, then they provide a very high-level data type, much like very high-level programming languages. Relational databases are conceptually just collections of tables: all the programmer is aware of is that the data is organized into tabular form. A fourth-generation programming language, which interfaces with a relational database system, usually contains high-level facilities for accessing stored data that are equivalent to many lines of conventional program code. For example, complex queries such as 'list all the products that we stock which are manufactured by Jones but which are out of stock', can be usually written in one line of program code.

- *Employ reusable software.* The theory behind this form of prototyping is relatively simple: if there is the possibility of keeping a library of reusable components, then a rapid version of a system can be developed by just bolting together the components, and writing some top-level program code which carries out the sequencing of the actions that are required. This, indeed, is the strategy that will be described in the remainder of this chapter. Object-oriented programming languages provide a number of facilities that make this form of prototyping feasible.

12.4   PROTOTYPING AND OBJECT-ORIENTED PROGRAMMING LANGUAGES

This book has only really concentrated on developing system from a fresh start with little other software being used. One of the features of object-oriented programming languages is that they contain facilities that enable the developer to build up a library of reusable objects and operations. In this case development would consist of identifying candidate objects, modifying them to match the perceived requirements of an application, and then writing the top-level program code which controls the time sequencing processing that affects the objects.

Indeed, when the developer has an extensive library, an object-oriented approach is suitable for prototyping. Before looking at how prototyping can be managed, monitored, and controlled on an object-oriented project, it is worth looking at the facilities that object-oriented languages offer for reusability.

The first facility is polymorphism. You will remember that polymorphism allows a developer to define a particular aggregate or composite object, and then instantiate that object for differing component types. For example, assume that we have defined a symbol table object which might normally contain identifiers for a compiler that we have written. Object-oriented programming languages allow the programmer to instantiate a new object which might, instead of containing identifiers, contain items of another type, e.g. names of products in a warehousing application, the names of accounts in a banking application, the names of planes in an air traffic control application, or the names of reactors in a chemical process control application.

The second facility that enables us to support prototyping from a reusable library of components is inheritance. Here objects are built up from base objects with the addition of further components, both data and operations. For example, a simple library system may have defined an object called a book, together with a number of operations on books such as those associated with borrowing, returning, and enquiring about the state of a book. Let us assume that the library decides to stock journals. It is a relatively easy thing to do to derive a new object that represents journals and which inherits many of the properties of books.

The reason why both inheritance and polymorphism enable prototyping to occur is that the derivation of objects and operations from already developed objects and operations often takes no more than a few lines of program code. In effect program code, which if written anew would be hundreds of lines long, can be developed by means of the programmer writing a small number of extra lines of program code.

In order to show how both polymorphism and inheritance work in a prototyping scenario, consider part of a purchase order system that we have decided to develop. Part of such a system will be a back-orders subsystem that consists of a queue of orders that cannot currently be satisfied from the stock held by the customer. This queue will be added to whenever an order or part order is placed which cannot be satisfied, and will be decreased whenever a delivery of products is made. Whenever a delivery occurs the system will scan the queue and take off any orders that can be satisfied from the delivered stock. Let us assume that we have identified a number of objects and operations required for the back-orders subsystem.

The objects are the queue and the orders that make up the queue. Let us also assume that we have found a queue object which was used in a communications system that has previously been developed, and a purchase order object which was developed for a simple invoicing system.

It is a relatively simple job to instantiate the queue so that it contains purchase orders. This, together with its operations, can then be quickly incorporated into a prototype and demonstrated to the customer. The customer will almost invariably be unhappy with what is demonstrated, and will make suggestions for amendment; the aim of the following paragraphs is to show how relatively easy it is to cater for many of these amendments using an object-oriented approach. Some of the remarks from customers for the back-order system are shown in italics below, and the actions taken by the developer reproduced in roman type.

We always keep track of the date on which an order was placed in the back-orders queue. This is fairly typical of a remark made during prototyping where the developer has forgotten to put some data in a record or in some aggregate data structure. This is a relatively straightforward change. It would involve using inheritance to derive a new object from the original purchase order object by adding a date component. A new operation to extract the date component from a purchase order would need to be written.

Usually we add items to the queue in the order in which we receive the purchase orders. However, there are some customers whose business we especially value and we tend to put them near to the head of the queue. Again this is a typical change that often emerges from the prototyping process when a customer asks for a modification to the access discipline that occurs. If the original queue that we used in the prototype was a first-in, first-out store, then the operation to add items to the queue would need to be changed. If important customers were to be added to the queue at its head, then an operation to do this would need to be written. However, if there was some form of priority mechanism where different customers were placed in the queue at a position dependent on their worth to the developer, then a more complicated operation would have to be written. Even so, because information hiding would have been used, this operation could have been written without affecting other operations.

We need to have a facility whereby we can remove orders from the queue, e.g. a customer could cancel the order. Again, if the original queue was only a first-in, first-out queue, then the only operation that removed orders from the queue would be one that removed the head of the queue. A new operation would need to be developed to scan the queue and remove the particular order that was cancelled. If the original queue provided an iterator operator, then this operation could be coded up relatively quickly. Again, since information hiding would be used, this would have no effect on the other operations on the queue.

These, then, are a sample of some of the changes that crop up during prototyping. As you can see they can normally be accommodated reasonably well by employing an object-oriented programming language. The next section will describe how such languages can be used within prototyping.

12.5   EVOLUTIONARY PROTOTYPING AND OBJECT-ORIENTED PROGRAMMING

Object-oriented programming languages, and many of the ideas presented in previous chapters, lend themselves well to evolutionary prototyping: the development of an initial prototype, followed by a series of improvements applied to the prototype in order to make it meet user requirements. The aim of this section is to see how the software development life-cycle presented in this book needs to be modified in order to cope with this rather dynamic form of software development.

In describing how to use evolutionary prototyping I shall assume that planning for a project that uses this technique has taken place. Given that this has happened, the next stage is to carry out a form of rapid analysis. This involves examining the statement of requirements of the system, and interviewing potential and actual users. The aim of the initial analysis is to gain a high-level view of the functions of a system, and also identify any objects and operations required. Initial analysis is an important task to carry out, since it provides a base for the prototyping effort and ensures that the initial prototype will not be too off beam.

The product of the initial analysis will be a high-level data flow diagram, usually no more than two or three levels—often just one level—and a list of the objects and operations that are needed. It is important to point out that initial analysis should not take too long—once it starts taking longer than a fortnight you should get worried. Remember if you do start spending a large amount of time on analysis, then there is the distinct possibility that large amounts of the specification you produce will be rendered obsolete by the prototyping process.

Once you think that you have captured the essence of the initial analysis, the next stage is to design and implement the first prototype. This consists of a number of activities.

- The existing database of objects and operations is scanned in order to discover any that match the objects discovered in the analysis. If the developer has previously carried out even a few projects using object-oriented technology, then this library will usually consist of general objects such as stacks, queues, sets, sequences, and functions.

- The objects are brought in and stored in a project file, any obvious differences are catered for by means of applying the polymorphism and inheritance facilities of the implementation language.

- The system is designed in terms of a program design language, with the designer using the top-level data flow diagram to drive the design process. The final level of the design will involve basic facilities such as input/output or calls on object operations.

- The design is then translated into program code and combined with the objects and operations identified in the first step.

- The final step is to create a test database of data which the first prototype, constructed in the previous step, can use.

The first prototype has now been constructed. The next step is prototype iteration. Here the prototype is demonstrated and changed until the user/customer is happy with what has been shown.

During this process the developer should ensure that the following criteria are met:

- The demonstration period is short. Normally one hour is advised. An hour is long enough for anyone to stare at a VDU. A demonstration lasting an hour will usually give rise to a large number of changes which often seriously affect the functionality and require implementation before further prototype evaluation can take place.

- That only one component, usually corresponding to a data flow bubble at the top level of a requirements specification, is examined at at time. For example, a natural candidate for an evaluation session for a purchasing system would be that part of the system which dealt with the back-orders queues.

- That a script is produced which details all the functions that are to be invoked together with the order in which they are invoked. This will include descriptions of the function execution, the data entry procedures, any report writing procedures, and any error messages or error reports that are generated.

- That the user be allowed to operate the prototype. This encourages the user to think possessively of the prototype and leads to a much better rapport between the developer and the customer.

After a demonstration, the developer should issue a report form which details the important events and concerns that the demonstration gave rise to. This report should detail the following: what new functions were exercised in the demonstration session, usually this would be specified in terms of data flow bubble numbers; what functions were exercised during the demonstration which were left over from a previous demonstration, e.g. a previous demonstration may have given rise to some change requests and the demonstration being documented may have shown these amended functions in action; the development staff who were involved in the demonstration; the customer staff involved; and any suggested modifications that arose from the customer's unhappiness with a particular demonstration of functionality.

Prototype iteration—the process of modification, demonstration, and elicitation of change requests from the customer—continues until the customer is happy with the system that has been shown. The time that this iterative cycle takes really depends on a number of factors: the experience of the developer with prototyping; the experience of the customer with prototyping; the tools that are used, some are quicker to apply modifications than others; and the quantity of requirements that are to be prototyped—a system where only a small number of functions are fuzzy will obviously take a shorter time to prototype than a system that requires full prototyping.

There are two important points to make about the modification, demonstration, and elicitation of change request process: first, the specification should be kept in step with the prototype. If this does not occur, then the developer will have major problems when further change requests are demanded by the customer—it will not be known what functions affect each other or what parts of the system correspond to the requests. The need for the requirements specification to be kept in step with the prototype virtually means that some form of CASE technology should be used in maintaining the requirements specification.

The second point is that it is optional whether the design that was produced during the derivation of the initial prototype should be kept in step with the prototype. This is less critical than keeping the requirements specification in step. Normally most companies who carry out evolutionary prototyping re-engineer the design from the final code of the prototype, merely by examining the code and discerning the overall structure.

After the customer has finally signed off the prototype, and if the design has not been kept in step with the prototype, the design is derived. The prototype is now at the stage where the developer has virtually carried out all the system testing of functionality that is required. The user has signed off the prototype and said that the functions that were demonstrated were those that were required. However, at this stage the developer may have delivered a prototype which, although functionally complete, has performance problems. The next stage in the development process is to tune the prototype.

Tuning involves the developer examining the implemented objects and applying local optimizations. For example, the developer may have used a singly linked sequence for holding a queue and the application required the customer to traverse this queue backwards and forwards, hence requiring a doubly linked list. In this case the list would be augmented with a backward link as well as a forward link. Another example of a local optimization might occur in a table which was searched linearly. The developer might find out that only a few items were normally searched for. An increase in response time can easily be achieved if when an item is found after a search, it is placed at the beginning of the table.

These are just a few of the large number of optimizations that can be carried out. What is important about the optimization process is that it should be carried out incrementally with the final set of stored data that the application will manipulate. By carrying out the optimization process incrementally—either an operation at a time, or a group of operations associated with an object at a time—the developer can ensure that if a programming error occurred during the optimization process, the location of the error can be discovered very easily.

When the optimization is complete, system testing starts. Now, as has already been stated, the prototype evaluation cycle involves the user signing off the functionality of the system. There is thus no need to test the functionality of the system during system testing: all that is required is to test for non-functional requirements such as response time and memory usage. The system testing will involve using real data for the application, both the data that is normally expected, and also data that occurs when the system is operating at peak load. When the system tests have been developed, the system can then be handed over to the user.

It is worth stating that, just as with conventional software projects, it is useful for evolutionary prototyping projects to have a number of reviews scheduled. Two useful reviews would be the rapid analysis review, to which a customer representative would be invited. The aim of this review is to check that the products of the rapid analysis phase matched, in concept, the system that was to be developed. Another review, or really set of reviews, would be the final prototype review, which occurs prior to the signing off of the final prototype. The main aim of this review is to ensure that all the functional requirements of the system have been demonstrated, and all the problems and changes notified by the customer have been taken into account by the developer.

There are major differences between this form of software development and conventional, phase-oriented development (Connell, 1989).

- The requirements analysis and requirements specification phases are replaced by the prototype iteration phase.
- There is an initial phase called rapid analysis which does not form part of a conventional software project.
- The prototype iteration phase takes much longer than the conventional requirements analysis and requirements specification phase. The reason for this is clear: in this phase the developer is carrying out requirements analysis, requirements specification, coding, some design, and functional system testing.
- Since the prototype iteration phase takes such a long time, all the subsequent phases in an evolutionary prototyping project will be shorter because they are telescoped together.
- System tuning replaces the conventional programming phase.
- The functional requirements of the system are not frozen until a very late stage in the evolutionary prototyping project.

12.6 SUMMARY

This chapter has shown how evolutionary prototyping can be achieved by the use of an object-oriented programming language. Such languages contain a number of facilities—inheritance, polymorphism, and information hiding—that enable the character of a system to be changed very quickly, and consequently can be used to develop rapidly a prototype that can easily be changed.

12.7 FURTHER READING

Connell (1989) is an excellent book which describes how evolutionary prototyping can be carried out on commercial data processing projects. Many of the ideas described in this chapter were taken from this book. Hekmatpour and Ince (1988) as well as describing a toolset for evolutionary prototyping, also contains an excellent review of the prototyping process.

BIBLIOGRAPHY

Connell, J. L. (1989) *Structured Rapid Prototyping*, Prentice-Hall, Englewood Cliffs, NJ.

Hekmatpour, S. and Ince, D. C. (1988) *Software Prototyping, Formal Methods and VDM*, Addison-Wesley, Reading, Mass.

13

THE WHOLE PROCESS

AIMS

- To bring together all the activities that have been described in the previous twelve chapters.
- To provide the framework necessary to access the case study presented in the next chapter.
- To describe some of the developmental models that are possible using an object-oriented approach.

13.1 INTRODUCTION

The last eleven chapters described a number of techniques that are used at different points in the software project. So far you have not seen them combined together. This is the role of the next chapter, which describes a case study that shows all the activities combined. The role of this chapter is to set the scene for this final chapter and describe, without using any examples, the sequencing and interrelationship between these tasks.

13.2 ENTITY ANALYSIS

The first event that occurs in a software project is the receipt of the statement of requirements. This document may be received after a contract between a developer and a customer has been signed, or may be received as part of the bidding process for a contract.

The statement of requirements is processed by the software developer and any problems with it identified. These problems will include ambiguities, contradictions, platitudes, design directives, and implementation directives. The developer will then examine any manual systems and interview members of staff from the customer's organization in order to get a feel for what system is required. The developer will make rough notes about the functions of the system, but will often delay specifying the functionality of the system in any detail. The major activity at this stage is to carry out an entity analysis. This process consists of the following:

- Discovering the entities in a system by looking at the base objects that the system manipulates.
- For each identified object, listing the items of data associated with these objects; these will be the entity attributes.
- Looking at the external events that occur in the application and discovering how these are communicated to the system.
- Defining the actions that need to respond to the events.
- Identifying the action attributes for each action.

THE WHOLE PROCESS   203

Once this process has been completed, the actions that have been identified are ordered in time using an entity life history. This notation shows the relationship between the actions that a particular entity suffers and specifies the ordering of these actions.

The final step in the process of entity analysis is the identification of the basic operations in the system. These are operations which cannot be split up into further operations, e.g. in a car hire system the operation of returning a car from a hiring. Once the entity analysis has concluded, the data model that has been produced is then reviewed for correctness. Also, at this stage, scenarios might be generated—a scenario being a sequence of actions which occur in the application, e.g. in a hotel booking application a typical scenario might be a customer booking a room and then cancelling it. These scenarios are used to validate the data model by checking that the entity life histories contain operations in the right order which correspond to a scenario.

13.3 DATA DESIGN

Once the data design has been completed, the next step in the development process is to design the data. This will be done in terms of abstract data types. In Chapter 6 the main abstract data types were described. They included sequences, maps, and sets. The design of the abstract data types is driven by a consideration of the relationship between data items in the application to be computerized. For example, if the data items are ordered, a queue would be the natural choice of abstract data type. At the end of the data design process the developer will have expressed the system in terms of a series of abstract data types which consists of a data description and a specification of a series of operations. These can now be implemented.

13.4 CLASS IMPLEMENTATION

Once the individual abstract data types in an application have been specified, the next step is to implement them. For a particular abstract data type there will be a large number of implementation options. For example, a queue can be implemented using linked list schemes or by using an array. The decision about the implementation will be based on factors such as memory limitations, response time, and the complexity of programming. The object-oriented language described in this book, C^{++}, contains a feature known as a class which enables an abstract data type to be implemented in terms of data declarations and functions. Each class will be implemented and class tested; each function is tested in isolation and then in combination with other functions in the class. The strategy for carrying out this class testing will be developed by the programmer charged with the construction of the class.

In the vast majority of applications, classes will be interrelated to each other: a class may use facilities provided by a number of other classes, which in turn use facilities provided by other classes, and so on. In this case, a form of integration testing will be carried out. The integration policy adopted will have been decided upon at a comparatively early stage in the project—usually during data design.

It is worth stating at this point that a software developer who has been carrying out a large amount of object-oriented software development will have built up a class library. Many of the

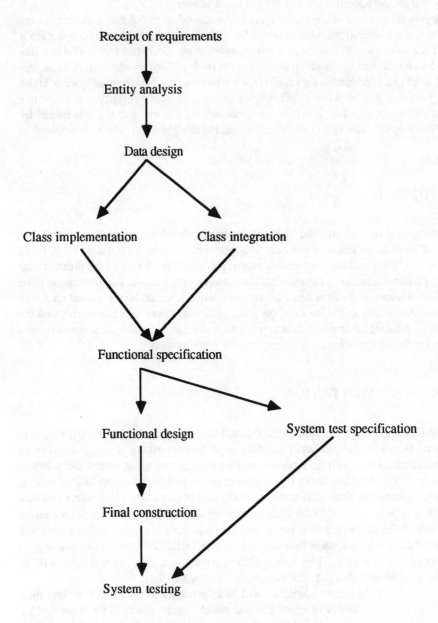

Figure 13.1 An object-oriented development model.

components in this library could be directly used in the system that is being built up rather than being implemented anew.

13.5 FUNCTIONAL SPECIFICATION

So far the functions of the system have been ignored in the development. By this stage of the project all the abstract data types will have been implemented, and all that is necessary is to determine the functions of the system and specify them. The notation used for this in the book is the data flow diagram. The developer will use the results of the early investigation of the system to build up a hierarchic graphic view of the flow of data in the system to be developed, together with a description of the processes in the system. Once this functional specification is complete, the developer can start work on the system test specification: the detailed description of the tests that are need to check out the functions of the system. An outline system test specification is usually constructed and expanded out in the later stages of the project.

One of the pleasant aspects of the functional specification process is that much of the work has already been carried out. A developer who uses an object-oriented approach will discover that much of the data flow diagram being constructed consists of bubbles that represent operations which form part of the classes that implement the system's abstract data types. The data flow diagram essentially only consists of a specification of the high-level processing in a system.

13.6 FUNCTIONAL DESIGN

The next step is to carry out a design of the system. At this stage all the classes corresponding to abstract data types will have been implemented. All that is required is to take the data flow diagrams developed during the functional specification phase and transform them into a design expressed in a program design language. Chapter 11 showed how this process, while not being a totally automatic process of transliteration from the data flow diagram is, nevertheless, relatively straightforward. Once the design is complete, all that is required is for the program design language statements to be translated into statements in the programming language used. During the functional design process, the system tests that have been expressed in outline during functional specification are expanded until they become detailed tests.

13.7 FINAL CONSTRUCTION

The final task is to bring together the coded part of the system which deals with control and the already implemented classes, and then apply the system tests which were refined during the functional design process. Once these tests have been successful, the system can then be delivered.

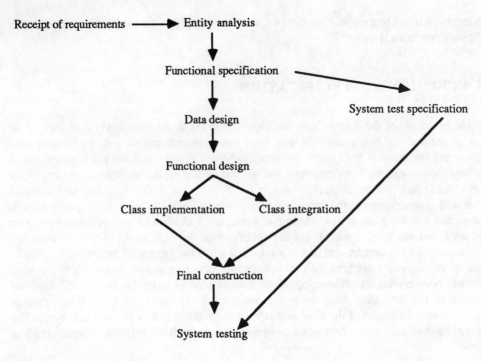

Figure 13.2 An alternative development model.

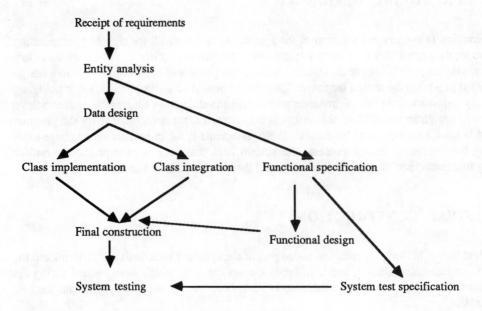

Figure 13.3 Another alternative development model

13.8 ALTERNATIVE DEVELOPMENT MODELS

The previous seven chapters have discussed a development model where the specification of functionality was delayed as late as possible. This mirrors practice of many commercial data processing projects which use relational data design methods. The process is shown in Fig. 13.1, where much of the front-end effort in the project involves data design. However, there may be a number of reasons for bringing forward the functional specification process, e.g. there may be a desire for a very accurate project costing early in the project, or the customer may only be happy discussing the functionality of the system during the analysis process. Two models of development that bring forward the functional specification process are shown as Figs 13.2 and 13.3. The first is strictly sequential, while the second model shows functional specification occurring in parallel to entity analysis and data design.

13.9 SUMMARY

This brief section has described how the various components presented in the previous chapters of this book can be integrated together to form one developmental whole. It has, thus, acted as a curtain raiser to the next and final chapter, which describes the ideas put into practice on a real application.

14

CASE STUDY

AIMS

- To describe the tools and techniques outlined in previous chapters within the context of a simple case study.
- To describe one of the models of object-oriented development described in the previous chapter within the context of a case study.

14.1 INTRODUCTION

Let us assume that we are a software developer and have received the following statement of requirements for a system for administering the booking of seats for an airline.

FLY EASY AIRLINES

The management of Fly Easy wish to have a system that administers the flight booking of its flights in the United Kingdom. The company schedules a number of flights between its London base and the main United Kingdom cities in one type of commuter aircraft which contains no more than 16 seats. The system will be operated by booking clerks who will either take flight bookings over the phone or at an airport. A number of functions are to be provided by the system:

BOOKING: the system should allow a booking clerk to book a flight for a particular passenger. The passenger would provide his or her name, their address, the flight date, and the flight required. The booking is then made. The customer is provided with the flight number of his or her flight.

LIST: the system should allow a booking clerk to provide a listing of passengers who are currently booked on a flight. The clerk should provide the flight number and its date.

CANCEL: the system should allow a booking clerk to cancel a particular flight that has already been booked for a particular customer. The customer should provide the flight number, the date of the flight, and his or her name and address.

The system should keep a list of customers who use our flights so that advertising material can be sent out with our latest offers.

The system should keep details of flights that are scheduled for up to 150 days into the future. On average we schedule eight flights per day.

Flight numbers are unique for a particular day. For example, although there might be a flight FE23 each day, there will be no two occurrences of that flight on any day.

14.2   ANALYSIS

This is quite a good, succinct statement of requirements. The only questions I would have are the following:

- Is it intended that the booking clerk carries out the purging of the customer file?
- There are no details of how the flight details are to be communicated to the system, should it be done by the system above or will there be a separate program for doing this?
- There is no mention about whether the system is continuous or should be closed down by a booking clerk?
- What happens to a flight record when the plane has taken off?

The answers to the question are the following: the system should allow a booking clerk to close it down at the end of the day; another system will carry out the purging of the customer file; a flight record will be archived after the flight has taken off on the next day following the flight; both this and the loading of the flight details should be carried out by another system.

This, then, is the system. The first stage is to identify the entities. In this example there are clearly four entities: a *flight*, a *seat*, a *customer*, and a *flight booking*. There are also a number of actions associated with the system and a series of attributes associated with each action.

- *Booking.* A customer provides his or her name and address, a destination city, and a date. The system then books a seat on a flight. The attributes for this are thus: customer name, customer address, destination, and date.
- *Check.* A customer provides a destination city and a date and the system determines whether there is an available seat. The attributes for this are thus destination and date.
- *Cancel.* A customer provides his or her name and address, date, and flight number. The system cancels the booking. The attributes for this are thus customer name, customer address, flight number, and date.
- *List.* A booking clerk provides the flight number of a flight and the date and the system lists all the passengers for that flight. The attributes for this are thus flight number and date.

Since the creation of flight details is not carried out by this system, actions associated with the processing of these details are, of course, not listed. We have now identified the entities, the actions, and their attributes; the only remaining task to carry out at this stage is to identify the entity attributes, i.e. the data that is associated with each entity. These are shown below:

- *Flight.* Attributes: flight number, destination, date, time of departure.
- *Customer.* Attributes: customer name, customer address.
- *Flight booking.* Attributes: flight number, date, customer name, customer address.
- *Seat.* Attributes: seat number.

The first two entities and the fourth entity together with their attributes are self-explanatory. The third entity, which this chapter concentrates on, provides the linking between flights and the customers who have booked a seat on a flight. Since customers are only uniquely identified by their name and their address, and flights are only uniquely identified by the flight number and date, all four items should form part of the entity.

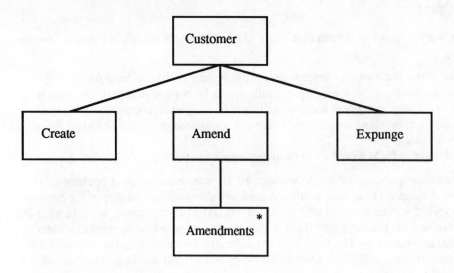

Figure 14.1 The life history of a customer.

The next stage is to derive the entity life histories. For this system these are comparatively simple. The entity life history of the flight entity is not required since the particular system we are considering does not carry out the creation, deletion, and amendment of the flight data. However, we shall assume that the system that does this provides us with a class that allows us to access flights in the final code of the system. The entity life history of a customer is shown in Fig. 14.1. The construction of this life history begs an important question: is the booking clerk allowed to modify a customer's details?

This might happen when a customer phones in to, say, cancel a flight and reports that his or her address has changed. After interviewing the airline company it is decided that the customer details should be amended. This means an extra action is required:

• *AmendCustomer*. This adjusts a customer address. This action requires the name of the customer, their old address, and a new address. The attributes for this action are thus: customer name, old address, and new customer address.

The life history for a booking is shown in Fig. 14.2. It involves a booking being created, and either cancelled or archived when the system is operated on the day after the flight has taken off. Notice that this life history does not directly cover the case of a customer who wished to amend a booking, e.g. to change a flight. This can be achieved, however, by cancelling a booking and creating a new booking.

Once these two life histories are established, the next stage is to determine the basic operations. The life history of a customer annotated with these operations is shown in Fig. 14.3.

The description of the operations is as follows:

1. CreateCustomer(Customername, Customeraddress). This operation creates a customer with a name *Customername* and address *Customeraddress*.

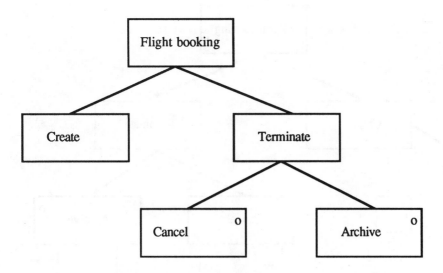

Figure 14.2 The life history of a booking.

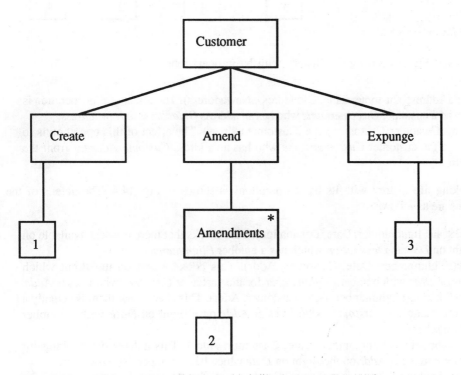

Figure 14.3 Customer life history with basic operations.

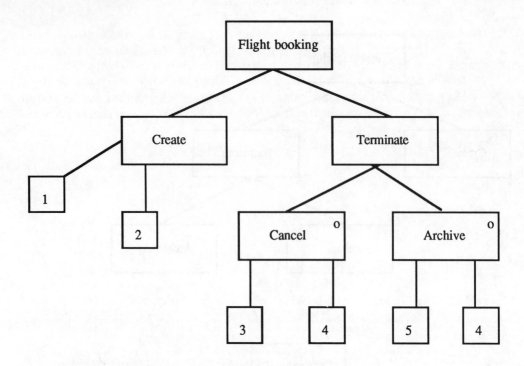

Figure 14.4 Flight booking life history with basic operations.

2. AmendAddress(Customername, Oldaddress, Newaddress). The effect of this operation is to amend a customer *Customername* who has an address *Oldaddress* to *Newaddress*.
3. ExpungeCustomer(Customername, Customeraddress). The effect of this operation is to expunge the customer *Customername* who has an address *CustomerAddress* from the system.

The booking life history with its basic operations is shown in Fig. 14.4. The details of the operations are as follows:

1. Checkseat(Flightnumber, Date, Destination). This checks that there is a seat available on a flight on *Date* to *Destination* which has a number *Flightnumber*.
2. Book(Flightnumber, Date, Customer, Addr). This books a seat on the flight which leaves on *Date* with number *Flightnumber* for the customer *Customer* who lives at *Addr*.
3. Checkbooking(Flightnumber, Date, Customer, Addr). This checks that there is actually a booking made for *Customer* who lives at *Addr* on a flight on *Date* with a number *Flightnumber*.
4. Removebooking(Flightnumber, Date, Customer, Addr). This deletes the booking for *Customer* living at *Addr* on the flight on *Date* which has a number *Flightnumber*.
5. Archivebooking(Flightnumber, Date, Customer, Addr). This archives the booking for *Customer* living at *Addr* travelling on *Flightnumber* on *Date*.

14.3 THE DESIGN OF THE ABSTRACT DATA TYPES

Once the entities have been identified, their life histories specified, and the basic operations added to the life histories, the next step is the design of the abstract data types that will correspond to the entities. For the remainder of this chapter we will concentrate on the main booking abstract data type which implements the relationship between a flight and the flight details. I shall assume that when the design of the system is being carried out the analyst discovers that the system can only hold *maxbookings* bookings. This is a good example of the type of data that is discovered during the design process.

The specification of the abstract data type is shown below:

Customerdetails ::   Name: custnames
                               Address: custaddresses

Seatallocations ::   MAP integer TO customerdetails

Bookings ::   MAP dates, flight numbers TO Seatallocations

INVARIANT There will be no more than *maxbookings* bookings and there will be no more than 16 items in the *Seatallocations* map and they will be associated with a seat number ranging from 1 to 16.

The operations on the data type are as shown below, and correspond to the basic operations identified during the analysis of entities.

OPERATION Checkseat(Flightnumber:flightnumbers, Date:dates, Destination:destinations, b:Boolean)

When this operation has been completed *b* will be true if there is an available seat on *Date* to *Destination*. *b* is set to false otherwise. If there is a seat then *Flightnumber* will be set to the number.

OPERATION Book(Flightnumber: flightnumbers, Date: dates, Customer: custnames, Addr: custaddresses)

For this operation to be defined there must be at least one seat available on the flight *Flightnumber* on *Date*. The effect of the operation is to book a seat on that flight for *Customer* at *Addr*.

OPERATION Checkbooking(Flightnumber:flightnumbers, Date:dates, Customer:custnames, Addr:custaddresses, b:Boolean)

When this operation has been completed *b* will be set to true if *Customer* living at *Addr* has booked a seat on *Flightnumber* on Date. *b* will be set to false otherwise.

OPERATION Removebooking(Flightnumber: flightnumbers, Date: dates, Customer: custnames, Addr: custaddresses)

For this operation to be defined there must be a booking for *Customer* living at *Addr* on flight *Flightnumber* on *Date*. The effect of this operation is to delete the booking.

OPERATION Archivebooking(Flightnumber: flightnumbers, Date: dates, Customer: customers, Addr: custaddresses)

This operation archives the booking for *Customer* living at *Addr* on *Flightnumber* to *Destination* on *Date*

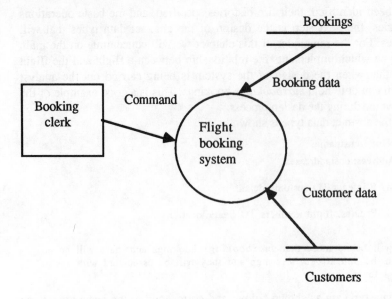

Figure 14.5 The top level of the functional specification.

Given this specification the classes corresponding to the various entities can be implemented. We do not show this, but shall assume that each entity provides a number of operations.

14.4 SPECIFYING FUNCTIONALITY

The next stage in development is the specification of functionality using data flow diagrams. Figure 14.5 shows the top-level specification.

This shows that a booking clerk will communicate commands to the system, and the system will require data from a store of customer data and from a store of bookings data. The expansion of the top-level bubble is shown in Fig. 14.6. This diagram shows the command typed in by a booking clerk being checked for correctness, i.e. that the command name is correct. It is then decoded (its identity discovered) and executed. The next stage is to expand bubbles 3, 4, 5, 6, and 7. The expansion of bubble 3 is shown in Fig. 14.7.

The diagram shows the use of the operations *CHECKSEAT*, *CREATECUSTOMER* and *BOOK* identified during analysis and specified during the identification of the abstract data types. It also shows the operation *GETFLIGHTNO* which is associated with the flight abstract data type. This gets a flight number of a particular destination and date and returns an error if no flight for that date exists. Bubble 3.6 is concerned with the management of the customer details and will not concern us here since we shall concentrate on the bookings subsystem and its associated abstract data type.

The expansion of bubble 4 is shown in Fig. 14.8.

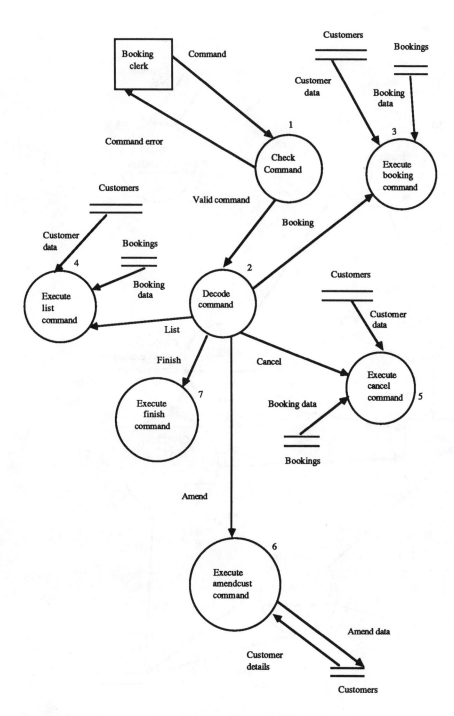

Figure 14.6 The expansion of the top-level data flow diagram.

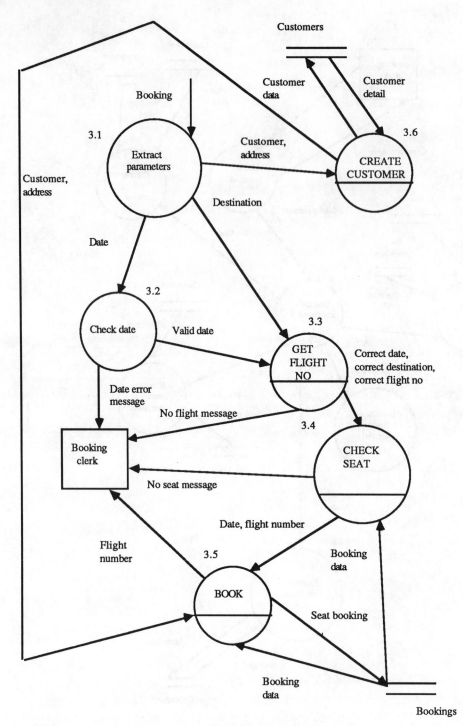

Figure 14.7 The expansion of bubble 3.

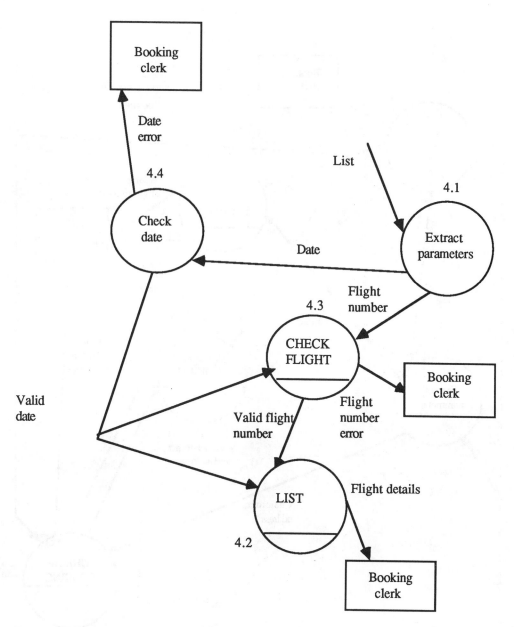

Figure 14.8 The expansion of bubble 4.

This data flow diagram uses the operation *LIST* which displays all the passengers associated with a particular flight and the operation *CHECK FLIGHT*, which checks that a valid flight number has been presented to the system. This operation is associated with the entity flight. The next data flow diagram represents the expansion of bubble 5 is shown in Fig. 14.9. It uses

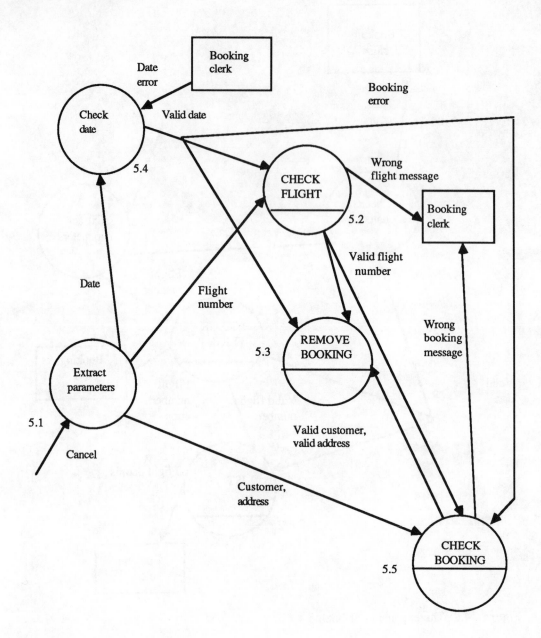

Figure 14.9 The expansion of bubble 5.

the operation *CHECK FLIGHT* associated with the flight entity. The expansion of the bubbles 6 and 7 are shown in Figs 14.10 and 14.11.

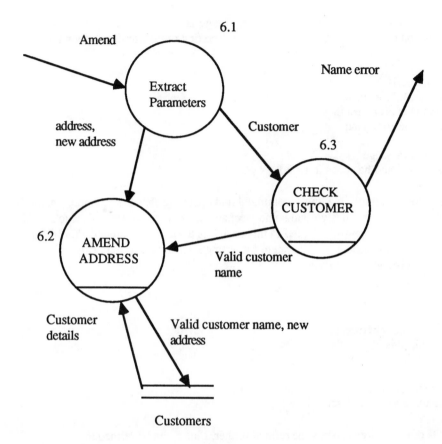

Figure 14.10 The expansion of bubble 6.

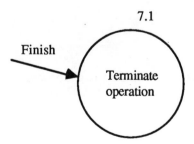

Figure 14.11 The expansion of bubble 7.

14.5 DESIGNING FUNCTIONALITY

Once the data flow diagrams are complete, the next stage is to design the system using the design decomposition method described in Chapter 11. The first outline design is shown below:

```
1   Repeat
2       Read a command
3       Check command for correctness
4       If the command is correct then
5           Execute the command
6       else
7       Issue an error message
8   Until the last command has been initiated
```

This continually loops around, reading a command and checking that the command name is correct. It is obvious from this design that some mechanism needs to be devised which senses the last command. The mechanism adopted in this design is to have a command *TERMINATE* that will terminate the processing of the system by setting a termination flag. This means that the design above can be modified to read:

```
1   Repeat
2       Read a command
3       Check command for correctness
4       If the command is correct then
5           Execute the command
6       else
7           Issue an error message
8.1 Until the termination flag is set
```

The components of this design can now be refined further. Line 5 can be refined to

```
5.1     Decode command
5.2     Case command of
5.3         Booking:Execute BOOKING
5.4         List: Execute LIST
5.5         Cancel: Execute CANCEL
5.6         Finish: Execute FINISH
5.7         Amend: Execute AMEND
```

where the command *FINISH* just sets the termination flag. Its refinement is straightforward

```
5.6.1       Set termination flag
```

This gives the design so far as being

```
1.      Repeat
2.          Read a command
3.          Check command for correctness
```

4.		If the command is correct then
5.1		Decode command
5.2		Case command of
5.3		Booking:Execute BOOKING
5.4		List: Execute LIST
5.5		Cancel: Execute CANCEL
5.6		Finish: Set termination flag
5.7		Amend: Execute AMEND
6	else	
7.		Issue an error message
8.	Until the termination flag is set	

The remaining commands can now be refined. As Chapter 11 indicated, much of this refinement can be extracted from the data flow diagrams of the commands. The refinement of the *BOOKING* command is shown below:

5.3	Booking:
5.3.1	Extract booking parameters(cust, addr, date, destination)
5.3.2	If the date is valid then
5.3.3	<u>Createcustomer(cust, addr)</u>
5.3.4	<u>Getflightno(date,destination, flightnumber, flightok)</u>
5.3.5	If flightok then
5.3.6	<u>Checkseat(flightnumber, date, destination, avail)</u>
5.3.7	If avail then
5.3.8	<u>Book(flightnumber, date, cust, addr)</u>
5.3.9	Display flightnumber to booking clerk
5.3.9	else
5.3.10	Inform the booking clerk no seats available
5.3.11	else
5.3.12	Inform the booking clerk that there is no such flight
5.3.13	else
5.3.14	Inform the booking clerk of a date error

Refinement 5.3.1 extracts the parameters of the booking command. *Getflightno* is an operation associated with the flight entity which places a flight number for a date and destination into *flightnumber*. The operations on the abstract data types are, of course, underlined. The refinement of step 5.4 is shown below:

5.4.1	Extract list parameters(flightnumber, date)
5.4.2	If the date is valid then
5.4.3	<u>Checkflight(flightnumber, date, ok)</u>
5.4.4	If ok then
5.4.5	<u>List(flightnumber, date)</u>
5.4.6	else
5.4.7	Issue a message informing the clerk that no such flight exists
5.4.8	else
5.4.9	Inform the booking clerk of a date error

Operation *Checkflight* checks that a particular flight number occurs on a particular day and the operation *List* lists out the passengers on a particular flight. The refinement of step 5.5 is shown below:

5.5.1	Extract cancel parameters(date, cust, addr, flightnumber)
5.5.2	<u>Checkflight(flightnumber,date, ok)</u>
5.5.3	If ok then
5.5.4	If date is valid then
5.5.5	<u>Checkbooking(flightnumber,date,cust,addr,okbooking)</u>
5.5.6	If okbooking then
5.5.7	<u>Removebooking(flightnumber,date,cust,addr)</u>
5.5.8	else
5.5.9	Inform the booking clerk that the customer has not booked such a flight
5.5.10	else
5.5.11	Inform the booking clerk of a date error
5.5.12	else
5.5.13	Inform the booking clerk the flight does not exist

The refinement of step 5.7 becomes

5.7.1	Extract amend parameters(cust, addr, newaddr)
5.7.2	<u>Checkcustomer(cust, addr, okcust)</u>
5.7.3	If okcust then
5.7.4	<u>Amendaddress(cust, addr, newaddr)</u>
5.7.5	else
5.7.6	Inform the booking clerk that the customer does not exist

where *Checkcustomer* and *Amendaddress* are functions associated with the customer entity. The whole design then becomes

1	Repeat
2	Read a command
3	Check command for correctness
4	If the command is correct then
5.1	Decode command
5.2	Case command of
5.3	Booking:
5.3.1	Extract booking parameters(cust, addr, date, destination)
5.3.2	If the date is valid then
5.3.3	Createcustomer(cust, addr)
5.3.4	<u>Getflightno(date,destination, flightnumber, flightok)</u>
5.3.5	If flightok then
5.3.6	<u>Checkseat(flightnumber, date, destination, avail)</u>
5.3.7	If avail then
5.3.8	<u>Book(flightnumber, date, cust, addr)</u>
5.3.9	Display flightnumber to booking clerk
5.3.9	else

5.3.10	Inform the booking clerk no seats available
5.3.11	else
	Inform the booking clerk that there is no
5.3.12	such flight
5.3.13	else
5.3.14	Inform the booking clerk of a date error

5.4	List:
5.4.1	Extract list parameters(flightnumber, date)
5.4.2	If the date is valid then
5.4.3	Checkflight(flightnumber, date, ok)
5.4.4	If ok then
5.4.5	List(flightnumber, date)
5.4.6	else
5.4.7	Issue a message informing the clerk that no such flight exists
5.4.8	else
5.4.9	Inform the booking clerk of a date error

5.5	Cancel:
5.5.1	Extract cancel parameters(date, cust, addr, flightnumber)
5.5.2	Checkflight(flightnumber,date, ok)
5.5.3	If ok then
5.5.4	If date is valid then
5.5.5	Checkbooking(flightnumber,date,cust,addr,okbooking)
5.5.6	If okbooking then
5.5.7	Removebooking(flightnumber,date,cust,addr)
5.5.8	else
5.5.9	Inform the booking clerk that the customer has not booked such a flight
5.5.10	else
5.5.11	Inform the booking clerk of a date error
5.5.12	else
5.5.13	Inform the booking clerk the flight does not exist

5.6.1	Finish:Set termination flag

5.7	Amend:
5.7.1	Extract amend parameters(cust, addr, newaddr)
5.7.2	Checkcustomer(cust, addr, okcust)
5.7.3	If okcust then
5.7.4	Amendaddress(cust,addr, newaddr)
5.7.5	else
5.7.6	Inform the booking clerk that the customer does not exist

6	else
7	Issue an error message
8	Until the termination flag is set

14.6 THE PROGRAM CODE

The program code for this design is shown below, and uses facilities provided by the implemented abstract data types described earlier:

```
main()
{

char *com,*cust, *addr,*newaddr,*date,*destination;

int flightnumber,okcommand,termflag = 1,
    ok,okbooking,okcust,flightok, avail;

customers s;
flights f;
bookings b;

do {
    readcom(com);
    okcommand =checkcom(com);
    if (okcommand >0){

        switch(okcommand) {

        case 1://book
        exbookparam(cust,addr,date,destination);
        if(valdate(date)){
          s.createcustomer(cust,addr);
          f.getflightnumber(date,destination,flightnumber,flightok);
          if(flightok){
              b.checkseat(flightnumber,date,destination, avail);
              if(avail){
                  b.book(flightnumber,date,cust,addr);
                  message("The flight number is");
                  dispfno(flightnumber);
              }
          else
              message("no seats available");
          }
          else
              message("No flight for this destination");
        }
        else
            message("You have mistyped the date");
    break;
```

```
case 2://list
exlistparam(flightnumber,date);
if (valdate(date)){
   f.checkflight(flightnumber,date,ok);
   if (ok)
      f.list(flightnumber,date);
   else
      message("no such flight exists");
}
else
   message("You have mistyped the date");
break;

case 3: //cancel
excancelparam(date,cust,addr,flightnumber);
f.checkflight(flightnumber,date,ok);
if(ok){
   if (valdate(date)){
      b.checkbooking(flightnumber,date,cust,addr,okbooking);
      if( okbooking)
         b.removebooking(flightnumber,date,cust,addr);
      else
         message("customer not booked this flight");
   }
   else
      message("You have mistyped the date");
}
else
   message("the flight does not exist");
break;

case 4: //finish
termflag= 0;
break;

case 5:// amend
examendparam(cust,addr,newaddr);
s.checkcustomer(cust,addr,okcust);
if (okcust)
   s.amendaddress(cust,addr,newaddr);
else
   message("Customer does not exist in our files");
break;

};
```

```
    }
}
while (termflag);
};
```

This program uses classes such as `bookings`, `flight`, and `customers` which are implementations of the entities identified during analysis. The system also uses a number of functions that are not associated with classes, e.g. `examendparam`, which extracts the parameters of the amend command. Most of the functioning of these functions can be gathered from reading the code and the design. However, it is worth detailing that the function `checkcom` checks that the command typed in is a valid one. If it is, then an integer in the range 1–5 is returned, which is then used to execute the switch statement that carries out the processing. If the command is unrecognized, then a zero is passed back and an error message displayed.

This, then, is the development of the system. It could have occurred in any of the orders implied by the models presented in the previous chapter. The important point is that the development placed concerns about data at the same level of importance as concerns about functionality.

abstract data type, 29, 30, 33, 74, 76,
    77, 78, 81, 86, 87, 88, 90, 91,
    123, 124, 125, 148, 203, 205, 213
abstraction, 11, 74, 75
acceptance test, 2, 6, 7, 8, 63
acceptance testing, 5, 6, 8, 43, 62, 70
accounting system, 9
action, 25, 45, 46, 47, 48, 56, 61, 202
action attribute, 24, 25, 46, 47, 202
Ada, 1, 4, 16, 75
adaptive maintenance, 9
address of operator, 100
admit, 61
agenda, 64
aggregate data type, 93
air defence system, 9
air-traffic control system, 14
airline booking system, 31
algebraic specification, 90, 91
algorithm, 4, 9
ambiguity, 10, 40, 42
analysis, 198, 207
analyst, 5, 67
APL, 71, 194
appendix, 42
application-oriented programming
    language, 71
arithmetic operator, 98
array, 30, 76, 97, 102, 103, 115, 124,
    132, 133, 134, 148
array address, 115
artificial intelligence, 195
ASCII, 95, 101
assembler, 1
assembler language, 4, 179
assignment statement, 105, 106
attribute, 46, 47, 48, 51, 67
AWK, 195
axiom, 91
axiomatic specification, 90

back order, 15
backtracking, 61

bag, 86
base class, 138, 146
basic operation, 26, 29, 56, 57, 58,
    59, 61, 203
basic type, 78
bitwise and, 100
bitwise exclusive or, 100
bitwise inclusive or, 100
bottom-up integration, 7
boundary data, 151
branch, 8, 183
branch coverage, 31
bubble, 156, 157, 158, 160, 163, 165,
    166, 167, 171, 214

C, 14, 16, 30, 31
C++, 14, 16, 30, 69, 87, 93, 95
case statement, 33, 53
CASE technology, 199
CASE tool, 161
char, 94
character array, 102, 103
character constant, 96
check-list, 64
chemical plant control system, 88
chemical plant monitoring system, 10
circuit design, 75
class, 14, 15, 16, 30, 31, 33, 69, 71,
    72, 123, 128, 136, 137, 139, 140,
    142, 143, 203
class integration, 151
class library, 203
COBOL, 194, 195
combined assignment operator, 100
comment, 97
commercial data processing, 71, 194
commercial data processing system, 5,
    16, 146
communications system, 15
compiler, 16, 76, 78, 101, 127
complex number, 140
complex type, 105